The Historic Cumberland Plateau

The Historic Cumberland Plateau

AN EXPLORER'S GUIDE

Second Edition

Russ Manning

Outdoor Tennessee Series
Jim Casada, Series Editor

THE UNIVERSITY OF TENNESSEE PRESS

Knoxville

To celebrate Tennessee's bicentennial in 1996, the Outdoor Tennessee Series covers a wide range of topics of interest to the general reader, including titles on the flora and fauna, the varied recreational activities, and the rich history of outdoor Tennessee. With a keen appreciation of the importance of protecting our state's natural resources and beauty, the University of Tennessee Press intends the series to emphasize environmental awareness and conservation.

Paper: 1st printing, 1999; 2nd printing, 2006

Frontispiece: Stinging Fork Falls. All photographs were taken by the author unless otherwise noted.

The paper used in this book meets the minimum requirements of ANSI/NISO Z39.48-1992 (R 1997) *(Permanence of Paper)*. The binding materials have been chosen for strength and durability. Printed on recycled paper.

Library of Congress Cataloging-in-Publication Data

Manning, Russ.
The historic Cumberland Plateau: an explorer's guide / Russ Manning.—2nd ed.
        p.   cm.— (Outdoor Tennessee Series)
Includes bibliographic references (p.) and index.
ISBN 1-57233-144-9 (paperback: alk. paper)
1. Cumberland Mountains—Guidebooks. I. Title. II. Series
        F457.C8 M36 1999
        917.69'10443—dc21

                                        98-40194

FOR SONDRA
who shares my joy of discovery

Contents

Illustrations

Foreword

As the late Louis L'Amour once wrote in his simple yet eloquent fashion, "The cities are for money but the high-up hills are purely for the soul." L'Amour was thinking of the West, but the sentiments underlying his words are equally applicable to the Cumberland Plateau. This geological outcropping, spreading over several states in the eastern heartland, remains a special place. Much of it is still wild, little touched by humanity's crass material caress. And in its fastnesses the wayfarer leaves behind the burdens and haste of our modern world. Here worries are forgotten amidst quiet, unhurried time for contemplation; and here one finds reminders, tangible and otherwise, of the strong links joining yesteryear with today.

Somehow, the Plateau has for the most part escaped the less welcome developments attendant on what we call, sometimes in singularly misguided fashion, "progress." There are coves and hollows as remote and unchanged as when the first pioneers ventured through the historic Cumberland Gap. Streams still flow clear and cold, and only on the periphery do bustling cities and towns such as Chattanooga and Crossville intrude in any meaningful fashion. In between is a vast tableland, intersected by deep canyons like so many laughter lines on an old man's face. Crossroads villages, peaceful inns, and old homesteads greet one at every turn. They are throwbacks to a world we have largely lost, reminders of a time when life moved at a more sedate and, arguably, more meaningful pace.

Certainly to enter the world of the Cumberland Plateau is to take a delightful step back in time. As Russ Manning says in his preface, the region is "full of wonder and surprise." With the insatiable curiosity to know the little known, which at times stirs in even the most cosmopolitan among us, the plateau cries out for exploration. To walk along the gently rounded spines of its hardwood forests, to gaze at its myriad waterfalls, to float its tumbling rivers, is to savor some small part of the thrill that must have stirred the souls of legendary pioneers in the region such as Daniel Boone and David Crockett.

My own introduction to the Cumberland Plateau was of the eclectic sort in which armchair adventurers rejoice. Zane Grey's *Spirit of the Border* captivated me as an adolescent, and I remain convinced that this work ranks right alongside his westerns in enduring appeal. It depicts, in fictional form laced with a solid underpinning of fact from the mind of a man who knew the outdoors intimately, the rough and ready life of the frontier as brave men breached the bulwark of the Appalachians in their inexorable push westward. Counterbalancing Grey's highly romanticized treatment were Harriette Simpson Arnow's seminal works, *Seedtime on the Cumberland* and *Flowering of the Cumberland.* Hers are enduring books, ones that I suspect many who follow the pathways delineated in the present volume will find attractive.

In time, thanks to pursuing both undergraduate and graduate studies at institutions situated on the periphery of the Cumberland Plateau, my previously vicarious acquaintance with the region became a first-hand one. There was much to attract an individual of my inclination (and turn me from my studies). Each year April's time of renewal brought wildflowers bursting forth in a way guaranteed to cure the malaise of spring fever as surely as sassafras tea or a dose of sulfur and molasses. Come summer, fat, feisty smallmouth bass, so aptly described by Tennessee writer Caroline Gordon as "chicken hawk and chain lightning," offered a welcome relief from long hours in the library at Vanderbilt. Fall and winter meant grouse and squirrel hunting along hardwood ridges and in sheltered coverts. In all seasons there was an abiding air of expectancy, for one never knew when the next ridge or forgotten cove would offer a joyful surprise. Most of all, though, the Cumberland Plateau was for me a place of escape.

So it remains today, and how I wish I had had Russ Manning's book to direct my footsteps when the Plateau lay at my back doorstep. He begins with an overview of the region's character, then offers, chapter by chapter, a guide to the plateau's principal regions and features. His is, in essence, a guidebook, but thankfully it goes far beyond the usual listings of trails and roads, contacts, and "must see" attractions. Each chapter includes a narrative section sufficient to give the reader a feel for the particular area being covered. By reading these sections, you can make your own decision whether the region has sufficient appeal to merit first-hand exploration.

Speaking of appeal, the Plateau and this book on it offer something for everyone who loves the outdoors, nature, and the American past. Browsing the place names alone is a treat. Who can resist the temptations inherent in names such as Kingdom Come State Park, Yahoo Falls, the Moonbow, Frozen Head, Ozone Falls, Savage Gulf, Bone Cave, or Fiery Gizzard? For those of an intellectual bent, there are Lincoln Memorial University, Sewanee and its University of the South, and the fascinating attempt to give America its version of the famed English public school, Rugby. Most of all, though, there is natural wonder. As Manning suggests, this is a region best seen on foot, for there is something about the lack of haste inherent in walking that lends itself to maximum enjoyment of the Plateau. Indeed, many of its most striking features can only be reached by shank's mare.

This is, as the title suggests, a book for explorers. It carries the reader (perhaps "user" would be a more appropriate description) into the unknown, and that is what exploration is all about. With the work as a companion, rest assured that there will be discoveries. They will vary with the individual, perhaps being fragile bluets blooming along the trail or the awe-inspiring plunge of a waterfall. Others will be attracted by the undying draw of the Civil War or by reminders of the vanished culture that was life on the frontier. For most, there will also be discoveries of a different sort. These will be dawning recognition of just how much the natural world can and should mean to us. As one walks and wonders, there comes realization that ecosystems such as those of the Cumberland Plateau have more lasting value than any product of worship at the altar of the false gods of materialism.

In short, as I suggested in the Louis L'Amour quotation with which I began, this is a book for the soul. As such it is a welcome addition to the Outdoor Tennessee Series of which it is a part. The author reminds us, quietly but convincingly, of just how important the good earth is to our physical and mental well being. In that regard, he does us a signal service as a conservationist even as he points the way to parts of the Plateau in five states. By all means use this work as the first-rate guidebook it is. But as its pages and the vast tableland described herein give you ample measure of pleasure, remember that yours is a privileged passage through a world richly deserving of protection and preservation.

Jim Casada
Series Editor
Rock Hill, South Carolina

Preface to the Second Edition

I continue to be amazed at the dedication and hard work of local citizens who, through their love and respect for the land, make great strides in preserving the Cumberland Plateau. Much has happened in the years since this book first appeared, mostly due to the work of such people.

Through the efforts of individuals and conservation groups, especially Tennessee Citizens for Wilderness Planning, five thousand acres preserving the canyon country of the Three Forks of the Wolf River have been added to Pickett State Forest. A dedicated group of hikers and trail builders from the Tennessee Trails Association has formed a Cumberland Trail Conference and has resurrected the Cumberland Trail, which will one day travel the length of the plateau through Tennessee. An association of groups and individuals is working determinedly as the Friends of Scotts Gulf to preserve the canyon country surrounding Virgin Falls Pocket Wilderness.

New areas have received official designation. Karlan State Park in Virginia near Cumberland Gap contains new trails and a campground. Big Ridge Small Wild Area on TVA lands near Chattanooga preserves old-growth forest. Bowaters has set aside Chickamauga Gulch north of Chattanooga as the North Chickamauga Pocket Wilderness. Little River Canyon in Alabama is now a national preserve.

But much remains to be done, including monitoring and opposing environmental threats. Save Our Cumberland Mountains, along with other groups, has filed a lands-unsuitable-for-mining application for the Fall Creek Falls watershed to prevent strip mining that is encroaching on Fall Creek Falls State Park. The potential for chip mills in the lower Sequatchie and existing chip mills in the Big South Fork region threaten the plateau forests with their requirement for vast quantities of trees. A proposed dam on Clear Creek, a major tributary of the Obed

Wild and Scenic River, would reduce water flow and add pollutants and silt to the waters of the river system. A dormant proposal could be resurrected for a pump storage facility in Sequatchie Valley that would add scars to the land.

The Cumberland Plateau has beckoned throughout history to come and explore and to help in preserving the natural wonders and the way of the life of the plateau region. The invitation still stands. See you there.

Russ Manning 1998

Preface to the First Edition

When I first came to East Tennessee in the late 1960s, my attention was first drawn to the Great Smoky Mountains. It was only natural that this much-publicized and most-visited national park in the country should attract first notice. But while I paid my initial visits to Clingmans Dome, Cades Cove, and the Chimneys, I heard rumors of a tableland to the west with canyons and waterfalls and isolated villages.

My first encounter with the Cumberland Plateau was while driving from Knoxville west on I-40 toward Nashville. Just as I rounded a curve and came abruptly upon the Harriman-Rockwood exit, the Plateau stood like a wall nearly a thousand feet high. From there the interstate climbed to the top of the Plateau, clinging precariously to the face of the eastern escarpment. However, I did not continue to the top of the Plateau with those first encounters. I pulled off at the exit and drove into Harriman where I was teaching school for one season before moving on to other careers.

At that stage of my life I had not spent much time in the outdoors except to walk the fields and woods of my father's land in south Alabama where I grew up. But eventually curiosity about the Plateau became more than I could endure, and I donned hiking boots and backpack and set out for what proved to be an adventure.

Over the years, a number of individuals and conservation groups introduced me to sites on the Plateau. Bill and Liane Russell of Tennessee Citizens for Wilderness Planning took me to the Obed River soon after their efforts helped establish the stream as a national Wild and Scenic River.

In Rugby, Dorothy Stagg welcomed me to an overnight stay at Roslyn, her old Victorian home, and told me of her son's efforts to preserve the small community that was the last English colony in the United States.

It was while attending a meeting of the Tennessee Chapter of the Sierra Club at Beersheba Springs that member Ken McDonald guided me in the drizzling rain to the Great Stone Door that drops into Savage Gulf, the preeminent Tennessee state natural area.

Gordon Grissom led several of us from the Sierra Club on an exploration of Big Bone Cave, a place where he played as a child and now sometimes serves as a guide after spending most of his life out of the region.

Randy Hedgepath, Ranger-Naturalist at the South Cumberland Recreation Area, showed me Ranger Falls in Big Creek Gulf and Greeter Falls on Firescald Creek. Ranger Wayne Morrison guided my wife, Sondra Jamieson, and me to Suter Falls in Collins Gulf. Sondra was a frequent companion who showed great patience when I had to find that one last iron furnace in Kentucky.

Jerry Gernt welcomed us to the Bruno Gernt House in Allardt, the German colony founded in the late 1880s, where Sondra and I were married amidst friends on an April afternoon in 1988.

My stepson, Jason Hankins, accompanied me on an exploration of Kentucky's Beaver Creek Wilderness and retrieved my walking stick when I dropped it after being swarmed by yellow jackets.

As I raced to keep up with men and women twice my age on a Smoky Mountains Hiking Club outing into Bowater's Honey Creek Pocket Wilderness, I encountered for the first time a piece of what would become the Big South Fork National River and Recreation Area, a land of arches and waterfalls and steep-walled canyons.

On a backpacking trip in Cumberland Gap National Historical Park years ago with Art Davis and some of the students from Knoxville's Bearden Junior High School Hiking Club, I wandered into Hensley Settlement, an early pioneer community perched on the mountain ridge.

I discovered 256-foot-high Fall Creek Falls myself one ecstatic day in early spring when few people were about; the mist from the falls rose around me, drenching my clothes and firing my spirit.

After pulling off I-59 in northern Alabama just to check out the sign that said "DeSoto State Park," I spent the night camped under a rock overhang on the edge of one of the deepest canyons east of the Rocky Mountains.

The Cumberland Plateau is like that, full of wonder and surprise, a place for exploring. This book is intended to get you started.

Acknowledgments

In addition to those who guided me to specific sites on the Plateau, several people aided me by reviewing the manuscript. I am grateful to Bob Fulcher, Regional Interpretative Specialist with the state of Tennessee, for his thorough and very helpful reading of early drafts of the entire manuscript; his comments and recommendations greatly improved the final product.

Thanks to Dr. Ed Clebsch, Professor of Botany, and Dr. Don Byerly, Associate Professor of Geology at The University of Tennessee, for reviewing Chapter 1, and to Dr. Molly F. Miller, Professor of Geology at Vanderbilt University for additional geological information.

In addition, I thank the following for perusing parts of the manuscript: Daniel Brown, Park Historian at Cumberland Gap National Historical Park for the material on Cumberland Gap; Rick Fuller, Naturalist at Pine Mountain State Resort Park, for the material on Pine Mountain; Robert K. Strosnider, Recreation and Land Management Staff Officer for the Daniel Boone National Forest, for the material on the Daniel Boone National Forest and the Red River Gorge Geological Area; Steve Kickert, Park Naturalist at Cumberland Falls State Resort Park, for the material on Cumberland Falls; Steven Seven, Chief of Interpretation at the Big South Fork National River and Recreation Area, Ron Cornelius, Chief of Resources Management at the BSFNRRA, and Don Forester, Site Manager of the Obed Wild and Scenic River, for the material on the Big South Fork and the Obed Rivers; Lee and Bill Russell of Tennessee Citizens for Wilderness Planning for the material on the Big South Fork National River and Recreation Area and the Obed Wild and Scenic River; Barbara Stagg, Executive Director of Historic Rugby, Inc., and Eileen Hurt, Director of Education, for the material on Rugby; Gerald Gernt, descendent of Bruno Gernt, for the material on

Allardt; Doyle Vaden, President of the Homesteads Tower Association, and Emma Jean Pedigo Vaden, both second-generation Homesteaders, for the material on the Cumberland Homesteads; Stuart Carroll, Interpretive Specialist for Fall Creek Falls State Resort Park, for the material on Fall Creek Falls; Randy Hedgepath, Ranger-Naturalist for the South Cumberland Recreation Area, and Herman Baggenstoss, Chairman of the Grundy County Conservation Board, for the material on Savage Gulf and the South Cumberland Recreation Area; and Talmadge Butler, Park Manager of DeSoto State Park, for the material on the Park and Little River Canyon.

How to Use This Book

The major attractions of the Cumberland Plateau are its history and its natural and cultural heritage. As a result, I have designed this book to serve two purposes: to introduce you to the Cumberland Plateau and its history and to help order your exploration if you want to see some of the natural wonders and participate in the cultural activities. Therefore, each chapter, with the exception of the first, is divided into two parts: a narrative that describes a section of the Plateau and tells its history, and a guide that gives directions, lists services, and locates hiking trails.

Exploring the entire Cumberland Plateau would make for an exciting spring or fall, the best seasons for being outdoors in the Southeast. But few people have an entire season to devote to travel. Since you will likely be visiting the Plateau sporadically—a week at a time or perhaps only a weekend at a time—and you will probably visit places on the Plateau in no particular order, I've written each chapter so that it stands alone as a description of a region. After looking over the first chapter, which gives you the geographical, geological, biological, and historical context, you will lose nothing by skipping around in the book to read about what interests you most.

To use the book as a guide, it's important to remember that each chapter is about a section of the Plateau. Although the place named in the chapter title is the main attraction, I also discuss other nearby places, so you may want to read an entire chapter and plan an itinerary before you begin to explore a certain area. I've also included a map for each chapter to help orient you to the major highways and sights.

I have divided the narrative section of each chapter with subheads, most of which refer to specific places. Since subheads can only catalog major attractions, other places and people mentioned in passing are listed in the index.

The Cumberland Plateau must be experienced outdoors, so at the end of each chapter you'll find short descriptions of hiking trails in the area. Although this is not a hiking guide, I include the trails to let you know what is available. For more details, talk to the staff of each park, who will be able to provide information and recommend hiking guides that cover the region you are exploring.

Although hiking is probably the best way to cover the Plateau, you don't have to be an avid hiker to find the Plateau interesting or the book useful. You can discover much of the Cumberland Plateau by touring historic sites; experiencing the Plateau's cultural diversity; sampling the food, inns, and celebrations; visiting national and state parks; and taking short walks to major geologic attractions.

In reading the book, you'll see various terms used to label the region. *Cumberland Plateau* and *Plateau* typically refer to the Cumberland Plateau region, which includes both a plateaulike area to the south and a more mountainous region to the north. When not capitalized, *plateau* indicates an actual tableland. Generally, *Cumberland Mountains* refers to the mountains that stand on the northern part of the Cumberland Plateau; but also *Cumberland Mountains* or *Cumberland Mountain* refers specifically to the mountains along the northeastern edge of the Plateau that are labeled as such on many maps.

While exploring the Cumberland Plateau, you're likely to encounter some current efforts to save the land from development and exploitation. In my years of wandering the Plateau, I've seen roads slash across mountainsides, strip mines erode the tableland, and various developments threaten untouched areas. This is a fragile land which, although still containing pristine areas, has seen more than its share of abuse and should be spared much that is planned for it. If you're so inclined, you can join the effort to protect the land. The conservation groups that are working to preserve the Cumberland Plateau as well as other areas in the Southeast welcome your interest and support. Addresses for some of these organizations are listed at the end of the book.

Chapter 1

The Plateau

A strip of land called the Cumberland Plateau runs southwest through eastern Kentucky while spilling eastward just over the border into Virginia. It then passes through Tennessee, grazes the northwest corner of Georgia, and extends into Alabama. It is a flat tableland in places; in others, mountains stand atop the capstone rock. Because of its irregular geological features, its remoteness, and its small population, much of the Plateau remains in a natural state. It is covered with forests, dotted with waterfalls, and spanned by stone arches. Its rivers and streams have carved great canyons.

Hundreds of thousands of acres of this unique area in the eastern United States have been set aside for preservation. Within this strip of land are a national park, 24 state parks, a national forest, a national river and recreation area, 19 state natural areas, numerous state forests and recreation sites and wildlife management areas, 2 nationally designated wilderness areas, a national wild and scenic river, 6 state wild and scenic rivers, 4 national natural landmarks, a national monument, a national preserve, and part of a national military park. Interspersed among these preserved lands are small mountain communities, some of which still wage battles to preserve their way of life against development interests. And in the backwoods, you'll find the remnants of a few visionary communities that once sought new beginnings.

The Delta Systems

On the North American continent, a sea once covered a huge depression, called the "Appalachian Basin," in what is now the southeastern

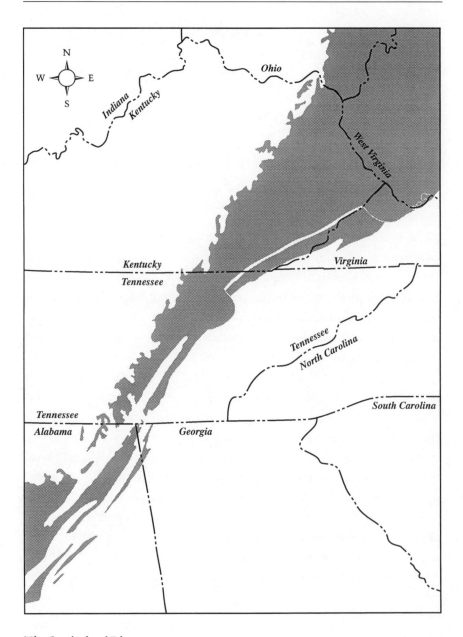

The Cumberland Plateau

United States. Rivers and streams flowing west from the Appalachian highlands to the east created vast delta systems at the sea's edge where thick swamps and marshes formed. This complex delta region consisted of meandering channels, natural levees, floodplains, bays, barrier islands, and lagoons.

The rivers and streams carried countless tons of sediment which deposited in the expanding deltas, often burying the vegetation that grew along the floodplains and in the swamps and lagoons. Occasional subsidence allowed the sea to temporarily reinvade the delta plain. The intermittent seas and swamps and converging streams left behind layer upon layer of sediment, vegetation, shell, and marine growth that under the increasing pressure of accumulating weight became slabs of sandstone, shale, and siltstone and occasional tiers of clay, limestone, and coal.

This filling of the Appalachian Basin marked the end of the inundation of this portion of the North American continent.

Mountain Building

Then began a final interval of mountain building to the east. This was the end of the Paleozoic Era, a time when the land rose. Great slabs of rock miles across pushed upward and tilted and sometimes folded on top of themselves, all happening in the slow motion of geologic time.

The forces that caused such upheaval originated somewhere to the southeast. Early geologic studies refer to a mysterious "force from the east"—the pattern of rocks showing irrefutably that some force had pushed in a northwesterly direction. It was only after the introduction of plate tectonic theory that the origin of the force had an explanation.

Only recently has the idea been accepted that features on the earth's surface, such as mountain ranges, could be the result of movement of the continents. The force behind continental drift is sea floor spreading, in which new rock emerges from the depths of the earth along fractures in the ocean floor and pushes aside old rock. Plate tectonic theory employs the image of continents supported by hard rock plates drifting on a sea of pliable rock in the earth's mantle and occasionally bumping into each other—the surface of the continents bulging under the impact to form mountains.

This last mountain building that occurred in eastern North America was probably the result of a collision between the African and North American continental plates. The force of the collision sent a rippling wave from the southeast to the northwest. The Appalachian mountains, worn down by erosion, rose again in this last episode of great mountain building called the "Allegheny Orogeny." The erosion of these new mountains sent another wave of sediment westward down the rivers to be deposited at the edge of the inland sea.

Mountain building to the east, followed by erosion and deposition to the west, repeated in a cycle of several pulses over millions of years during a time geologists call the "Pennsylvanian Period" and likely continued until as late as 250 million years ago. The accumulating weight of overlying layers of sediment caused the layers of sand and gravel to consolidate into rock. One particularly thick layer solidified into an erosion-resistant rock that came to be called "Pennsylvanian sandstone." Later pulses of the Allegheny Orogeny deformed this rock, in places fracturing and folding the sandstone while it was still buried by overlying sediment.

Much later, the delta area where the rivers had met the inland sea, now filled, rose above sea level in a secondary uplift. This occurred through the process of isostatic adjustment in which rain and the subsequent streams swept away the top sedimentary deposits; the weight was thus reduced and the land rose, pushed up by surrounding dense rock. There were probably several intervals of secondary uplift, between which the mountains eroded down again, until eventually the Pennsylvanian sandstone was uncovered. When this resistant sandstone rose, it slowed the erosion and so formed a capstone that protected the uplifted land, essentially ending the period of secondary uplift. Just to the east, where there was no protective sandstone, erosion dipped out troughs between parallel hard rock ridges, creating so many low mountains and shallow valleys that the region is now called the "Valley and Ridge Province."

The Plateau

After millions of years of erosion, this region to the west of the Valley and Ridge Province still remains a tableland 2,000 feet above sea level. In places it was once thousands of feet higher and miles wider. The overall region, called the "Appalachian Plateaus Province," stretches from the southern border of New York to central Alabama.

The Plateaus Province runs northeast to southwest, the ripples in the earth's surface having formed perpendicular to the force pushing from the southeast. The eastern edge in the southeastern United States is clearly a wall, an escarpment, at places a steep mountainside and at other places a long rock cliff standing atop a wooded slope. The appearance of such a clearly defined wall is due to the hard Pennsylvanian sandstone that resists erosion and so has kept the eastern wall of the Plateau intact.

White Rocks at Cumberland Gap National Historical Park

In contrast, the western wall is not so clearly defined. Drainage on the Plateau is generally to the west, helping to break up the western escarpment. Although the western wall is also capped by Pennsylvanian sandstone, the persistent streams have cut it for millions of years, carving the Plateau's western edge in to a rambling, jagged line.

The Cumberland Plateau

One of the early explorers of Kentucky, Thomas Walker, named the Cumberland River in Kentucky and Tennessee for William Augustus, Duke of Cumberland, son of Britain's George II. Many objected to the new name, for while leading the English army in the 1746 Battle of Culloden Moor, in which he defeated the Scottish clans under Bonnie Prince Charlie (Charles Edward Stuart), the Duke showed so little mercy to wounded enemy that he was nicknamed "the Butcher." The Duke's successful campaign was partly responsible for the influx of Scottish immigrants into the American colonies.

Since the Cumberland River is one of the primary waterways that drain the southern portion of the Appalachian Plateaus Province, the surrounding region also soon acquired the name "Cumberland." As a result, Walker bequeathed to future generations a name many consider dishonorable—a name now used for everything from mountain, river, and county to schools, churches, and subdivisions.

Generally, the names "Cumberland Plateau" and "Cumberland Mountains," sometimes used synonymously, apply to that portion of the Appalachian Plateaus Province that runs through Kentucky and Tennessee and into Alabama, where it breaks up and descends to the Gulf Coastal Plain. To the north of Kentucky, this same Plateaus Province is referred to as simply the "Appalachian Plateau" in West Virginia and the "Allegheny Plateau" in Pennsylvania.

Stretching northeast to southwest, the Cumberland Plateau is as an uplifted tableland with broad plains dissected by river canyons. As the Plateau enters Tennessee along the Kentucky-Virginia line it is 55 miles wide. Where it leaves the state, near Chattanooga, it narrows to around 38 miles.

This Plateau was once overlain with eroded beds; while these partially remain as the Cumberland Mountains on much of the northern Plateau, this material has mostly eroded away to the south, leaving the flat sandstone as the surface rock. Standing in many areas of the southern Plateau with nothing more than a rolling hill in the distance, you would have little idea you are in a mountainous region.

Because it rises a thousand feet above the surrounding valley, the Cumberland Plateau was an obstacle to westward migration in the country's early years. Before roads were built, the only passageways were through a few gaps in the ridge, especially Cumberland Gap, or along the Tennessee River where it cuts through the Plateau to form the Grand Canyon of the Tennessee near Chattanooga.

Geography and Geology

As the force that formed the Cumberland Plateau moved from southeast to northwest it bent the hard capstone rock, producing such tension that sometimes the rock snapped, relieving the stress. Part of the Plateau was thus shoved northwest. Like tearing a piece of paper and letting the bottom half overlap the top, older rock that was deep in the earth in the southeast was laid over younger rock that was on the surface in the northwest. Geologists call this the "Cumberland Plateau Overthrust fault"—a fault being a place where rock has broken and moved.

To the southwest on the Cumberland Plateau, one of the subsidiary breaks of the overthrust system formed a great arch, part of which remains as the Crab Orchard Mountains in Tennessee, which rise a thousand feet above the plateau surface. Southwest of these mountains the rock was so broken that erosion was able to wear away the mountain ridge and then dip out a long, straight depression following the line of the arch, creating the 70-mile-long Sequatchie Valley which divides the southern part of the Plateau. The name "Sequatchie" was taken from the name of a Cherokee chief, Sequachee. The valley extends across the Tennessee border into Alabama for about another 70 miles, but there it is called "Browns Valley" or sometimes simply the "Tennessee River

The Big South Fork Canyon

Valley" because the Tennessee River flows southwest down the valley after cutting through the eastern portion of the Plateau at Chattanooga.

The northwest side of Sequatchie Valley is referred to as the "Cumberland Plateau" while the southeast side is called "Walden Ridge," named for Elijah (or Elisha) Walden, an early explorer of the region. Nearly the entire length of the eastern escarpment of the Plateau in Tennessee and into Kentucky is now called "Walden Ridge." Farther north, it is known as the "Allegheny Front." At many places along its length, such as at Sequatchie Valley, Walden Ridge is separate from the plateau, sometimes appearing as a low mountain range in front of the Plateau proper.

Throughout what is now the Cumberland Plateau, thick vegetation buried in the ancient past was transformed into peat, then lignite, and finally coal, under the heavy layers of sediment deposited by the rivers that descended to the sea. The sediment layers themselves contained coal that had formed long ago and were washed down from the highlands. Later, when men discovered that the coal found beneath the surface layers of the Plateau could be burned, they ripped open the earth to get to the black rock, leaving behind gaping wounds and girdled mountaintops. The mountains still bear the scars of strip mines. Where the earth is left exposed, it releases acids as rainwater percolates through the rocks and flows across the land, killing vegetation and the fish and other aquatic species that inhabit nearby streams. In places, what had been considered a boon has became a blight on the land.

Such mining scars can be repaired, and the work is proceeding in many places on the Plateau. Indian Mountain State Park is a demonstration reclamation area at Jellico, Tennessee, which lies near the Kentucky border within Elk Valley (like the larger Sequatchie Valley, a long, straight valley in the Plateau running northeast to southwest). Once a strip mine, with mines still obvious on the surrounding mountains, the land that makes up the Park has been covered and reseeded and now encircles a small pond.

The most important coal mining region on the Plateau is the Cumberland Mountains, which spread across the northern part of Tennessee on the Plateau's eastern edge and into Kentucky. During World War II, a

radar station was placed atop Cross Mountain in the Tennessee Cumberlands to detect any German planes that might have penetrated that far
and posed a threat to the federal installations in Oak Ridge, Tennessee.
Scientists in Oak Ridge were working to enrich uranium to fuel the first
atomic bombs. The radar station never saw an enemy plane but
remained in operation until 1957. At the top of the mountain, which is
situated near Briceville, Tennessee, are the ghostly remains—foundations, a few walls, and the platform for a tram that brought supplies to
the mountain retreat.

In the region of the Cumberland Mountains near Lake City,
Tennessee, is an offset in the Plateau. The eastern escarpment turns
northwest along this offset as far as Caryville, where it resumes its usual
direction, running northeast. The offset resulted from the separation
from the Plateau of a block 125 miles by 15 miles that was created
during the plateau-building episode by faults on all four sides. The force
from the southeast pushed this massive block to the northwest, creating
the offset of about 10 miles. This "Cumberland Block," or "Pine
Mountain Block," extends for most of its length along the Kentucky-
Virginia border.

To the east of the Cumberland Mountains and separate from the Plateau stand Lone Mountain and Powell Mountain. Because they are capped
with the same sandstone as the Plateau, these mountains provide evidence
that the Cumberland Plateau once covered a much broader expanse. Erosion has not only lowered the tableland but has narrowed it, leaving behind
outliers. These mountains to the east, and Lookout Mountain, Raccoon
Mountain, and Sand Mountain running south into northern Alabama, and
numerous pieces off the more ragged western escarpment are all capped
with Pennsylvanian sandstone.

For much of the remainder of the Plateau, the hard cap rock is still
intact, in places reaching a thickness of hundreds of feet. The various
depositional layers of this Pennsylvanian sandstone are called "Crossville,"
"Lee," "Rockcastle," "Newton," "Sewanee," and "Warren Point." These
are the cliff-forming sandstones that cap the top of the plateau. To the
north, the cliffs are most often the Rockcastle conglomerate, a fine- to

coarse-grained sandstone; while to the south, the cliffs are most often the Sewanee conglomerate, a medium- to coarse-grained sandstone. The various sandstone layers are often separated by layers of shale that sometimes contain coal seams.

Below these Pennsylvanian layers are rocks of the Mississippian age. These are layers of shale, limestone, and calcareous sandstone. The Mississippian rocks are exposed only in the deepest canyons of the Plateau, where the streams have eroded below the Pennsylvanian strata.

Because the Pennsylvanian sandstone layers that form the top of the Plateau resist erosion, streams and rivers cut deep, steep-walled canyons as they run their courses. From the edge of a canyon, it is a 100- or 200-foot drop to the forest and rubble zone that slopes steeply to the edge of the stream in the center of the gorge.

The main drainage of the Plateau consists of the Tennessee, Cumberland, Kentucky, Licking, and Big Sandy Rivers. In Tennessee, the Obed and Emory Rivers and the Sequatchie flow east and south to join the Tennessee River. The Big South Fork, Calfkiller, Caney Fork, and Collins Rivers flow north and west to the Cumberland River. In Kentucky, the Rockcastle and Laurel Rivers flow south and west into the Cumberland River, while the Red River flows west toward the Kentucky River, and numerous creeks converge on the Licking River. The Russell Fork, Levisa Fork, and Tug Fork move north to form the Big Sandy River. Each of the main rivers eventually flows into the Ohio River and finally the Mississippi.

Where the water flows over breaks in the sandstone, it quickly scoops out softer layers beneath and waterfalls are formed. But because of the hard capstone, the lip of a waterfall resists breaking off, and so erosion usually continues downward and behind the waterfall until an amphitheater is formed. This is why you can walk behind many waterfalls on the Plateau. Eventually the lip is no longer supported by the underlying layers and it breaks off, the waterfall retreating upstream.

Groundwater dissolves softer limestone layers beneath the sandstone, creating a network of caves in the Plateau. Because surface erosion with its heavier load proceeds faster, the surrounding landscape has

Bridal Veil Falls on the University of the South Domain. Photograph by Sondra Jamieson

been lowered and the openings to these caves now usually appear as gaping holes in rock walls. Within are large rooms, created by breakdown of the cave ceilings. Water seeps from the ceilings and evaporates, leaving deposits of calcium carbonate, the beginnings of stalactites. If the water drips to the floor, a temporary pool of water creates a rimstone dam. Eventually a stalagmite forms. Left undisturbed for thousands of years these stalactites and stalagmites grow together, forming columns of calcium carbonate.

Most of these caves were partially or completely filled with silt at one time. Drying and compaction of the silt or erosion by a stream flowing through the cave has once more opened many of these passages. What remains of the cave fill often contains nitrates, which have been mined from numerous caves on the Plateau for use in gunpowder.

In exposed hillsides and ridges of the Plateau, erosion sweeps away soft layers underlying hard sandstone, creating the numerous stone arches and natural bridges. The process might be by headward erosion, in which an active gully erodes up a slope, sometimes on both sides of a ridge. At first a rockhouse is formed, a depression under the hard sandstone along the ridgetop. Eventually erosion breaks through to form a "lighthouse," a hole in the cliff. By slow erosion and weathering, a symmetrical tension dome develops, allowing the arch to become a graceful arc of stone.

Less symmetrical arches form by gravity, in which a rock falls from a cliff and spans a depression when it lands, or underlying layers creep downhill or simply sag to open an arch under the more resistant upper layers. Many large bridges form by the widening of a joint, in which headward erosion or some other process forms a cavity and then a joint cutting across the cavity is widened by erosion to separate the top of the opening from the ridge, forming an arch. Also, natural tunnels are created by water eroding through less-resistant rock layers or by caves being exposed at both ends by the downward eroding of surrounding lands.

All of these geologic processes have contributed to forming a dramatic landscape on the Cumberland Plateau. It is a land of steep-walled canyons, sandstone arches, deep caves, and numerous waterfalls.

South Arch of the Twin Arches at the Big South Fork

The Biota

The forest of the Cumberland Plateau is composed of communities that comprise two distinct woodlands—the Uplands Forest and the Ravine Forest. While the vegetation of the Plateau is sorted into these two types of forest by variation in microclimatic and soil conditions, nearly all of the Plateau forests have been altered by logging, fire, coal mining, resort development, and agriculture. Only a few virgin stands remain in inaccessible canyons.

The Uplands Forest inhabits the surface area of the Plateau. The segregation of tree associations that make up this forest results from differences in slope exposure, soil composition, and availability of moisture. As a result, segregation of dominant species is more common in the Cumberland Mountains to the north, while the forest is more uniform on the southern part of the Plateau, which is relatively flat.

In the mountainous region of the Plateau, pine and oak grow on the shallow, sandy soils along dry, rocky summits and in eroded draws. Chestnut oak, white oak, and shortleaf pine dominate the mountain slopes, with occasional sugar maple, basswood, buckeye, tulip poplar, and beech.

The tableland region of the Plateau surface is covered with a dominant mixed-oak forest. Occasional swales, streams, and marshy areas have tulip poplar, red maple, black gum, sourwood, and white oak. Old fields have come back in oak and Virginia pine.

The Ravine Forest of the Plateau's canyons is affected like the Upland Forest by exposure, soil condition, and moisture level. The canopy layer of the Ravine Forest consists of beech, sugar maple, red oak, tulip poplar, white oak, chestnut oak, basswood, sweet buckeye, white pine, hemlock, and formerly, chestnut, which once made up 15 percent of the forest canopy but has now been depleted by the chestnut blight. Also abundant are yellow birch, black cherry, white ash, red maple, and umbrella and cucumber magnolias. Less frequently found are sour gum, black walnut, and hickory. Along the streams grow willow, sycamore, sweet gum, and river birch. Where lumbering and erosion have scarred the land, oak-hickory forests predominate, and Virginia pine grows on slopes where white oak and beech once flourished.

The understory of the Ravine Forest includes dogwood, hop horn-beam, sourwood, striped maple, holly, redbud, ironwood, serviceberry, and sassafras. Rhododendron, mountain-laurel, and occasional wild aza-lea are a few of the shrubs. Mayapple and a variety of ferns gather on the forest floor, and in spring the ground is scattered with showy flowers, including trillium, violets, delphinium, phacelia, phlox, blood-root, spring beauty, fire pink, wild iris, anemone, and in late summer and fall, asters and goldenrods.

Not all plant species occur in any one area. Distinct communities have developed in which only some of these species are present. The rapid change in elevation in the canyons, with accompanying changes in soil, nutrients, exposure, and moisture, create the different habitats that support the different communities. From any perch on the edge of a river canyon, thickets of pine, chestnut oak, sourwood, and various shrubs begin the progression of forest communities that make up the Ravine Forest as the canyon walls descend and reach the river's edge.

But these different communities are not just associations of trees and plants; they are also habitats for animals. White-tailed deer patrol the mixed pine forest on the rim of the canyon. The pine warbler and red-breasted nuthatch forage for conifer seeds and insects. Hawks and crows nest in the trees. In the mixed pine-oak habitats, hairy woodpeck-ers, common flickers, and pileated woodpeckers search the trees for insects. The pine seeds are also food for the red crossbill, evening grosbeak, bob-white, turkey, gray squirrel, eastern chipmunk, and white-footed mouse. The eastern cottontail frequents areas where foliage grows near the ground.

The massive walls of the canyon stand bare except for a few irregu-larities in the rock surface that provide footholds for alum root, a few ferns, and small wind-swept pines. Vultures, eastern phoebes, and swal-lows nest in precarious crevices in the cliff face, and an occasional bat clings to the underside of a rock overhang. The red-tailed hawk surveys the canyon from a perch, and the timber rattlesnake and northern cop-perhead bask in the bright sun.

From the base of the rock walls, the south-facing slopes descend, clothed in mixed-oak communities where turkey, gray squirrel, and opossum are attracted to the mast and thick undergrowth. The wood thrush, hooded warbler, and downy woodpecker frequent the understory, while the red-eyed vireo, scarlet tanager, and tufted titmouse feed in the canopy.

In the heads of canyons and shaded coves of the north-facing slopes, where understory and groundcover are inhibited, hemlock and rhododendron predominate in a quiet forest that sees only an occasional passing deer, bobcat, or fox. Pine and blackpoll warblers and the golden-crowned kinglet search for seeds and insects in the canopy.

On the lower slopes, where the soil is deep, moist, and nutrient rich, several species congregate to create the classical mixed mesophytic forest, a complex association in which several hardwood species are dominant. This community of beech, tulip poplar, sugar maple, basswood, ash, and buckeye is a refuge for gray fox, skunk, and raccoon. The barred owl and red-shouldered hawk search for the smoky shrew, eastern mole, eastern woodrat, white-footed mouse, and eastern chipmunk.

Along the floor of the canyon persists an alluvial forest of red maple, sycamore, river birch, and American holly with wild oats and dense stands of cane; beaver and muskrat, maybe even mink and otter, live in harmony with the river. The Louisiana water thrush, spotted sandpiper, and American woodcock explore the wet sand.

A sand, gravel, and rubble zone including a few shrubs edges the river. The strip is inhabited by the bullfrog, southern leopard frog, pickerel frog, water snake, and midland painted turtle. Deer and other large species come to the stream for water as wood ducks paddle by.

The river breathes with its rapids and riffles, giving life to the riverweed growing on the flooded rocks with diatoms and algae in association. These support the zooplankton and aquatic insects that are food for the bluebreast darter, rainbow trout, longear sunfish, and smallmouth bass. Belted kingfishers skim the river's surface, and green herons lunge for fish and amphibians. Rough-winged swallows, eastern phoebes, and bats feed on the congregating insects.

Recent floods leave debris hanging in the limbs of shrubs and trees along the river's edge. Small ponds left by the retreating floodwaters and replenished by recent rains are filled with life in spring. Salamanders and turtles grope through the cattails, rushes, and occasional peat moss of the larger water holes. Swallows and eastern bluebirds flit across the ponds as they feed on the numerous insects attracted to the water. Puddles serve as nurseries for amphibians that hurry toward maturity before the warming summer sun dries the pools to dusty bowls on the forest floor.

From the overlook of the canyon the different communities meld into one, and what appears is not distinct boundaries but a wholeness and a balance that can only be achieved by undisturbed nature.

Early Human Habitation

For thousands of years the remoteness of the Plateau protected the wildlife. Once elk, deer, and bison grazed placidly in grassland openings between the hills covered with ancient forests and the canyons with their streams and waterfalls.

A succession of prehistoric peoples that lived in what is now Kentucky, Tennessee, and Alabama—from the Paleo-Indians, through the Archaic and Woodland cultures, to the Mississippian tradition—considered the Plateau a prime hunting ground. The Shawnees in Kentucky and Ohio later called the Plateau "Ouasioto," or perhaps "Wasioto," meaning "mountains where the deer are plentiful."

The early inhabitants were originally big game hunters. By about 1000 B.C., they had developed a more refined existence, living along the rivers when the walleye were running and shellfish could be found, and in season, living in the numerous rock shelters in the forest where they could easily gather hickory nuts and chestnuts to supplement the game they killed. By 900 A.D., they were growing some of their own food and during the next hundred years became experienced horticulturists, with corn and squash a primary part of their diet. This development led the people to move to the broad, fertile river valleys away from the plateau country which was not very good for growing crops.

By the time white men encountered the American Indians of the southeastern United States, the Indians had coalesced into the historic tribes, including the Cherokees, Creeks, Chickasaws, Choctaws, and Shawnees. The Cherokees and Shawnees dominated the Plateau region. The Cherokee towns were concentrated in what is now East Tennessee, the Carolinas, and Georgia; and the Shawnees lived mostly north of the Ohio River, after having been driven from modern-day Tennessee by the Cherokees with the help of the Chickasaws. However, both groups considered the Plateau a part of their hunting grounds. Hunting parties from both sides made frequent forays into the area along with occasional groups of the minor tribes. Fighting probably ensued whenever one group encountered another. The hunters intermittently used rock shelters as camps.

Pressure from encroaching Europeans, who had settled in the east and filtered west, eventually caused the Cherokees and the Shawnees to depend more heavily on the Plateau as a source of game. But it was inevitable that even in the interior of the Plateau the native Indians would eventually have to compete with whites, beginning about the time of the longhunters of the Daniel Boone era.

Early Immigration

Some of the first white people to enter what is now eastern Tennessee and Kentucky were plantation workers who had left the drudgery of the fields in search of freedom and a new life. Many had been sent to the New World as indentured servants; some had been debtors, criminals, or orphans with nowhere else to go.

Many others were immigrants of Scotch-Irish and German ancestry who came with few possessions, having sold their small farms and moved west in the prospect of new lands and new fortunes. Many of the settlers were veterans of the French and Indian Wars and the Revolutionary War who received land grants in payment for their service first to Great Britain and then to the newly formed United States. The Military Reservation Act of 1782 granted millions of acres of Cumberland lands for Revolutionary War veterans.

The immigrants came alone or with families and were sometimes already settled in when adventurers entered what they thought was un-explored territory. At first the new settlers lived in the rock shelters the Indians had frequented, closing off the openings with leaning poles. They soon built pole cabins with mud floors. Over the next few decades, typically, floors were covered by split-log flooring; walls became thick, hewn logs; lofts or second stories were placed atop the original struc-tures; and stone chimneys were added. The settlers cleared small plots of land for growing crops and raising livestock while continuing to add wild game to their diet, as the native peoples had done. Some of the men who came alone took Indian women as wives, and today many families claim a distant ancestor of Native-American descent.

In the beginning, few people settled on the Plateau because they were attracted to the more fertile areas farther to the west. They floated down the Tennessee River to get to the Cumberland River Valley in Middle Tennessee or traveled through Cumberland Gap to reach the Bluegrass region of Kentucky. These early immigrants referred to the

The Litton Farm at the Big South Fork

Plateau that separated their new settlements in the west from the older settlements in the east as "the Wilderness."

In later years, new settlers passed over old Indian trails that crossed the tableland. The most important of these was an old Cherokee trail, called "Tallonteeskee" after a Cherokee chief; the trail climbed the eastern escarpment near the present-day town of Rockwood, Tennessee, and passed near Crab Orchard, Crossville, and Monterey before it descended the western side of the Plateau.

Although most of the Plateau in Tennessee belonged to the Cherokees, as affirmed by the Treaty of Hopewell in 1785, the migrating settlers presumed to have the right to travel through the area and to hunt wherever they wished. In 1787, the North Carolina legislature called for a lottery to finance a road across the Plateau, linking the settlements in the Washington District in the east with those in the Mero District to the west. (At that time, what is now Tennessee constituted the western lands of North Carolina.) Peter Avery was chosen to head the group of men who blazed the road across the Plateau. They followed essentially the old Tallonteeskee Trail, widening it to 10 feet.

But the Cherokees objected to this new road, which illegally crossed their lands. Therefore, in the first attempt to preserve the Plateau from further abuse and in a spirit of accommodation, the Cherokees asked for a federal road to which travelers would be restricted. This was agreed to in the Treaty of Holston in 1791, which also gave much upper East Tennessee land to the whites. By now Tennessee had become the Territory of the United States South of the River Ohio, after North Carolina had turned over its western lands to the U.S. government in 1790. Work on the road was not begun until 1799; meanwhile, in 1796, the territory became the state of Tennessee.

When it was completed in 1802, the Walton Road, named for one of the commissioners overseeing the construction, followed roughly the Avery Trace across the Plateau and was the first toll road in the state. Sections of US70 and I-40 and the rail lines of the Southern Railway now coincide with the route. To the chagrin of the Cherokees, small settlements began to appear along the new road.

Increasing pressure from those who had settled in Tennessee and who wanted all the lands still belonging to the Cherokees opened for settlement led to several treaties. The Cherokee Nation was forced into these agreements by persuasion that most of the time included bribery to get a Cherokee leader's signature on a piece of paper.

In the Treaty of Tellico in 1798, the Cherokee hunting grounds in upper East Tennessee were restricted to the Plateau. Then, in the Tellico Treaty of 1805, Dearborn's Treaty of 1806, the Jackson and McMinn Treaty of 1817, and Calhoun's Treaty of 1819, the Cherokees gave up their people's claim to the highland.

After these treaties, the only land retained by the Cherokees was that on which permanent settlements had always existed in lower East Tennessee, Georgia, and a few holdings in North Carolina and Alabama. This last Cherokee land was signed over by a few Cherokees in the Treaty of New Echota in 1835, which was approved by the U.S. Congress in 1836. This treaty was rejected by a Cherokee National Council, and the U.S. Supreme Court had earlier recognized the Cherokees' rights to the land in the 1832 case, *Worcester v. Georgia*. Nonetheless, the federal government, with the encouragement of President Andrew Jackson, moved against the Cherokees. Except for those few who escaped and several families that had relinquished connection with the Cherokee Nation and had become citizens of North Carolina, the Cherokees still remaining on their lands in 1838 were forcibly rounded up and moved to Oklahoma. Some traveled by boat, but most moved on foot along the Trail of Tears, crossing the southern part of the Cumberland Plateau. Approximately 4,000 Cherokees, nearly a fourth of those removed, died along the way.

The Shawnees and other northern tribes also lost their claim to the Plateau by a similar intrusion of the whites. In 1768, the Iroquois gave up any claim they had to the Kentucky region in the Treaty of Fort Stanwix, which totally ignored the Shawnees' claim to the region. The Shawnees, along with several minor tribes, continued to raid settlements and attack whites who invaded the region these Indians still considered their own. Armies were raised and sent against the Indians, who were defeated at the Battle of Point Pleasant in 1774. In the Treaty of Camp Charlotte, negotiated after the battle, and the Treaty of Pittsburgh, the following year, the Shawnees and the minor tribes were forced to agree to stay north of the Ohio River.

During the ensuing American Revolution, British agents encouraged the disgruntled Indians to continue their attacks on settlements in the Kentucky region. Even after the war, the hostilities continued until in 1794 the Indians were defeated at the Battle of Fallen Timbers in Ohio by troops under "Mad" Anthony Wayne, a Revolutionary War general who had earned his nickname by reckless exploits.

The Plateau Today

In the years since the taking of the Plateau, villages and towns arose, many in response to the discovery of coal and subsequent mining in the region. Coal underlies about 4,400 of the Plateau's 5,400 square miles in Tennessee and is ubiquitous in eastern Kentucky. Since 1973, Kentucky has led the nation in coal production.

Archaeological evidence indicates that during the period from about 1812–65 much saltpeter mining occurred on the Plateau. An ingredient in gunpowder, the saltpeter was a precious commodity during the War of 1812 and the Civil War.

The economic growth of the Cumberland Plateau stagnated for a time during the Civil War; Cumberland Gap to the north and Lookout Mountain near Chattanooga to the south had strategic significance and experienced major engagements. The rest of the Plateau saw minor skirmishes. After the war, the people renewed their efforts to establish their highland homes.

Lumber was an early attraction, and with the arrival of the railroads, most of the Plateau forests were exploited. Timber is still an important resource, with 75 percent of the land area still forested, although now in second-growth timber. To increase lumber production, large portions of Upland Forest are being converted to pine monocultures.

Stone used in building also became important to the Plateau economy. In later years oil and gas were discovered.

Today, small farms can be found over the entire range of the Plateau; the sandy soil is said to be good for Irish potatoes, livestock, vegetables, and fruit trees. However, until the adoption of modern agricultural methods that used fertilizer, crop farming was only profitable in Sequatchie Valley and the small coves where the soil is more fertile.

Due to its remote and rugged nature and the initial reluctance for immigrants to settle on the Plateau, the tableland remains sparsely peopled; the population is less than a third of the average for this southeast region as a whole. Thus, today the explorer can still find many uninhabited forests and river canyons—a biological and geological prize that many are working to preserve and protect.

This effort to save what remains of the Cumberland Plateau should include the designation of the region as a Zone of Cooperation for the establishment of an International Biosphere Reserve under the UNESCO Man and the Biosphere Program. A Cumberland Plateau Biosphere Reserve could include such areas as Daniel Boone National Forest and Lilley Cornett Woods in Kentucky, and in Tennessee, the Big South Fork National River and Recreation Area, Obed River system, and Savage Gulf. Biosphere reserve designation would allow for cooperative management and environmental education programs to help ensure that such areas on the Cumberland Plateau will remain for the benefit and enjoyment of all.

References

Barr, Thomas C., Jr. *Caves of Tennessee.* Nashville: Tennessee Dept. of Conservation and Commerce, 1961.

Braun, E. Lucy. *Deciduous Forests of Eastern North America.* Philadelphia: Blakiston, 1950.

Bullard, Helen, and Joseph Marshall Krechniak. *Cumberland County's First Hundred Years.* Crossville, TN: Centennial Committee, 1956.

Caplenor, Donald. "The Vegetation of the Gorges of the Fall Creek Falls State Park in Tennessee." *Journal of the Tennessee Academy of Science* 40, no. 1 (Jan. 1965): 27–39.

Caudill, Harry M. *Night Comes to the Cumberlands.* Boston: Atlantic Monthly Press, 1962.

Corgan, James X., and John T. Parks. *Natural Bridges of Tennessee.* Bulletin 80. Nashville: Tennessee Division of Geology, 1979.

Corlew, Robert E. *Tennessee, A Short History.* 1969. 2d ed. Knoxville: Univ. of Tennessee Press, 1990.

DesJean, Tom, National Park Service archaeologist, Big South Fork National River and Recreation Area. Interview with author. July 20, 1989.

Folmsbee, Stanley J., Robert E. Corlew, and Enoch L. Mitchell. *History of Tennessee.* New York: Lewis Historical Pub. Co., 1960.

Fullerton, Ralph O., et al. *Tennessee, Geographical Patterns and Regions.* Dubuque, IA: Kendall/Hunt Pub. Co., 1977.

Hinkle, C. Ross. "Forest Communities of the Cumberland Plateau of Tennessee." *Journal of the Tennessee Academy of Science* 64, no. 3 (July 1989): 123–29.

———. "The Relationship of Forest Communities and Selected Species to Edaphic and Topographic Factors on the Cumberland Plateau of Tennessee." Ph.D. thesis, Univ. of Tennessee, Knoxville, 1978.

Jones, Ronald L. "A Floristic Study of Wetlands on the Cumberland Plateau of Tennessee." *Journal of the Tennessee Academy of Science* 64, no. 3 (July 1989): 131–34.

Kincaid, Robert L. *The Wilderness Road.* Middlesboro, TN: Mrs. Robert L. Kincaid, 1973.

King, Duane H., ed. *The Cherokee Nation: A Troubled History.* Knoxville: Univ. of Tennessee Press, 1979.

Law, Harry L. *Brief Geography of Tennessee.* Clarksville, TN: Queen City Book Co., 1949.

Lewis, Thomas M., and Madeline Kneberg. *Tribes that Slumber.* Knoxville: Univ. of Tennessee Press, 1958.

Luther, Edward T. *Our Restless Earth: The Geologic Regions of Tennessee.* Knoxville: Univ. of Tennessee Press, 1977.

McFarlan, Arthur C. *Geology of Kentucky.* Lexington: Univ. of Kentucky, 1943.

Miller, Robert A. *The Geologic History of Tennessee.* Bulletin 74. Nashville: Tennessee Division of Geology, 1974.

Minkin, Steven Clinton. "Pennsylvanian Deltaic Sediments of the Northern Cumberland Plateau, Tennessee." M.S. thesis, Univ. of Tennessee, Knoxville. 1977.

Mitchell, John G. "The Mountains, the Miners, and Mister Caudill." *Audubon,* Nov. 1988, 78–102.

Ramsey, J. G. M. *The Annals of Tennessee to the End of the Eighteenth Century.* Charleston, SC: Walker & Jones, 1853. Rpt. Knoxville: East Tennessee Historical Society, 1967.

Raulston, J. Leonard, and James W. Livingood. *Sequatchie: A Story of the Southern Cumberlands.* Knoxville: Univ. of Tennessee Press, 1974.

Rice, Otis K. *Frontier Kentucky.* Lexington: Univ. Press of Kentucky, 1975.

Roberts, Thomas Adolph. "Transitional Lower Delta Plain—Upper Delta Plain Sediments in

Middle Pennsylvanian Coal-Bearing Strata, Eastern Wartburg Basin, Tennessee." M.S. thesis, Univ. of Tennessee, Knoxville, 1978.

Safford, James M. *Geology of Tennessee.* Nashville: State of Tennessee, 1869.

Schmalzer, Paul A. "Classification and Analysis of Forest Communities in Several Coves of the Cumberland Plateau in Tennessee." M.S. thesis, Univ. of Tennessee, Knoxville, 1978.

————. "Vegetation of the Obed River Gorge System, Cumberland Plateau, Tennessee." *Castanea* 53, no. 1 (Mar. 1988): 1–32.

Seeber, R. Clifford. "A History of Anderson County, Tennessee." M.S. thesis, Univ. of Tennessee, Knoxville, 1928.

Shekarchi, Ebraham. "Heavy Accessory Minerals of the Pennsylvanian Formation of Walden Ridge, Tennessee." M.S. thesis, Univ. of Tennessee, Knoxville, 1951.

Sherman, Michael D. "Community Composition, Species Diversity, Forest Structure and Dynamics as Affected by Soil and Site Factors and Selective Logging in Savage Gulf, Tennessee." M.S. thesis, Univ. of Tennessee, Knoxville, 1978.

Smith, Lawrence Roy. "The Swamp and Mesic Forests of the Cumberland Plateau in Tennessee." M.S. thesis, Univ. of Tennessee, Knoxville, 1977.

Stanley, Steven M. *Earth and Life Through Time.* New York: W. H. Freeman and Co., 1986.

Stearns, Richard G. *The Cumberland Plateau Overthrust and Geology of the Crab Orchard Mountains Area, Tennessee.* Bulletin 60. Nashville: Tennessee Division of Geology, 1954.

U.S. Army Corps of Engineers. *Big South Fork Final Environmental Impact Statement.* Nashville, 1976.

Wade, Gary Leon. "Dry Phase Vegetation of the Uplands of the Cumberland Plateau of Tennessee." M.S. thesis, Univ. of Tennessee, Knoxville, 1977.

White, Fullington John. "Depositional Environments of Pennsylvanian Redoak Mountain Formation, Northern Cumberland Plateau, Tennessee." M.S. thesis, Univ. of Tennessee, Knoxville, 1975.

Williams, Samuel Cole. *Early Travels in the Tennessee Country.* Johnson City, TN: Watauga Press, 1928.

Wilson, Charles W., Jr., et al. *Pennsylvanian Geology of the Cumberland Plateau.* Nashville: Tennessee State Dept. of Conservation, 1956.

Chapter 2

Cumberland Gap

In 1674, Gabriel Arthur trudged along a well-worn path that headed southwest across what would later be the state of Kentucky. The Shawnees had said the path would lead him back to the lands of the Cherokees on the other side of the mountains that paralleled the trail. But as the rolling peaks loomed in the distance, he wondered how he was to cross the mountain range that seemed to run to the horizon without a break.

Even as he grumbled about his uncertain route, Arthur felt relieved that he had been able to convince the Shawnees to let him go. He had told the Indians that the English settlers on the eastern coast of the continent would be very eager to trade guns and axes for the Shawnees' beaver skins if only they would let him return to set up the trade. Thinking it was worth a try, the Shawnees gave Arthur some food and set him on a path heading south to the Cherokee lands, from where Arthur could make his way east to his own people.

A year before, Arthur had accompanied James Needham as assistant in an exploration of the unknown lands that would eventually become the states of Tennessee and North Carolina. Needham and Arthur had been sent out by Abraham Wood, who ran Fort Henry on the Virginia frontier, to help set up a trade with the Indians. Meeting a group of friendly natives, Needham and Arthur were escorted across the Blue Ridge Mountains to the lands of the "Tomahitans," thought to be the Cherokees along the Little Tennessee River.

Eager to make a report, Needham left Arthur with the Cherokees to make his way back east. Before Needham could return, he was shot and killed in an argument with his guide.

Cumberland Gap

Arthur remained with the Cherokees during the ensuing year, accompanying them on several war expeditions. After traveling north into the Virginia country, the Cherokees with Arthur tagging along turned west into Kentucky to do battle with their traditional enemies, the Shawnees along the Ohio River. The fighting did not go quite as intended, and Arthur was taken prisoner and held until the time his captors set him on the southward path to pursue a lucrative trade with the white men.

To Arthur's surprise, the well-worn trail he was traveling eventually turned southeast through foothills and arrived at a large break in the mountain chain. Clambering to the top, he found the Shawnees had been correct; this was the way east. From the high mountain gap, Arthur was able to make his way south to the Cherokees and from there returned to the English settlements in Virginia.

The Shawnees had placed Arthur on the great Warriors' Path that connected the Shawnee and Cherokee civilizations. The path was originally a game trail, worn by buffalo and deer. By the time Arthur walked the trail, it had been used for centuries by the northern and southern Indians as a way to and from the hunting lands in Kentucky and as a trade route and warpath between the two peoples. It was called by the Indians, "Athawominee," or "Path of the Armed Ones."

Gabriel Arthur thus became the first white man known to travel this route, which is the easiest passage through the Cumberland Mountains on the eastern edge of the Cumberland Plateau into the interior of the Plateau and beyond. The Warriors' Path Arthur traveled eventually became the western half of the route for settlers traveling from the east. The eastern half was originally the Great Warpath that connected the Iroquois Confederacy in the north with the Cherokees in the south. What became known as "the Wilderness Road" followed these two trails—southwest on the Great Warpath through Virginia, then turning northwest onto the Warriors' Path through this gap in the Cumberland Mountains into Kentucky.

Cave Gap

On foot and by horse, wagon, and car, many people have since retraced Gabriel Arthur's route through the gap, passing in the shadow of the Pinnacle, the great stone wall that forms the eastern side of the pass. But Arthur was illiterate and so left no written account of his discovery. That opportunity was left to Thomas Walker, a physician and explorer, who with his small party was sent into the wilderness in 1750 by the Loyal Land Company to investigate lands suitable for settlement. He found the Warriors' Path that passed through the mountain gap, the same route traversed by Arthur 76 years before.

Walker named the pass through the mountains "Cave Gap," for the cave he described in his journal: "On the North side of the Gap is a large Spring, which falls very fast, and just above the Spring is a small Entrance to a large Cave, which the Spring runs through, and there is a constant Stream of Cool air issuing out."

Walker continued his explorations in Kentucky, renaming the Shawnee River the "Cumberland River" for the Duke of Cumberland. Later explorers—perhaps Walker himself on an expedition in 1760—attached the name "Cumberland" to the mountain plateau, and the pass through the mountains eventually became "Cumberland Gap."

Cudjo Caverns

The spring Thomas Walker noted as emerging from the mountainside at Cumberland Gap is the outlet for an underground river in the depths of the mountain under the Pinnacle. The river runs along the bottom level of a vast five-tiered cave system, the entrance to which Walker noted in his diary.

Once the mountains became known as the "Cumberlands," the cave was generally referred to as "Cumberland Gap Cave." For a brief time in the 1840s, it was known locally as the "John A. Murrell Cave," for the Tennessee outlaw who may have used the cave. During the boom era in the late 1800s the name was changed to "King Solomon's Cave," presumably because of the riches to be found in the natural resources of the area.

Finally, in 1935 the name "Cudjo's Cave" was borrowed from a Civil War novel of the same name written by J. T. Trowbridge and published in 1863. Although Trowbridge supposedly never visited Cumberland Gap, the description of the cave in his novel fit the Cumberland Gap Cave. In Trowbridge's story, an escaped East Tennessee slave, Cudjo, hid in the cave.

Wilderness Road

The first suggestion of a road through Cumberland Gap was made by Judge Richard Henderson. In 1775, having recently retired from the North Carolina bench, Henderson formed the Transylvania Land Company, which purchased from the Cherokees, for goods valued at the relatively piddling sum of 10,000 English pounds, all the land south of the Ohio River bounded by the Tennessee, Cumberland, and Kentucky Rivers—approximately 20 million acres. The transaction was, in fact, illegal since at the time only the British crown could purchase land from the Indians and, thus far, settlement had been restricted to the region east of the Appalachian Mountains. The Virginia Colony later refused to recognize Henderson's claim to the land, and so the new colony he envisioned with himself as proprietor never materialized. Thereafter, Henderson promoted settlement of the Cumberland River Valley in Middle Tennessee.

The land concession to Henderson was considered traitorous to some of the Cherokees; Chief Dragging Canoe is reported to have told Henderson, "You have bought a fair land, but will find its settlement dark and bloody." In 1777, a splinter group opposed to land deals was formed under the leadership of Dragging Canoe, who with his people withdrew to Chickamauga Creek east of Lookout Mountain near Chattanooga to continue to fight for their lands. The group became known as the "Chickamaugas." The British agent John McDonald had established his headquarters in the Lookout Mountain region, and so the Chickamaugas had located there so the British could supply them during the years of the American Revolution. When the British lost that war, the Spanish supplied the Chickamaugas for a time, with McDonald as their agent. After the Chickamauga villages were destroyed in 1779 by a force under Evan Shelby, and facing continuing attacks by whites at that location, the Chickamaugas moved southwest of present-day Chattanooga and founded the Five Lower Towns. The Chickamaugas remained the center of Cherokee resistance until 1794 when an unofficial force under Major James Ore attacked and destroyed the towns of Nickajack and Running Water on the Tennessee River; Dragging Canoe had died in 1792. At a peace conference in 1794 at the Tellico Blockhouse on the Little Tennessee River, in talks between the Cherokees and William Blount, Governor of the Southwest Territory, the Chickamaugas rejoined the Cherokee Nation.

In the meantime, Henderson proceeded with settling the Kentucky region, ignoring the objections of the Chickamaugas and any claim the Shawnees might have had. He hired Daniel Boone to cut a path to Kentucky. As a longhunter, Boone had passed through Cumberland Gap on earlier explorations. The early explorers of the American interior were called "longhunters" because they hunted for long periods of time, but they also had long guns and long knives and traveled long distances.

Boone led a group of 30 axmen who blazed the old Warriors' Path so settlers following could find the way. He then passed into Kentucky where he later erected a fort on the site that became Boonesborough. Once the way was open, both the poor and the rich streamed over the mountains, seeking lands to make a new start. But for years the trail was nothing more than a path for pack horses.

Kentucky became a state in 1792, and the new governor, Isaac Shelby, the son of Evan Shelby, argued that the trail from Virginia should be expanded to accommodate wagons. He succeeded in getting legislation that authorized construction. Boone wanted to build the road that he had blazed years before, but by then he was 62 years old and was passed over by Governor Shelby when men were chosen to build the road from Crab Orchard, Kentucky, to Cumberland Gap, partly following Boone's Trace. The road was completed in 1796 and for the first time was officially called "the Wilderness Road."

Civil War

Because the Wilderness Road was the main thoroughfare from northwest to southeast, it was of strategic importance during the Civil War. And whoever controlled Cumberland Gap controlled the road.

Although Tennessee joined the Confederacy during the war, a substantial portion of the population in East Tennessee remained loyal to the Union. In mountainous East Tennessee, few plantations existed; so there were relatively few slaves and little interest in fighting for planters in other states to have the right to own slaves. Virginia, to the north of Tennessee and east of the mountains, declared itself Confederate; and Kentucky, also to the north but west of the mountains, remained out of the Confederacy. Therefore, the route for Union armies to go to the relief of Union sympathizers in East Tennessee was south through Kentucky, primarily over the Wilderness Road and through Cumberland Gap. Of course, the Confederacy had no intention of letting the Union army into East Tennessee to rally the local populace; many Tennesseans had already fled over the mountains into Kentucky to join the Union army.

During the war, Cumberland Gap changed hands four times. Both the Confederate and Union armies placed cannons on the mountain ridges on either side of the gap when they had possession, and at one time a bridge spanned the gap to get guns and supplies to the other side. Each time one army realized it could not hold the gap any longer, it retreated, destroying what it could not carry so as not to leave anything of value for the other. Even today, mounds of earth where the troops dug in and large holes created by explosions used to destroy buildings and supplies when armies evacuated are scattered around the gap area.

For two decades following the war, the land was allowed to rest and rejuvenate.

Old Headquarters of the American Association, Ltd.

American Association, Ltd.

When Alexander Alan Arthur came to Cumberland Gap in 1886, he looked out across the Cumberland Mountains at what seemed to be unlimited natural resources—rolling mountains blanketed with timber, thick coal seams below the surface, and pockets of iron ore in a virtually uninhabited countryside. Here was a clean slate upon which to design a prosperous beginning.

This second Arthur had come to Cumberland Gap to explore the feasibility of building a railroad from Morristown, Tennessee, to haul out the coal buried in the Kentucky mountains. Convinced that the area had great potential, Arthur expanded his vision and sought financial backing to develop the area. He found support in young men of wealthy families in New York and Baltimore, and they organized into the "Gap Associates" to capitalize on the resources of the Cumberland Gap region.

Representing the group, Arthur traveled to London in search of more financial backing. Investors in England, including the British Steel Syndicate, became convinced of the potential of Arthur's dream, and they formed the "American Association, Ltd.," with Arthur in charge of turning their investments into fortunes.

The first task was a rail line connecting East Tennessee with the Kentucky coal fields. This meant a tunnel through the mountains. The town of Cumberland Gap, Tennessee, was built to house the workers who were to build the tunnel. After 18 months of digging from both ends, workmen broke through to complete the tunnel on August 8, 1889.

Middlesboro

Although the community of Cumberland Gap was the first of Arthur's developments, he envisioned a metropolis on the Kentucky side of the mountains that would be his base of operations. Money from the investors poured in to construct Middlesboro, Kentucky, named for Middlesbrough,

England, which had recently become a great commercial success. Arthur and his associates obviously hoped their Middlesboro would be as successful.

The site for Alexander Arthur's model city was a natural choice— Middlesboro rests in a bowl in the midst of the mountains. The Middlesboro Basin is thought to have been created by the impact of a meteorite millions of years ago.

Many people came to the region, seeking to make fortunes in Arthur's promising scheme. Some came from the English colony of Rugby, Tennessee. Founded in 1880 by English author Thomas Hughes to provide a start for Englishmen seeking a new life, the colony foundered from the beginning; some settlers left with the prospect of more success at Cumberland Gap.

Two fires in 1890 that wiped out parts of Middlesboro were the harbingers of the collapse that was to come. Investors in England began to wonder about returns on their investments; the money so far had been used for development and not in active production of coal, timber, and iron. There was even talk that the iron ore in the region was not of high quality.

Arthur was accused of mismanagement. Although an investigation absolved him of any wrongdoing, he was ousted from direction of the enterprise. But even with new management, investment from England stopped in 1891, and the depression of 1893 in the United States brought about a final collapse. The American Association, Ltd., was liquidated; its 80,000 acres sold for $15,000. Investment in the region had been around $20 million.

Arthur tried once more to realize his dream by founding the community of Arthur on the railroad line a few miles southwest of Cumberland Gap. But the community never grew beyond some farm homes and a few stores.

Middlesboro eventually became a successful community once the mines and the railroad were taken over by other private interests and began operating. After a time in New York, Arthur returned to live in Middlesboro, where he died in 1912; he is buried on a hill in the Middlesboro Cemetery north of the city center.

Lincoln Memorial University

To the south of Cumberland Gap on the other side of Poor Valley Ridge lies Lincoln Memorial University. The site was originally the location of another of Alexander Arthur's schemes. He convinced investors that a resort community would thrive there if they touted the health benefits of the local mountain water. In 1892, they constructed a 700-room "Four Seasons" hotel along with a sanatorium. The venture was a failure from the start. Three years after its construction, the hotel was torn down and sold as salvage.

The Reverend A. A. Myers wanted the land the hotel had stood on for an expansion of his Harrow School, which he had founded for the education of the local mountain children. Having no funds, he turned to retired Union Gen. Oliver O. Howard who happened to be traveling through the area. By coincidence, General Howard had had a conversation with President Lincoln during the war, in which Lincoln expressed concern for the people of East Tennessee and the mountains surrounding Cumberland Gap. Lincoln asked General Howard during their meeting to see what he could do to help the "mountain people who have been shut out of the world all these years."

The founding of the school was General Howard's opportunity to respond to the president's request. The general asked that the school be a memorial to President Lincoln, and thus it became "Lincoln Memorial University."

Enough funds were raised to purchase the hotel land before the sanatorium was also torn down; the building became the headquarters of the new college and was named "Grant-Lee Hall." Although the original building burned, the hall was rebuilt using the original stonework for the bottom half of the building, and today it is still in use. Alexander Arthur's home during the boom years was also located on what is now the grounds of LMU, but it also burned; the spot is marked by a stone tower that was on the Arthur property.

Cumberland Gap National Historical Park

When there was talk of some way to commemorate the historical significance of Cumberland Gap, one proposal was for a carving on the Pinnacle similar to that on Mount Rushmore. Another was for a 200-foot statue of Abraham Lincoln on the mountain ridge. Fortunately cooler heads prevailed, and Cumberland Gap National Historical Park was authorized in 1940. The land was purchased by the three states involved, and deeds were transferred to the Department of Interior in 1955.

The park is one of the largest historical parks in the country; second only to the C&O Canal National Historical Park that runs from Washington, D.C., to Cumberland, Maryland. Cumberland Gap National Historical Park contains over 20,000 acres on both sides of Cumberland Gap, but mostly along the ridgeline northeast of the gap which is the boundary between Kentucky and Virginia. The park is a memorial to the significance of the Wilderness Road, the battles fought during the Civil War, and the way of life of the mountain people, as represented by Hensley Settlement, a pioneer village, now a historic exhibit, that rests on the mountain ridge in the backcountry of the national park.

In 1903, Sherman Hensley with his wife and small son moved to the site that was to become Hensley Settlement. Other Hensleys soon joined the Sherman Hensley family, as did other families—especially the Gibbonses whom many of the Hensleys married.

No road led to the settlement, only a few trails; horse-drawn wooden sleds were used to get supplies and furniture up the mountain. Electricity never reached the village, even in later years. So the settlement had to be self-sustaining. Eventually there were two water-powered grist mills, a sorghum mill, a blacksmith and carpenter shop, whiskey stills, and a school. In addition to the houses and barns, the larger farms had chicken houses, hog houses, smokehouses, corncribs, springhouses, and sometimes sheep barns.

As the children married and settled their own farms, the community grew larger; at the peak there were perhaps 40 buildings and 140 people. Eventually, as the younger people began to look for jobs off the

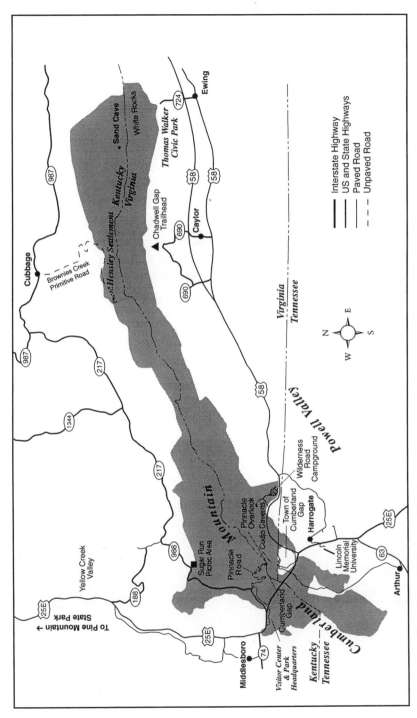

Cumberland Gap National Historical Park

Bert Hensley House

mountain and married people outside of the community, fewer were willing to live in the settlement.

When the national park was authorized, the families began selling their farms to the Cumberland Gap National Park Commission, funded by the states of Kentucky and Virginia, and left the mountain. After spending two years alone at the settlement, Sherman Hensley departed in 1951, the first to come and the last to leave. When he died in 1979, he was brought back to the mountain and buried in the Hensley Settlement cemetery.

The settlement remains nearly as isolated today as it has always been. The community consists of log cabins and barns made of oak and chestnut, now weathered a uniform gray. The old schoolhouse remains. Intricate wooden latches adorn gates and doors. Graceful fence lines flow over the rolling pastureland.

Tunnels

Although the Wilderness Road, now US25E, had proven to be the best route through the Cumberland Mountains, it was a difficult route, traversing Cumberland Gap over what in the 1800s was still a dirt road that often mired wagons and broke wheel axles.

Robert P. Baker, chief engineer for the commonwealth of Kentucky, sought to find a solution to the high road over the mountain pass. In 1836, he proposed to the state legislature an incredible scheme to divert water from the Cumberland River and Yellow Creek and, by a series of canals and locks and dams, to send that water through a tunnel to be drilled through the mountain at Cumberland Gap to join with the Powell River on the other side. This would allow for easy transportation through the mountains.

Baker's fantastic scheme was never approved, although many people sympathized with the need to have an alternative route through the mountains. It was not until Alexander Arthur's great enterprise that a tunnel was cut through the mountain for a railroad.

During the 1970s, as more and more cars and trucks poured over the mountain down treacherous US25E, reputed to be the most perilous stretch of road for its length in the United States, there was talk of a second tunnel to reroute the highway through the mountain. The National Park Service first proposed the tunnel in 1977; this move, it said, would allow the present route of US25E to be converted to a historic trail resembling the original Wilderness Road. Funding was finally approved by the U.S. Congress, and a test bore was begun in 1985 on the park grounds behind the visitor center in Kentucky. Construction of the 4,100-foot tunnel was completed by the Federal Highway Administration and opened to traffic in 1996. The Park Service expects to reclaim the gap by 2010 and return the Wilderness Road to the way it looked around 1800.

Directions and Services

US25E now passes through the Cumberland Gap tunnel, with the visitor center for **Cumberland Gap National Historical Park** on the Kentucky side of Cumberland Mountain. Motels and restaurants are available in Middlesboro, Kentucky, and on the Tennessee side along US25E. A paved bicycle path connects the visitor center with Middlesboro.

Within the national park, the 160-site Thomas B. Fugate Wilderness Road Area Campground is located on US58, which turns east into Virginia on the Tennessee side of Cumberland Mountain into Powell Valley. The campground is named after one of the early supporters of the park, who was later a U.S. representative from Virginia. Although the campsites are large, there are no hookups. Backcountry camping in the park is by permit only at designated campsites, including a backcountry cabin at Martins Fork that sleeps eight and rents for $10 a night. You'll find the Sugar Run Picnic Area on KY988 on the northwest boundary of the park.

In **Powell Valley** a number of large white clapboard and red brick houses were built over the years along the eastern half of the Wilderness Road and can still be seen along US58, which generally follows the route of the old road. At 5.0 miles along US58, you can turn right to find the ruins of an old mill on Indian Creek. The mill is on private property, but you can see it from the road. At 8.2 miles, turn north on VA690 to **Karlan**, an 1847 home, now included in a 200-acre Virginia state park with picnicking, camping, and trails on the grounds.

Taking in the view from the **Pinnacle** is the best way to get your bearings in the national park. From the park visitor center, take the 3.7-mile Pinnacle Road, a scenic highway that doubles back through the park and climbs the eastern side of the gap to a parking area at the top. At 2.4 miles along the way, you can stop at the Civil War site of **Fort McCook** on the right, where you can climb some stairs to a cannon emplacement; the fort was named for Robert L. McCook, a prominent Brigadier General in the Union army; McCook never served at the gap. While the Confederates held the Gap, they called this fortification "Fort Rains," after Col. J. E. Rains who at one time had the command of the Confederate garrison in the gap.

At the end of the Pinnacle Road, a short walk of 200 yards takes you to the Pinnacle Overlook. From the overlook, you can see directly below the town of **Cumberland Gap,** a quaint little village that is just southwest of US25E on the Tennessee side of the mountain. You can see the railroad tracks heading to the base of the mountain on the northwest corner of the community and into the tunnel through the mountain. If you park at the tracks at the edge of town, it's a short walk to the opening of the tunnel. Since the tunnel is about a mile long, the tracks disappear into darkness. The tunnel is still used by the railroad; so you should not enter the tunnel.

In the town, a preserved pre-Civil War **Iron Furnace** marks the southern end of the Wilderness Road Trail that descends from Cumberland Gap. The Iron Furnace is located at the northern side of the community just off Pennlyn Avenue across from an "Old Mill." Just beyond this turnoff to the furnace, keep straight to get to the railroad tracks and the railroad tunnel.

Iron production at this site began in the early 1820s; the furnace was rebuilt in 1870. During the nineteenth century, these iron furnaces were found throughout the frontier, producing the iron for rifle barrels, ax blades, and pots needed by the settlers and later for rails and car wheels needed by the railroads. The furnaces were located where iron ore, limestone to remove the impurities, and charcoal for heating the mixture could be had. By 1880, the operation had become uneconomical and was abandoned.

Gap Creek runs alongside the iron furnace. The creek emerges from below old US25E; its source is the spring Thomas Walker noted when he traversed the gap in 1750. The highway was built over the spring, which emerged from the Pinnacle wall. The spring should be uncovered during the gap restoration. At various times water-powered mills were located along the creek. Both the Union and Confederate troops during their occupations erected mills to grind corn and wheat.

From the Pinnacle Overlook you can see just beyond the town of Cumberland Gap to the route of US25E, where the highway emerges from the new tunnel through the mountain. To the far right, you can see **Middlesboro,** located west of US25E north of Cumberland Gap. KY74 takes you through the heart of the town. Some of the original buildings, churches, and large Victorian homes can still be found in the city, including the old headquarters of the American Association, Ltd., built in the early 1890s at 2215 Cumberland Avenue, which is also KY74, between 21st and 24th Streets. You can get additional information on the city from the Bell County Chamber of Commerce, which is housed in a small building constructed of coal in 1926 on 20th Street north of Cumberland Avenue.

Lincoln Memorial University is located in Harrogate, Tennessee, on US25E as the road approaches Cumberland Gap from the south. Grant-Lee Hall stands on a hill at the back of the campus, on the site of the sanatorium built by Alexander Arthur; the stone tower that marks the site of Arthur's home is to the left of the main entrance. You'll also find on the pastoral campus the **Lincoln Museum,** which houses over 25,000 historical artifacts, books, paintings, and sculptures having to do with Abraham Lincoln and the Civil War period. There is a small admission fee to the museum.

Cudjo Caverns, located in the heart of the mountain at Cumberland Gap on the old route of US25E, will reopen to the public in 1999 after being closed for a time with the rerouting of the highway. Reopening of the cave, which has an entrance in the rock wall below the Pinnacle, is the first step in the restoration of the gap. Rangers will lead visitors on wilderness cave trips by way of lantern light. Electric lighting has been removed from the time when it was a commercial cave operated by Lincoln Memorial University; the university still gets its drinking water from the river that flows through the lower level of the cave.

The cave system of Cudjo Caverns is so extensive that some parts have yet to be explored. The ceilings are festooned with stalactites, and stalagmites rise from the floors to meet them, often forming pillars. On the second level of the cave stands the "Pillar of Hercules," 65 feet high and 35 feet in circumference. Although it appears to be a complete column, a small gap separates the pillar from the cave ceiling, making it a stalagmite. Currently the formation is inactive; so it will never develop into a complete column unless the drainage patterns change and water once again drips from the ceiling. The pillar is believed to be the largest stalagmite in the world; considering the size, the claim may well be true.

Trails

The 200-yard path you take from the parking lot at the top of Cumberland Gap to the Pinnacle Overlook is part of a 400-yard loop trail that passes by the site of **Fort Lyon,** a position held by Union troops for a short time during the Civil War. Surrounded by Confederate troops who cut off supplies, Captain Sidney S. Lyon, topographical engineer under Brig. Gen. George W. Morgan, led the Union troops on a 200-mile retreat along the old Warrior's Path to Ohio. Before they departed, they destroyed what was left behind so it would be of no use to the Confederates.

Big guns that had been placed on the cliff were pushed off. Meeting this fate for the second time was "Long Tom," a giant gun, 18 feet long, which the Confederates had first installed and then pushed over the precipice when they had to evacuate. The Union troops had managed to get the gun back to the top of the mountain during their occupation of the gap but now had to return it to the bottom of the mountain before their own retreat. The site of the fort is now marked with a single Civil War cannon.

A short side trail near the site of the fort leads to an overlook of **Powell Valley.** The Powell River, and thus Powell Valley, got their names from Ambrose Powell, who accompanied Thomas Walker on his early exploration of the area. Elijah Walden, for whom Walden Ridge is named, led a party of longhunters into the area in 1761. They kept finding "A. Powell" carved on trees along what Thomas Walker had called the "Beargrass River" and at times "Powell's River." Walden's group called it the "Powell River" and thus fixed the name. It was also perhaps Walden and his men who changed the name of "Cave Gap" to "Cumberland Gap"; by that time the mountains were already being referred to as the "Cumberlands." The Virginia county from which Walden and his men apparently came was also "Cumberland."

Near the Powell Valley Overlook you'll find the beginning of the 16-mile **Ridge Trail**, which follows the mountain ridge through the national park, passes Hensley Settlement, and ends with the White Rocks Lookout, which provides panoramic views of Powell Valley at the northeast end of the park. You can also get to the Ridge Trail by taking the 1.7-mile **Lewis Hollow/Skylight Cave Trail** or the 5.0-mile **Gibson Gap Trail,** which climbs the southeast side of the mountain from the park camping and picnic area off US58, or the 2.3-mile **Sugar Run Trail** on the Kentucky side of the mountain, which starts at the picnic area on Sugar Run Road.

Hensley Settlement is a walk of about 11 miles one way if you follow the Ridge Trail from the Pinnacle; you'll probably want to camp overnight at the designated campsites near the settlement. The buildings at Hensley quickly deteriorated once they were abandoned by the families, but the Park Service has restored three of the farms. The settlement is open year-round, and in the summer months guided tours are offered.

To get to the settlement in a dayhike, use the steep 2.1-mile **Chadwell Gap Trail** from the Virginia side of the mountains to the top of the ridge and then 1.1 miles west along the Ridge Trail to the settlement. To get to the Chadwell Gap trailhead, follow US58 east along Powell Valley, pass the first intersection with VA690 on your left, and then at 9.6 miles turn left at Caylor, Virginia, on the other end of VA690, which has formed a loop. In

1.7 miles, you'll come to a junction; bear to the right and it will become a dirt road. Soon, a small sign on the left indicating the trail will direct you onto what appears to be a private driveway, which it is—the Park Service has permission for hikers to park at the end of this driveway for access to the Chadwell Gap Trail. Walk through the property to a gate at which the trail begins. At Chadwell Gap along the Ridge Trail, watch for the Old Stone Face on the left, a rock formation in the cliff that appears to be a person's profile, and also a junction with the **Martins Fork Trail** that leads about a mile down to the Brownies Creek Primitive Road.

During the summer, the park provides transportation to Hensley Settlement in a van along the 5-mile **Shillalah Creek Trail,** which is a gated service road that ascends the ridge from the Kentucky side of the mountains. It may be possible to also reach Hensley Settlement along the 5-mile Brownies Creek Primitive Road from Cubbage, Kentucky. The road can be negotiated only by 4-wheel drive vehicles, but even that is getting difficult; check with the park about the current condition of the road.

Toward the northeast end of the Ridge Trail, you'll find Sand Cave, one of the largest "rockhouses" in the eastern United States. A rockhouse is usually distinguished by its large opening and shallow depth, as if it were a room open on one side; most were used as shelters at one time or another by Cherokees and other native tribes. In the back of some of these shelters, you'll find round depressions that are thought to have been used by the Woodland Indians to grind seeds and nuts.

Sand Cave is an acre in size. Over the millennia during which the cave formed, sand dribbled from the roof so that today the floor of the cave is covered with a deep layer of sand. A small waterfall forms a creek on the left side of the entrance.

You can see Sand Cave and the White Rocks at the end of the Ridge Trail in a dayhike by coming in from Ewing, Virginia. Travel east along Powell Valley on US58 past the turnoff for the Chadwell Gap Trail. You'll see the White Rocks towering above the valley long before Ewing. The rocks were a landmark for travelers along the Wilderness Road. Just beyond Ewing on old US58 lies Rose Hill, Virginia, the site of Martin's Station, one of the early stopovers for the pioneers. Turn left in Ewing on VA724. Or on the new US58, exit left on VA724. The road becomes gravel in 0.7 mile and then splits with the left fork leading to the Thomas Walker Civic Park, where you can leave your vehicle. From there, the 3.9-mile **Ewing Trail** leads through the woods to a junction with the right fork of road on which you entered the area; this fork of the road is blocked just beyond where you turned left to enter the civic park, so you could not have driven this far.

Follow the road, which becomes a trail once you reach the mountain ridge. It loops to the left and first takes you by Sand Cave. From there the Ridge Trail takes you east along the ridgeline to the top of the White Rocks. A section of trail descends from the Ridge Trail near the White Rocks to eventually intersect with the dirt road on which you came up. It's about 8 miles round-trip.

The Ewing Trail is used for horseback riding to Hensley, Sand Cave, and White Rocks. Follow the old road up the mountain past the Thomas Walker Civic Park to join the foot path up from the park. Horses are not allowed in the settlement, at the cave, or on the rocks; you'll have to tie and leave them to enter the three scenic areas.

Sand Cave

In Cumberland Gap itself, on the Kentucky side, you can access the trailhead for the **Tri-State Trail** by walking up the old roadbed of US25E. The Tri-State Trail takes you a little less than a mile to the top of the ridge where the three states of Tennessee, Kentucky, and Virginia come together. The trail passes by the sites of Union army fortifications, including the site of Fort Foote.

Near the beginning of the Tri-State Trail, the 0.5-mile **Wilderness Road Trail** branches to the south, following the original route of the Wilderness Road as it crossed the mountain pass. A stone monument honoring Daniel Boone marks the beginning of the trail. The path descends to the town of Cumberland Gap at the site of the Iron Furnace.

The tri-state marker at the end of the Tri-State Trail is also the beginning of the **Cumberland Trail,** which heads south for a couple of miles along the Plateau. Not far beyond the tri-state marker the trail passes through Fort Farragut, another Civil War earthen fortification.

Some parts of the Cumberland Trail, a Tennessee State Scenic Trail, are not yet constructed, but eventually the trail will pass 220 miles along the Plateau, terminating near the Tennessee-Alabama border. About one-third of the trail has been developed, most crossing private land by lease agreement.

The Cumberland Trail was proposed in 1968 by conservationists who organized into the Tennessee Trails Association (TTA); one of these founding members, Bob Brown, took the lead in establishing the trail. The state of Tennessee initially supported the trail with staff and trail maintenance, but the state withdrew funds some years ago. In the absence of official support, dedicated members of TTA in 1997 formed a Cumberland Trail Conference (CTC), under the leadership of Rob Weber with Bob Brown as advisor, to work for the completion of the trail with the support of local communities and much volunteer work. This effort led to the state becoming involved again with the declaration in 1998 of a new Cumberland Trail State Park; the state has agreed to work with the CTC in establishing the trail.

You can now hike parts of the northern portion of the Cumberland Trail. Some information is available at **Cove Lake State Park** on US25W at Caryville, Tennessee, at the foot of the Plateau. The park has camping and recreation facilities, including a bicycle trail and tennis courts. You can get to the state park from Cumberland Gap along TN63, which parallels the eastern escarpment of the Plateau. Or the state park can be reached off I-75. The park's facilities overlook a lake where flocks of ducks and geese spend the winter.

Taking the Cumberland Trail north from Cove Lake, you'll ascend to the plateau to a left side path leading to rock pinnacles, the "Devil's Race Track." These massive rock plates standing upright are evidence of the great force that pushed from the southeast during the Allegheny Orogeny; the best view is from I-75 where it climbs a cleft in the plateau. North along the trail another 3 miles, you'll reach Eagle Bluff, which overlooks the valley to the east of the plateau.

South from Cove Lake, the Cumberland Trail crosses over I-75, climbs the ridge, and heads toward Lake City, which was once called "Coal Creek." State troops were sent there in 1891 to stop a protest and insurrection by miners who objected to the use of convicts to work the mines. The conflict, which lasted two years, was called the "Coal Creek Wars." The miners on several occasions marched on the stockades and released the prisoners, and the militia was sent in to restore order. Although the miners were eventually forced to accept the presence of the convict miners, the convict lease system was abolished by the state legislature when the contracts with the coal companies to use convict labor expired in 1896. Coal Creek was renamed "Lake City" after nearby Norris Lake was created by Norris Dam, built by the Tennessee Valley Authority in the 1930s.

South from Lake City, the Cumberland Trail follows the spine of Walden Ridge with numerous overlooks of Dutch Valley to the east, which was settled by Germans around 1800. If you travel down Dutch Valley Road from Lake City, you can turn west on Walden Ridge Road, which becomes gravel as it takes you to the top of the ridge and the popular Laurel Grove Access to the trail.

While walking this section of trail, you can see to the west Cross Mountain—at 3,534 feet, the tallest mountain in the Tennessee Cumberlands. Coal mining is still the major occupation, and so strip mines have drawn horizontal lines across the slopes of the mountain. At the northeast end of the valley between Walden Ridge and the Cumberland Mountains lies Fraterville, where a mine disaster on May 19, 1902, killed 184 miners, the worst mine disaster in Tennessee and one of the worst in the nation. With the accident, only three adult men were left alive in the town. A monument in the Leach Cemetery at the Clear Branch Baptist Church on New Clear Branch Road off US25W commemorates the miners, men and boys, that died at Fraterville; many are buried there, with gravestones arranged in concentric circles around the monument. At Briceville, which is also in the valley, a mine accident at the Cross Mountain Mine in 1911 took 84 men.

From the Dutch Valley section, the Cumberland Trail heads southwest toward Oliver Springs.

Camp only in designated campsites along the trail. Carry water with you because water is scarce on some sections of the trail. Any water you find should be purified before use.

References

Brown, Bob. Interview with author. Oct. 27, 1991.

———. "The Tennessee Trails Assn.: Its Formation and Aims." *Tennessee Trails,* May 1986, 1–2.

Brown, Dan, historian, Cumberland Gap National Historic Park. Interview with author. Oct. 16, 1990.

Cox, William E. *Hensley Settlement*. Philadelphia: Eastern National Parks & Monument Assn., 1978.

Cumberland Gap National Historical Park. "Cumberland Gap Tunnel Project." Brochure. Middlesboro, TN, no date.

———. "Hensley Settlement." Brochure. Middlesboro, TN, no date.

———. "The Iron Industry at Cumberland Gap." Brochure. Middlesboro, TN, no date.

———. "The Pinnacle." Brochure. Middlesboro, TN, no date.

Kincaid, Robert L. *The Wilderness Road*. Middlesboro, TN: Mrs. Robert L. Kincaid, 1973.

King, Duane H., ed. *The Cherokee Nation: A Troubled History*. Knoxville: Univ. of Tennessee Press, 1979.

Lander, Arthur B., Jr. *A Guide to the Backpacking and Day-Hiking Trails of Kentucky*. Ann Arbor, MI: Thomas Press, 1979.

Lincoln Memorial Univ. "Lincoln Museum." Brochure. Harrogate, TN, no date.

Luckett, William W. "Cumberland Gap National Historical Park." In *Landmarks of Tennessee History*, ed. William T. Alderson and Robert M. McBride. Nashville: Tennessee Historical Society, 1965.

Overholt, James. *Anderson County, Tennessee: A Pictorial History*. Norfolk: Donning Co., 1989.

Rice, Otis K. *Frontier Kentucky*. Lexington: Univ. Press of Kentucky, 1975.

U.S. Dept. of the Interior, National Park Service. *Cumberland Gap National Historical Park Master Plan*. Washington, DC, 1979.

U.S. Dept. of the Interior, National Park Service. "Cumberland Gap." Brochure. Washington, D.C., 1989.

Walker, Thomas. *Thomas Walker's Journal*. Barbourville, KY: Dr. Thomas Walker State Park, 1750.

Williams, Samuel Cole. *Early Travels in the Tennessee Country*. Johnson City, TN: Watauga Press, 1928.

Chapter 3

Pine Mountain

Although Cumberland Gap provided passage through the primary obstacle for westward migration, Cumberland Mountain on the eastern edge of the Plateau, other geologic features also contributed to this being the best passage to the interior of Kentucky. Once the pioneers had passed through Cumberland Gap, they could then proceed northwest through the Middlesboro Basin and then north along the Yellow Creek Valley where Yellow Creek and its tributaries drain the north slope of the Cumberland, eventually flowing into the Cumberland River. Beyond this valley, travelers encountered another long mountain ridge.

Early in the formation of the Cumberland Plateau, a huge block, 15 by 125 miles, separated from the Plateau and was pushed northwest. This offset in the Plateau, now known as the "Pine Mountain Block," is crowned by Pine Mountain, which lies northwest of Cumberland Mountain. Pine Mountain is a long ridge that runs the length of the Pine Mountain Block from a region just northwest of Caryville, Tennessee, to Potter Flats near Elkhorn City, Kentucky. The ridge parallels the eastern escarpment of the Plateau, having been pushed up by the force from the southeast at the time the Plateau was formed.

Early travelers through the region found that the Cumberland River, on its way west to eventually join the Ohio River, had fortunately cut its way through Pine Mountain at a place called "the Narrows." Thus the combination of Cumberland Gap, the Middlesboro Basin, Yellow Creek Valley, and the Pine Mountain Narrows created a natural passageway through the Cumberland Mountains to the Kentucky interior. It is these four geologic features that made this region so important for early settlers traveling west. Today, US25E passes over the old route of the Wilderness Road through Cumberland Gap into the

Middlesboro Basin and along Yellow Creek Valley and through the Pine Mountain Narrows.

Pine Mountain State Resort Park

Southwest of the Narrows, Pine Mountain State Resort Park rests in the mountains overlooking Pineville, Kentucky, which is the site where pioneers traveling the Wilderness Road forded the Cumberland River. Today, Pineville is protected from the flooding of the river by a massive flood wall along US25E through the community.

Established in 1925, the 2,500-acre state park is famous for its Chained Rock. Early travelers through the area noticed that a large rock, separated from the mountain cliff and hanging ominously over the town, looked like it might soon fall, cutting a broad swath through the houses and buildings of the community before coming to rest on the valley floor. One story has it that a traveler tried to convince the towns-people they needed to have the rock chained to the mountainside so it would not fall. He gladly offered to do the job for a small fee, but the people of Pineville were not taken in by the stranger.

Perhaps that was the origin of the idea of chaining the rock to the mountain. But whether the idea came from the stranger or not, the townspeople began to assure travelers facetiously that the rock could not fall because it was chained to the mountainside. The only trouble was, visitors to the area wanted to go up and see the fictitious chain. The townspeople then decided that a chained rock would make a good tour-ist attraction. So in 1933 the Pine Mountain Chained Rock Club, along with the Boy Scouts and members of the Civilian Conservation Corps who were at work on developing the park, actually chained the rock to the mountain. Although the chain is huge—100 feet long, with each link weighing 7 pounds—it would probably snap easily or pull loose from its anchor if the rock were to fall. In any case, the rock probably separated from the mountain thousands of years ago and is likely to re-main there several thousand more, chain or no chain. If it were to fall, it would probably miss the town.

Pine Mountain

The Chained Rock

Breaks Interstate Park

Toward the northeast end of Pine Mountain, Breaks Interstate Park sits astride the Kentucky-Virginia border, with most of the park in Virginia. The states of Kentucky and Virginia jointly established the 4,500-acre state park in 1954. The park boasts that it has the deepest canyon east of the Mississippi. Although Breaks Canyon, sometimes called the "Grand Canyon of the South," is 1,000 feet deep, there are other canyons on the Plateau that are comparable—the Tennessee River Gorge and Savage Gulf in Tennessee and Little River Canyon in Alabama. The Breaks Canyon is formed as the Russell Fork of the Big Sandy River "breaks" through Pine Mountain.

The region was probably first explored by Daniel Boone in the 1700s. Most of the land that became the park was settled by Richard Potter, who came to the region around 1820. The Breaks served as a thoroughfare during the Civil War; Union Lt. James A. Garfield, who later became President of the United States, fought in the region. In 1902, the Clinchfield Railroad chose the Breaks as the best route for a rail line through the area. By 1915, the Clinchfield line was completed through the Breaks, with 20 tunnels in 35 miles of track.

By 1930 lumbering operations had taken most of the trees, which were floated down the Russell Fork by the use of splash dams. Today, the park land has reforested with second-growth timber.

Kingdom Come State Park

About halfway between Pine Mountain State Park and Breaks Interstate Park lies Kingdom Come State Park. The names for the park and the Little Shepherd Trail—which passes through the park and has been proposed to connect eventually the three parks atop Pine Mountain—are taken from the Civil War novel, *The Little Shepherd of Kingdom Come,* written by John Fox Jr., a Kentucky writer who chose the area as the

The Breaks of the Russell Fork of the Big Sandy River

setting for his fiction. In the period 1893–1919, Fox wrote 11 novels, also including *Trail of the Lonesome Pine and Hell for Sartain.*

"Kingdom Come" is actually the name of a creek. The local explanation for the name has it that a man named "King" was the first to settle in the area. When later settlers arrived, they were told "King done come," which later became "Kingdom Come."

Lilley Cornett Woods

Just north of Kingdom Come State Park is a little-known forest enclave that is a remnant of the original forest once inhabiting the coves of the Cumberland Plateau in Kentucky.

The Lilley Cornett Woods is a 554-acre forest and is the Appalachian Ecological Research Station of Eastern Kentucky University. The tract of land was purchased in 1919 by a Virginia coal miner, Lilley Cornett, who preserved it until his death, when it was acquired by the commonwealth of Kentucky. The old-growth woods found there make up the largest preserved remnant of mixed-mesophytic forest in Kentucky. The term "mixed mesophytic" was first used by Lucy Braun in the early 1900s to describe a forest in which several species are dominant. In such a forest, dominance is shared by sugar maple, basswood, and tulip poplar with other species associated, such as buckeye, white oak, hemlock, chestnut oak, and beech.

Once, many of the coves and river canyons of the Cumberland Plateau were inhabited by a mixed-mesophytic forest. Only a very few undisturbed stands remain, such as Lilley Cornett Woods.

Dr. Thomas Walker State Historic Site

Northwest from Pine Mountain lies the Dr. Thomas Walker State Historic Site near Barbourville, Kentucky, which commemorates the early explorations of Thomas Walker and the five men who accompanied him: Ambrose Powell, William Tomlinson, Colby Chew, Henry Lawless, and John Hughes. On their explorations west from Cumberland Gap, they found a fertile area in Kentucky where Walker left three of his men to build a cabin and plant crops. He and two others continued westward, apparently stopping short of reaching the Bluegrass region to the northwest, for he found the land relatively poor. The cabin Walker erected to establish claim to the land was the first known house in Kentucky and stood in the general area of the state historic site.

Replica of the Thomas Walker Cabin

Directions and Services

Pine Mountain State Resort Park lies off US25E at Pineville, Kentucky, 13 miles north of Middlesboro. Turn west on KY190 and then continue straight ahead as 190 turns to the left; you'll pass through the Clear Creek Baptist Bible College campus before reaching the state park. A 30-room lodge with restaurant and 20 cottages are open year-round. You'll see from the restaurant windows a magnificent view of the mountains. You can reserve rooms at the lodge and the cottages, but there is no advance reservation for the 36-site campground, which is closed in winter. Development at the park, Kentucky's first state park, began with the work of the Civilian Conservation Corps in 1933. The lodge built by the CCC out of sandstone and chestnut logs is now the upper lobby of the present lodge. Some of the cottages are log cabins that were also built at that time. The more recent resort development occurred in the 1960s. Golf, swimming, and fishing are some of the recreational activities. The last weekend in May, you can attend the Mountain Laurel Festival. The park is bordered by the 10,000-acre **Kentucky Ridge State Forest** where hunting and backpacking are permitted.

You'll find the entrance to **Breaks Interstate Park** 6.8 miles south of Elkhorn City, Kentucky, on VA80. The park has camping, cottages, and a lodge and restaurant. You can make reservations for the lodge and cottages. Several overlooks along the drive through the park provide views of the canyon, including a view of the Towers, a 0.5-mile long ridge of rocks that stands at a bend in the river. There are also two overlooks southwest of the park entrance on VA80; one of these is Lovers' Leap, where an Indian couple supposedly leaped to their death; the story is no more likely to be true here than at many other places called "Lovers' Leap." You can fish on the 12-acre Laurel Lake and swim in a pool. The Russell Fork River is becoming known for whitewater rafting; guided trips from private outfitters are available in the fall. While you are at Breaks Interstate Park, you may want to visit the Corps of Engineers' **Fishtrap Lake,** which is just 12 miles north of Elkhorn City east on KY1789. To the northwest and southwest, the park borders **Jefferson National Forest,** which also offers outdoor recreation; the national forest is primarily a Virginia forest that does reach far enough west to encompass Plateau lands, including some in Kentucky.

To get to **Kingdom Come State Park,** watch for signs on US119 east of Cumberland, Kentucky. You'll turn off on KY1926 headed into town. In 0.8 mile, turn right up a very steep hill 1.4 miles to the park. Picnic areas abound in the 945-acre park. There are a few tent campsites but no lodging.

The forests of **Lilley Cornett Woods** are accessible only by guided tours from the visitor center. From Cumberland, Kentucky, and Kingdom Come State Park, take KY160 north and then northeast when you reach the beginning of KY463. In 4.6 miles farther along KY160, turn left, and then left again in another 1.6 miles. It's then 6 miles to Lilley Cornett Woods; the road becomes gravel along the way. If you're

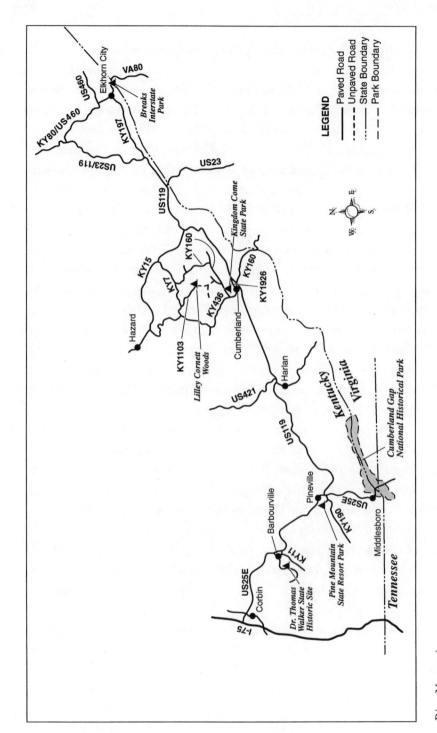

Pine Mountain

coming south from Hazard, Kentucky, take KY7 until you can turn south on KY1103; it's then 13.3 miles to the visitor center. The guided tours are conducted daily May 15 through August 15; on weekends in April, May, September, and October; and by appointment at other times.

Just to the west of Lilley Cornett Woods and Kingdom Come State Park, lies the **Bad Branch State Nature Preserve** on the southeast slope of Pine Mountain. Established by the Nature Conservancy, the 1626-acre area protects a sandstone gorge with a 60-foot waterfall and several rare plants and animals in a second-growth mixed-mesophytic forest. On US119 south of Whitesburg, turn east on KY932 2 miles to the mouth of Bad Branch where you'll see a small parking area with a sign-in box. A trail leads into a 436-acre section of the preserve now owned by the state.

A facsimile of log cabins of the time of Thomas Walker's exploration stands at **Dr. Thomas Walker State Historic Site** off US25E near Barbourville. Turn west on KY11 in Barbourville; keep straight as 11 turns left; and in about 5 miles you'll reach the state historic site. A monument to Walker's memory also is on the grounds of the historic site, which includes a 12-acre recreational park. No camping or lodging is available.

Trails

At Pine Mountain State Resort Park, you can reach the Chained Rock along the 0.5-mile **Chained Rock Trail,** which leads through a forest of hemlock, pines, and tulip poplar. The road to the trailhead passes along the spine of Pine Mountain and affords views of the surrounding country. From the rock, you'll have a panoramic view of Pineville. A sign there says the present chain replaced an older one, but that statement was made just to maintain the myth that the town early on had the rock chained. Other trails in the park take you to **Hemlock Garden,** a valley of virgin hemlock trees with an old stone shelter con-

structed by the CCC (0.7-mile loop); **Honeymoon Falls,** 25 feet high
(1.5-mile loop); the **Living Stairway,** a still-living tulip poplar that has
had steps cut in it and once served as a stairway on the trail (0.5-mile
loop); an old moonshine still on the 0.5-mile **Lost Trail; Fern Garden,**
which has large royal and cinnamon ferns (1.4-mile loop); **Rock Hotel,**
the largest rock shelter in the park (1.0 mile); and **Laurel Cove,** where
you'll pass by a small natural arch (1.8 miles).

Breaks Interstate Park has 10 miles of hiking trails. The **Chestnut
Ridge Nature Trail** is a mile-long, self-guided nature trail that uses
sections of other trails. You'll find typical forest species of the Plateau
along the **Ridge Trail;** pass through the Notches, a narrow portion of
the Laurel Branch Canyon on the **Laurel Branch Trail;** and return
along the **Geological Trail,** which has examples of rock formations and
faults. You can get a pamphlet guide to the nature trail at the visitor
center. The **Overlook Trail** provides almost continuous views as it
hugs the rim of the canyon for 0.8 mile.

At Kingdom Come State Park, several short hiking paths that total
about 5 miles wander past **Log Rock,** a 70-foot long sandstone arch,
and **Raven Rock,** a large outcropping of stone in the heart of the park
from which you have views across the valley to Big Black Mountain—at
4,140 feet, the highest in Kentucky. At the base of Raven Rock, you'll
find the Cave Amphitheater, a rockhouse that is sometimes used for
meetings.

The original proposal for the **Little Shepherd Trail** called for it to
eventually run 100 miles along the ridge of Pine Mountain, connecting
Pine Mountain State Park with Breaks Interstate Park. At this writing,
only a middle portion exists, about 40 miles long. This portion, which
is actually a fire road suitable only for 4-wheel drive vehicles, runs from
US421 near Harlan, Kentucky, north to US119 near Whitesburg, Kentucky, passing through Kingdom Come State Park along the way. It
seems the remainder of the trail is unlikely to be constructed any time
soon.

The 22.8-mile **Cumberland Mountain Trail** crosses Jefferson National Forest lands atop Pine Mountain, from Forest Service Road 201
off US27 at Pound Gap, Virginia, northeast to VA80 near Breaks Interstate Park.

References

Braun, E. Lucy. *Deciduous Forests of Eastern North America.* Philadelphia: Blakiston, 1950.

Breaks Interstate Park. "Breaks Interstate Park." Brochure. Breaks, VA, 1987.

———. "Chestnut Ridge Nature Trail." Brochure. Breaks, VA, no date.

———. "Hiking Trails." Flier. Breaks, VA, no date.

Jefferson National Forest, Clinch Ranger District. "Trail Descriptions." Brochure. Wise, Va., no date.

Kentucky Dept. of Parks. "Kentucky State Parks." Brochure. Frankfort, KY, 1990.

———. "Pine Mountain State Resort Park." Brochure. Frankfort, KY, 1990.

Kentucky Dept. of Public Information. "Kentucky Shrines." Brochure. Frankfort, KY, no date.

Lander, Arthur B., Jr. *A Guide to the Backpacking and Day-Hiking Trails of Kentucky.* Ann Arbor, MI: Thomas Press, 1979.

Pine Mountain State Resort Park. "Guide to Hiking Trails." Brochure. Pineville, KY, no date.

———. "Visitors Guide." Brochure. Pineville, KY, no date.

Walker, Thomas. *Thomas Walker's Journal.* Barbourville, KY: Dr. Thomas Walker State Park, 1750.

Chapter 4

The Kentucky Interior

Once early settlers had passed through Cumberland Gap and then the Narrows of Pine Mountain and crossed the Cumberland River, they had emerged into the interior of Kentucky. The Cumberland Plateau lies across this eastern part of the state, a mountainous region with high ridges, steep slopes, and narrow stream bottoms. It is a land of waterfalls, cascades, stone arches, and deep river canyons. Most of the original forest that covered the Plateau at the time of the early settlers has since been destroyed by lumbering, fire, and coal mining, but second-growth forest has come back in many places.

The interior of the Kentucky Plateau is a coal-producing region, especially the southern section, and is often referred to as the "Eastern Coal Field." This is the famed Appalachian coal country, where families live in isolated communities tucked between mountain ridges, often in poverty. Huge coal trucks dominate the roads, and the mountains show the results of past strip mining—highwalls, benches, and bare hillsides.

But scattered throughout this eastern Kentucky region are protected parks and forests that glisten amid a scarred land.

Daniel Boone National Forest

For 140 miles, the Daniel Boone National Forest stretches along the western edge of Kentucky's Cumberland Plateau. To the east of this strip lies another section of the national forest, the Redbird Purchase Unit.

The older section of the national forest, along the western escarpment of the Plateau, was established in 1937; it appears on some older maps as

"Cumberland National Forest." The name was changed in 1966 to recognize Daniel Boone's early exploration of the Kentucky wilderness.

The Redbird Purchase Unit was established in 1964. It surrounds the Redbird Wildlife Management Area and borders the Kentenia State Forest to the south. The Unit takes its name from the Redbird River, which is a major tributary of the South Fork of the Kentucky River. The river is named for Chief Redbird, an Indian who was friendly with early settlers and allowed them to hunt in the area.

Of the 2 million acres within the boundaries of the two sections of the national forest, only 670,000 acres are actually under federal control. Maps that show only the federal holdings have splotches of green, rather than a continuous forest. From time to time new acreage is added as purchase money becomes available or land exchanges are negotiated. For example, the Nature Conservancy in the 1980s purchased 1,126 acres along the Rockcastle River, some of which will be added to the national forest, to protect ten rare plants, three threatened fish species, and three imperiled species of mussels; the 140-acre Mrs. Baylor O. Hickman Memorial Preserve, a Conservancy inholding within the national forest, protects a newly discovered plant, the Rockcastle aster.

Even with such additions, the U.S. Forest Service will never acquire the entire acreage within the boundaries of the national forest because the patches of forest are interspersed with towns, roads, and farming communities, not just forested land.

As with all national forests, Daniel Boone National Forest is a multi-use area where mining, logging, hunting, camping, hiking, fishing, cross-country skiing, whitewater canoeing, and rafting occur side by side and supposedly in harmony. Although logging of second-growth oak, pine, and hemlock and mining of gas, oil, and coal are major activities in the national forest, special areas are set aside for outdoor recreation.

Cave Run Lake Recreation Area at the northern end of the national forest near Morehead, Kentucky, contains a water impoundment of over 8,000 acres. Next to the lake lies the Pioneer Weapons Hunting Area where only old-style weapons are permitted for hunting. Nearby is the Red River Gorge Geological Area, noted for its numerous sandstone arches. To the south near Corbin, Kentucky, Laurel River Lake Recreation Area includes an artificial lake of about 6,000 acres on the Laurel River. Nearby lies the Natural Arch Scenic Area that contains one of the largest natural stone arches on the Plateau. In addition to these major areas, there are also many smaller recreation areas that provide for picnicking and camping.

Within the national forest are stretches of five Kentucky Wild Rivers: the Cumberland River, the Little South Fork of the Cumberland, the Red River, the Rockcastle River, and Rock Creek.

Kentucky State Parks

The commonwealth of Kentucky has established several state parks within the Kentucky portion of the Cumberland Plateau to preserve special areas and to provide outdoor recreation for the public. To the north, within the boundaries of the Daniel Boone National Forest, lies Natural Bridge State Resort Park, which surrounds one of the largest natural bridges on the Cumberland Plateau; and to the south lies Cumberland Falls State Resort Park, which contains a waterfall often called the "Niagara of the South."

Midway between the main part of Daniel Boone National Forest and the national forest's Redbird Purchase Unit is the Levi Jackson Wilderness Road State Park. In 1803, John Freeman, who received acreage along the Wilderness Road in payment for his Revolutionary War service, established a tavern in the area. His daughter, Rebecca, married Levi Jackson, who took over the tavern and farm when Freeman died and who was later the county's first judge. In 1937, the surviving children of the Jacksons, Ella and Garrett, donated 307 acres for a state park. Named for Jackson and the Wilderness Road, the park has since been expanded to more than 800 acres. Ella Jackson also gave the park many family heirlooms, which along with other donations, are housed in the Mountain-Life Museum on the park grounds. The museum, with its seven log buildings, is a replica of early pioneer life. The park also includes the McHargue Mill, which has a large collection of old millstones.

McHargue Mill

Fern Bridge

The park also contains marked graves of pioneers who died along the Wilderness Road. On the evening of October 3, 1786, a group of about 30 settlers traveling west, called the "McNitt party," stopped to camp along Little Laurel River that runs through the park. During the night a group of Chickamaugas attacked the group, killing nearly all the settlers. One woman escaped by hiding in the hollow of a tree and, according to the story told, gave birth to a daughter during the night. One or two men, including the husband of the woman, also escaped by fleeing into the forest. The men who came looking for the party and buried its victims called the site, "Defeated Camp." The burial ground is now inside a low stone-wall enclosure on the grounds of the state park. Since the bodies were buried en masse, the stones inside the walls cannot mark actual graves.

In the northern part of the Redbird Purchase Unit lies Buckhorn Lake State Resort Park. To the northeast of the Unit is Jenny Wiley State Resort Park; and, farther north, Paintsville and Grayson Lake State Parks and Carter Caves and Greenbo Lake State Resort Parks.

The special attraction of Carter Caves State Resort Park is, of course, the caves; there are at least 125 caves in this region that includes the park. In 1902 J. F. Lewis acquired part of the property that would become the state park and named the caves collectively, "Carter Caves." But in fact, there is no cave named "Carter." In 1924 the Lewis family formed the Carter Caves Corporation to promote tours of the caves, and by 1933 at least one cave had electric lighting. In the 1940s, the commonwealth of Kentucky acquired the land for a state park.

Today, the state park offers guided tours of X Cave, which has the form of an X; Saltpeter Cave, with the remains of saltpeter operations used in the production of gunpowder; Bat Cave, which in winter harbors the endangered Indiana bat; and Cascade Cave, with its underground waterfall. With a permit, visitors to the park can explore Laurel and Horn Hollow Caves on their own.

In addition, the Carter Caves Park has several large natural arches and bridges. Smoky Bridge and Natural Bridge in the park are more accurately called "natural tunnels," a term used when the width (the distance through)

Paintsville Lake

is more than three times the span. Smoky Bridge, with a 40-foot span and a clearance of 90 feet, has a width of 220 feet. The Carter Caves Natural Bridge, with a 40-foot span and a 45-foot clearance, passes 180 feet through a ridge; the park road runs across the top and a creek flows through it. The park also has true natural bridges, or arches: Raven Bridge (40-foot span, 15-foot clearance), Cascade Bridge (60-foot span, 30-foot clearance and barely separated from the rock wall), and Fern Bridge (100-foot span, 90-foot clearance). The extraordinary dimensions of Fern Bridge are due to a gully underneath created by a wet-weather creek.

Corps of Engineers' Recreation Lakes

Also scattered through the Kentucky Plateau region are lakes constructed by the U.S. Army Corps of Engineers, primarily for flood control, navigation, and forest and wildlife management. A secondary benefit to the region is recreation. Most of the lakes have picnicking and camping facilities and provide opportunities for fishing, hunting, boating, and water skiing.

In four instances, Corps land is leased to the state for state parks—Jenny Wiley (Dewey Lake), Buckhorn Lake, Paintsville Lake, and Grayson Lake State Parks. The Corps-developed recreational facilities at these lakes complement the state park facilities. Cave Run Lake at the National Forest's Cave Run Lake Recreation Area is a Corps of Engineers Lake, although the Forest Service has recreation-management responsibility.

Fishtrap Lake Dam

In addition, there are Corps recreation lakes not associated with state parks or national forest lands. To the south are Fishtrap Lake, Carr Fork Lake, and Martins Fork Lake; and to the north, Yatesville Lake, the newest lake, impounded in 1992.

Iron Furnaces

In the 1800s the Cumberland Plateau region of Kentucky was a major center of iron production. In the 1830s, Kentucky was the third largest producer in the country. Primitive by today's standards, the iron plant of the nineteenth century was dominated by a tall stone furnace in which iron ore was smelted to produce pig iron and to make utensils. The surrounding wooden buildings, which constituted self-contained communities, have long since disappeared, and only the old stone furnaces remain.

Kentucky's first furnace was the Bourbon Furnace, built in 1791 south of present-day Owingsville. It produced iron for kettles, pots, and various tools. During the War of 1812, the furnace supplied cannonballs, canisters, and grapeshot for the army. The Bourbon Furnace operated until 1838.

The remains of the Buffalo Furnace stand on the grounds of the Greenbo Lake State Resort Park. It was a major producer in the Hanging Rock region of Kentucky in the period 1851–75. The stack was originally 36.5 feet high, had a steam-powered air blast, and could produce 15 tons of iron in 24 hours.

The Clear Creek Furnace, located in the Clear Creek Picnic Area at the Cave Run Lake Recreation Area, operated 1839–75. The stone furnace was 40 feet high. The iron was used primarily to make railroad car wheels.

The remains of the Estill Furnace rests at the community of Furnace, Kentucky; built in 1829, the stack was originally 34 feet high and produced its last iron in 1874. It was one of the first to use steam to power its blast rather than water power. The pig iron produced was shipped to the forges at Clay City to be made into finished products.

In the same region, on national forest land, the Cottage Furnace is a relatively intact furnace which during the 1800s was used to produce the iron

Cottage Furnace

for tools and utensils and pig iron that was shipped to the Clay City iron foundries for forming wheels and rails for the railroads. Built in 1854, the Cottage Furnace operated until 1879. The stack was 38 feet high.

Also in the same region is the Fitchburg Furnace, a rare double furnace located in an isolated tract of the national forest. The furnace was known at the time as the "Red River Furnace." A rectangular structure

60 feet high, it contains two stacks, called "Blackstone" and "Chandler," which had a capacity of 25 tons of pig iron a day. During its short operation, 1869 to 1874, the furnace produced 16,072 tons of iron, which was shipped to places like Cincinnati where it was made into railroad car wheels and rails. A financial panic in 1873, due mostly to overspeculation in western railroads, foreshadowed financial disaster. The discovery of rich iron ore beds around Birmingham, Alabama, and also the development of an iron industry in the northern Great Lakes region made mining the Kentucky ore impractical. Also by then, the process used in these stone furnaces had become obsolete. The Fitchburg Furnace closed. It is now on the National Register of Historic Places. The community of Fitchburg, chartered in 1871, no longer exists but in its time contained 100 families, all involved in smelting iron ore or support activities.

Directions and Services

The portion of the **Daniel Boone National Forest** along the Kentucky Plateau's western edge, called the "Pottsville Escarpment," can be reached south of Lexington on I-75 and east of Lexington on I-64. To the east, the Daniel Boone Parkway, a toll road, crosses the **Redbird Purchase Unit.** Many designated campsites in the national forest may be used for free, but a few have a minimal charge; some are available by reservation, but most are on a first-come, first-served basis. In addition, you are allowed to camp virtually anywhere on federally owned land—a practice characteristic of most national forests. Occasionally you'll see a sign that says "no camping," usually erected because an area has been overused, vandals frequent the area, or some geologic feature needs to be preserved. But where it's not specifically prohibited and you know you are not on private land, you are free to pull off anywhere and camp. However, the U.S. Forest Service asks that you set up out of sight of roads and trails. Contact the Daniel Boone National Forest headquarters in Winchester, Kentucky, for maps and more information on camping and trails in the various recreation sites throughout the forest. In

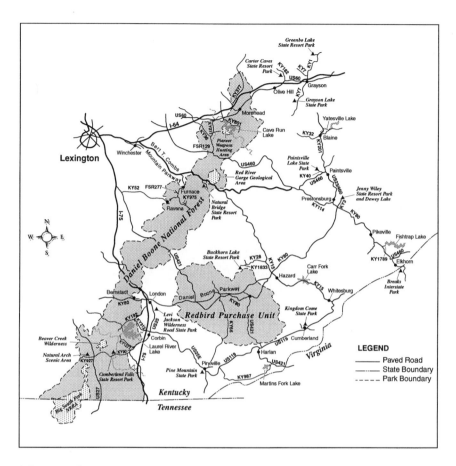

The Kentucky Interior

addition, motels provide accommodations in the larger communities surrounding the forest lands.

Cave Run Lake Recreation Area, in the northern part of the national forest, includes campgrounds, picnic areas, boat ramps, two marinas, swimming beaches, hiking trails, and numerous places to fish. One of the campgrounds, Claylick, is accessible only by boat. The 8,270-acre lake is a Corps of Engineers' impoundment on the Licking River. It contains largemouth bass, bluegill, crappie, and catfish but is especially known for muskie. You can enter the area on KY801 south of I-64 and the community of Salt Lick. The road to the Zilpo Campground and Recreation Area, with views along the way of the forest and lake, is designated a National Scenic Byway.

In the 7,600-acre **Pioneer Weapons Hunting Area,** adjacent to Cave Run, only pioneer weapons may be used for hunting—flintlock rifle, percussion cap rifle, crossbow, long bow, recurve bow, and compound bow. The timber-management practices here benefit wildlife, and so the area abounds in white-tailed deer and wild turkey. As the numbers of animals increase, they migrate out of the area to surrounding parts of the national forest where modern weapons are allowed. All hunting is subject to the regulations of the commonwealth of Kentucky. Enter the hunting area along KY129 and KY918.

Also in the northern part of the national forest is the **Rodburn Hollow** picnic and camping area, just outside Morehead off US60 on Rodburn Hollow Road. Go past the Morehead Ranger District Office and follow the signs. The area has 12 camping spaces and a picnic shelter.

At the **Red River Gorge Geological Area,** known for its many natural sandstone arches, camping is available in the Koomer Ridge Campground. You can enter the area along the Bert T. Combs Mountain Parkway and KY15.

Camping, boating, and fishing are the attractions of **Laurel River Lake Recreation Area,** in the southern end of the national forest. Two of the campgrounds have access only by boat—Grove Boat-In and White Oak Boat-In. The Holly and Grove Campgrounds have electricity and water hookups. The lake supports largemouth bass, rainbow trout, bluegill, crappie, and catfish. The area encompasses the **Cane Creek Wildlife Management Area**. You can approach the recreation area along KY192, KY770 to KY312, and US25/KY1277 west off I-75. The recreation area also has two marinas.

Just west of Laurel River Lake lies the **Rock Creek Natural Area,** a 190-acre preserve that contains an old-growth forest of hemlock and hardwood in the upper reaches of Rock Creek, which flows into the Rockcastle River. This is a small creek, not the Rock Creek that is a Kentucky Wild River. It's estimated that some of the trees in the natural area are 200 years old. There is no established trail into the area in order to limit the impact of visitors, but if you especially want to see the old trees, contact the London District of the Daniel Boone National Forest for specific directions to the natural area.

The **Natural Arch Scenic Area,** which contains one of the largest arches on the Plateau, lies off US27 south of Parkers Lake. It has a picnic area, but no lodging or camping. North of Parkers Lake, you'll find the **Beaver Creek Wilderness,** which has primitive camping and a single hiking trail.

In addition, there are several campsites in the southern part of the national forest. **Turkey Foot** is a 15-unit area near McKee, Kentucky. Take KY89 north from McKee 3 miles to Forest Service Road 4; turn east and follow the signs.

S-Tree is also near McKee. North from McKee on US421, take KY89 south for 3 miles; turn west on FSR43 for 1 mile, and then south on FSR20; follow the signs. The campground has 10 spaces.

On Lake Cumberland is **Sawyer,** a 5-unit campground. Take KY90 west from Cumberland Falls State Resort Park for 5 miles. Turn north on KY896 for 7 miles and follow the signs.

At the mouth of the Rockcastle River on Lake Cumberland, you'll find **Rockcastle,** an 18-unit area; a fee is charged here. Take KY192 southwest from London for 16 miles, and then go south on KY1193 for 5 miles.

Near Lake Cumberland is **Little Lick,** a 7-unit area. Take KY192 east from Somerset for 21 miles, then turn south on FSR122 and follow the signs on FSR816B.

There is also **Bell Farm,** a 5-unit campground in the southern part of the forest, which you reach by taking KY92 west from Stearns for 6 miles and then going left on KY1363 for 12 miles. From Bell Farm, turn southeast on FSR137 and go 5 miles to **Great Meadows,** a 20-unit campground. On the way you'll pass **Hemlock Grove Picnic Area,** which has a stand of large hemlocks and hardwoods.

Bon Hollow is a picnic area on the site of an old mining town. You can reach the area southwest of Williamsburg on KY92 to KY554. The picnic area is now operated by the city of Williamsburg.

The Redbird Purchase Unit has only one recreation area, **Big**

Double Creek, which is for day-use only. In the heart of the Redbird Unit, take KY66 south from the Daniel Boone Parkway 3.2 miles to the Redbird Ranger Station. Just past the station, turn right on a small road that becomes gravel and reaches the picnic area in 2.8 miles.

You can reach **Buckhorn Lake State Resort Park** in the northeast corner of the national forest's Redbird Purchase Unit by taking KY15 north from the Daniel Boone Parkway near Hazard, Kentucky. Bear left on KY28 and then left again on KY1833 for a total of 20 miles from the parkway. The state park has a 36-room lodge overlooking Buckhorn Lake, which is a Corps of Engineers' impoundment on the Middle Fork of the Kentucky River. Fishing, boating, and swimming are the attractions. The park has no campground, but the private Gays Creek Campground with minimal facilities is located at a distance from the park. You'll also find primitive camping near the Corps of Engineers' dam and at the Trace Branch boat launch area. At nearby Buckhorn, Kentucky, you'll find the Buckhorn Log Church, a building remaining from the Witherspoon College; the church is on the National Register of Historic Places. Each September, nearby Hazard, Kentucky, hosts the Black Gold Festival in recognition of the value of coal to the region's economy.

Natural Bridge State Resort Park is located adjacent to the Red River Gorge Geological Area and can also be reached off the Bert T. Combs Mountain Parkway; the state park has two campgrounds and a 35-room lodge.

You will also find a campground and a lodge and restaurant at **Cumberland Falls State Resort Park** on KY90 in the southern portion of the Daniel Boone National Forest. The park is known for its broad waterfall on the Cumberland River.

The **Levi Jackson Wilderness Road State Park** is on KY1006 east of US25 just south of London and north of Corbin, Kentucky. There is no lodge, but the park has one of the largest campgrounds—146 sites with electricity and water hookups and a 15-cabin group camp. Trails in the park follow the routes of the old Wilderness Road and Boone's Trace, the blazed trail that was the forerunner of the road.

West of London on KY80, you can visit **Bernstadt,** settled in 1881 by families from Switzerland on 4,000 acres of land. More than 100 families joined the colony to escape economic hardship in Europe at the time. In Kentucky, they started small farms with vineyards and orchards and produced milk, cheese, and vegetables for the surrounding communities. Bernstadt was the largest foreign colony ever established in Kentucky; a small white church established in 1884 marks the site of the settlement.

On KY1004 west of KY1955 and north of London lies the **Great Saltpeter Cave,** a commercial cave that at this writing is closed. Discovered in 1790, the 0.5-mile-long cave was a source of saltpeter for the manufacture of gunpowder used in the War of 1812, the Mexican War, and the Civil War. Corbin, Kentucky, south of London, still has the **Harland Sanders Cafe** on US25 where Col. Harland Sanders developed his Kentucky Fried Chicken; the restaurant with a museum is on the National Register of Historic Places.

To the east of the national forest, **Jenny Wiley State Resort Park** has a 49-room lodge, 17 cottages, and 126 camping sites and is the southern terminus for the Jenny Wiley National Recreation Trail. The campground is open April 1 to October 31. The park is named for a woman who in the eighteenth century was captured by Shawnees and taken to their settlements along the Ohio River where she remained for 11 months until she escaped. The park lies along the Corps of Engineers' 1,100-acre Dewey Lake, which is an impoundment of Johns Creek, a tributary of the Levisa Fork of the Big Sandy River. From the Redbird Purchase Unit, you can reach the park and lake by taking KY80 northeast, which is the extension of the Daniel Boone Parkway, to Prestonsburg, Kentucky; when KY80 turns right, keep straight on KY3 for 4 miles to the park. To the north of the park you'll find Dewey Dam and Recreation Area, and to the east, you'll find additional camping at the Corps' German Bridge Area that is open Memorial Day to Labor Day.

To the northeast on the Plateau, you'll find **Carter Caves State Resort Park** by taking the Carter Caves exit off I-64 on US60 at Olive Hill, Kentucky, and then turning north on KY182. The park has 90 camping sites, a 28-room Caveland Lodge, and 15 cottages. Camping is seasonal, but lodging is year-round; you can reserve rooms and cottages.

There's swimming, tennis, fishing, and golf. Stop at the welcome center for information and tickets for the guided cave tours. The last weekend in January, the park holds the annual Carter Caves Crawlathon, with tours of the caves, explorations in undeveloped caves, and a workshop for beginners. The park charges a registration fee for the Crawlathon. Accommodations fill up fast during the weekend, so make reservations well in advance. Additional outdoor recreation is available in the adjacent **Tygart State Forest.**

To the northeast, you'll also find **Grayson Lake State Park** and **Greenbo Lake State Resort Park.** Grayson Lake State Park has 71 campsites; there is no lodging, only central service buildings for campers. The park, off KY7 south of Grayson, is on the shore of the 1,500-acre Grayson Lake, a Corps of Engineers' impoundment on the Little Sandy River where you can boat and fish. Greenbo Lake State Park on KY1 north of I-64 has 63 camping sites and the 36-room Jesse Stuart Lodge, named after the Kentucky writer who in his fiction and poetry wrote about the hills and people of Kentucky. Canoeing and boating are popular on the 225-acre Greenbo Lake. Nearby is the **Jesse Stuart Nature Preserve.**

Paintsville Lake State Park is located on the shore of 1,139-acre Paintsville Lake, a Corps of Engineers' impoundment of Paint Creek, a tributary of the Levisa Fork of the Big Sandy River. The park is north of Jenny Wiley State Park on US23/460. Stay with US460 when it separates left from 23 after Paintsville; soon after, turn right on KY40 and go 1.6 miles to KY2275; turn right 0.6 miles to Paintsville Lake. You'll find a Corps of Engineers' visitor center on a hill overlooking the lake, and state park facilities that include a marina and picnic area. There is no camping or lodging; the primary activities are boating and fishing. The nearby community of Paintsville hosts the Kentucky Apple Festival each fall.

To the north in Lawrence County is where you'll find the Corps of Engineers' **Yatesville Lake,** an impoundment of Blaine Creek, a tributary of the Big Sandy River. Take KY201 north from Paintsville to Blaine and turn east on KY32. A marina at **Yatesville Lake State Park** on KY1185 offers boating and fishing.

To the southeast, you'll find the 1,131-acre **Fishtrap Lake,** a Corps of Engineers' impoundment on the Levisa Fork of the Big Sandy River. You'll find the lake off US460/KY80 south of Pikeville, Kentucky, and north of Elkhorn City. Turn east on KY1789 and go 2.2 miles to the Corps' visitor center. Boating and fishing are again the main attractions, but there are also picnicking and, during the summer months, camping at the Grapevine Creek area. Fishtrap Lake is close to Breaks Interstate Park on Pine Mountain, so you may want to visit these on the same trip.

Also on the southern portion of the Kentucky Plateau, you'll find the 1120-acre **Carr Fork Lake,** a Corps of Engineers' impoundment on the Carr Fork, a tributary of the North Fork of the Kentucky River. The lake and **Carr Creek State Park** lie along KY15 east of Hazard and northwest of Whitesburg, Kentucky. The facilities include two campgrounds, picnicking areas, a marina, and a swimming beach. Carr Fork takes its name from William Carr, an early longhunter in the 1700s. Early settlement of the area is represented in a group of reconstructed pioneer houses maintained by the Letcher, Knott, Leslie, and Perry County Community Action Council. You'll find the pioneer village off KY15 at the east end of the lake; watch for a sign that says "Pioneer Village Gift Shop." Crafts are sold in one of the log houses that are set back in a narrow hollow. Behind the gift shop, you'll see the Johnson Place that dates from 1789 and is believed to be the oldest log cabin in eastern Kentucky.

Farther to the south rests **Martins Fork Lake,** another Corps impoundment, this one on the Martins Fork of the Cumberland River. You'll find the lake along KY987 west of US421 south of Harlan, Kentucky. For the public, this is a day-use area with fishing, swimming, boating, and picnicking; there is no camping. Nearby is the Cranks Creek Wildlife Management Area.

The remains of the **Bourbon Furnace** stand beside KY36 just south of Owingsville and south of I-64. In addition to the **Buffalo Furnace** at Greenbo Lake State Resort Park, furnaces can be found within the boundaries of the national forest. Winding backwoods roads are sometimes the only way to get to these locations, so you must be persistent and have a special interest in the iron industry in the 1800s to carry you through to the sites.

To get to the **Clear Creek Furnace,** take KY211 south from Salt Lick for 4 miles and then go east on FSR129 for 2 miles. You must turn into the picnic area and bear right to get to the furnace.

The **Estill Furnace** sits at the junction of KY213 and 1057 in the community of Furnace.

To get to the **Cottage Furnace,** take KY213 south from Furnace, Kentucky, for 2.5 miles. Turn west on a gravel road where you'll see a sign for the furnace. In 2.7 miles stay straight on FSR227 and then turn left at a fork. At the end of the road are a turnaround loop and picnic tables. At the back of the loop is the trail to the furnace.

For the **Fitchburg Furnace,** continue south on KY213 for 3.3 miles from the Cottage Furnace turnoff to a junction with KY52, or take KY52 north from Ravena, Kentucky, to this same junction. Head east on KY52 from this junction; you'll drop down into a valley to a sharp left on KY1182, which is 7.8 miles east from Ravena. After turning on 1182, take an immediate left on KY975. It's then 3.3 miles to the furnace, reputed to be the largest of its kind in the world.

There are remains of other furnaces scattered along back roads in this region of Kentucky. But they are hard to find; you'll need to ask the local people if they know of any before you go searching for them.

Trails

About 500 miles of hiking trails wander throughout the Daniel Boone National Forest, with some concentration in particularly scenic areas. The **Sheltowee Trace National Recreation Trail** passes through the entire length of the national forest, north to south.

In February 1778, while Daniel Boone was bringing additional supplies from Boonesborough to the men who were making salt at Blue Licks, a band of Shawnees captured him. Boone was taken to a Shawnee town in Ohio, from which he later escaped and returned to Boonesborough. During his four-month sojourn with the Shawnees, he was favored by the war chief, Black Fish, who gave him the name "Sheltowee," which means "Big Turtle."

The Forest Service has used the outline of a turtle, along with a diamond blaze, to mark the 257-mile Sheltowee Trace. From its northern end, which begins on KY377 above Morehead, the trail meanders through the forests and river canyons of the national forest to its southern terminus in Tennessee's Pickett State Park. The trail skirts Cave Run Lake and the Pioneer Weapons Hunting Area and passes through the Red River Gorge Geological Area and Natural Bridge State Park. South, it passes near Wind Cave in Jackson County north of the McKee community. In Laurel County you'll hike through the Wildcat Mountain Battlefield, where a skirmish in the Civil War took place in which Confederate forces attempted to stop a Union advance toward Cumberland Gap on October 21, 1861. The Confederates lost the battle, but the Union army withdrew for the time being. Neither Wind Cave nor Wildcat Mountain are easily accessible by car.

Farther to the south, the trace travels along Laurel River Lake, passes through Cumberland Falls State Resort Park, and enters the Big South Fork National River and Recreation Area that straddles the Kentucky-Tennessee border. The trail ends at Tennessee's Pickett State Rustic Park on the western border of the BSFNRRA. Water along the trail should be considered unsafe until boiled or purified; water is scarce along some sections, so carry extra water with you if you're backpacking.

About 9 miles south from the northern end of the Sheltowee Trace, a side trail of about 2 miles connects with the **Jenny Wiley National Recreation Trail,** which follows the approximate route taken by the Shawnees when they brought Jenny Wiley north to the Ohio in the late 1700s. The trail was constructed by the FIVCO (Five County) Area Development District and the Jenny Wiley Trail Conference, with the help of over 200 landowners who allowed the trail to be placed across their lands. The 185-mile backpacking trail extends from near South Shore, Kentucky, which is opposite Portsmouth on the Ohio River, south and east to Jenny Wiley State Resort Park on Dewey Lake near Prestonsburg, Kentucky; to the north, the trail can be used to reach the North Country Trail in Ohio. The Jenny Wiley Trail has shelters and cistern water supplies approximately every 10 miles. The water should be purified before drinking. The trail is entirely outside the Daniel Boone National Forest, except for the **Dry Branch Connector** that links the Jenny Wiley Trail with the Sheltowee Trace.

The 9-mile **Simon Kenton Trail** joins the Jenny Wiley Trail with Kentucky's Carter Caves State Resort Park, passing through Tygart State Forest before entering the park and, once within the park, passing through Shangri La Arch. Simon Kenton, a frontier scout, saved Daniel Boone's life during a siege of Fort Boonesborough in 1777. The 3.5-mile **Red Trail** at Carter Caves passes by Smoky Bridge, Raven Bridge, and Fern Bridge, all of which have short access from various points along the trail, which circles the park facilities. The 0.5-mile **Natural Bridge Trail** leads down a walkway behind the welcome center to the Carter Caves Natural Bridge. The 1-mile **Cascade Bridge Loop** in the Cascades Cave area of the park swings by Cascade Bridge and an impressive box canyon.

The **Michael Tygart Trail,** named for an eighteenth-century explorer and scout, is a 24-mile connecting trail that joins the Jenny Wiley Trail with Greenbo Lake State Resort Park. At the state park, the 1.1-mile **Fern Valley Interpretive Trail** lets you experience nature and the 7-mile **Michael Tygart Loop** takes you by old homesites.

The Redbird Purchase Unit of the Daniel Boone National Forest contains the **Redbird Crest Trail,** a 66-mile trail blazed with a green diamond that begins at the Redbird Ranger Station and forms a loop through the Redbird Wildlife Management Area.

References

Carter Caves State Resort Park. "Cave Tour Information." Brochure. Olive Hill, KY, 1979.

———. "Visitor's Guide." Brochure. Frankfort, KY, 1990.

Collins, Robert F. *A History of the Daniel Boone National Forest.* Washington, DC: U.S. Dept. of Agriculture, Forest Service, 1975.

Daniel Boone National Forest. *Recreation on the Daniel Boone National Forest.* Newspaper. Winchester, KY, no date.

Kentucky Dept. of Parks. "Buckhorn Lake." Brochure. Frankfort, KY, 1990.

———— "Carter Caves State Resort Park." Brochure. Frankfort, KY, 1990.

————. "Greenbo Lake." Brochure. Frankfort, KY, 1990.

————. "Jenny Wiley." Brochure. Frankfort, KY, 1990.

————. "Jenny Wiley Trail." Flier. Frankfort, KY, no date.

————. "Levi Jackson Wilderness Road." Brochure. Frankfort, KY, 1990.

"Land Marks." *Nature Conservancy Magazine,* Jan.–Feb. 1990, 24.

Lander, Arthur B., Jr. *A Guide to the Backpacking and Day-Hiking Trails of Kentucky.* Ann Arbor, MI: Thomas Press, 1979.

Laurel County Historical Society. "Battle of Wildcat Mountain." Brochure. London, KY, no date.

Levi Jackson Wilderness Road State Park. "History of the McNitt Massacre." Flier. London, KY, no date.

————. "Levi Jackson Wilderness Road State Park" Flier. London, KY, no date.

McFarlan, Arthur C. *Geology of Kentucky.* Lexington: Univ. of Kentucky, 1943.

"New Projects." *Nature Conservancy Magazine,* Sept.–Oct. 1989, 22.

U.S. Army Corps of Engineers, Huntingdon District. "Dewey Lake." Brochure. Huntingdon, WV, no date.

————. "Fishtrap Lake." Brochure. Huntingdon, WV, no date.

————. "Grayson Lake." Brochure. Huntingdon, WV, no date.

U.S. Army Corps of Engineers, Louisville District. "Buckhorn Lake." Brochure. Louisville, KY, no date.

————. "Carr Fork Lake." Brochure. Louisville, KY, no date.

————. "Cave Run Lake." Brochure. Louisville, KY, no date.

U.S. Army Corps of Engineers, Nashville District. "Martins Fork Lake." Brochure. Nashville, no date.

U.S. Dept. of Agriculture, Forest Service, Southern Region. "Daniel Boone National Forest." Brochure. Washington, DC, 1983.

————. "Laurel River Lake." Brochure. Washington, DC, 1983.

————. "Pioneer Weapons Hunting Area." Brochure. Washington, DC, 1983.

————. "Recreation Guide to the Daniel Boone National Forest." Brochure. Washington, DC, 1985.

————. "Sheltowee Trace National Recreation Trail." Brochure. Washington, DC, no date.

Chapter 5

Red River Gorge

Before continental forces raised the Cumberland Plateau, rivers spilled down from surrounding highlands, fanning out into broad deltas as they met the shallow inland sea that reached into the interior of what was to become Tennessee and Kentucky. The rivers dumped sand and rock particles which hardened into the ponderous sandstone that eventually became the top layer of the Plateau.

The remnant of this hard capstone, in the Kentucky portion of the Plateau usually called the "Rockcastle Conglomerate," created dramatic relief on the Plateau. Rivers plowed canyons with steep rock walls. Waterfalls often formed great amphitheaters. And just below ridgetops, wind and water together dug out softer layers, usually from both sides of the mountain at once, leaving behind great spans of suspended sandstone.

Natural sandstone arches are found throughout the Cumberland Plateau, but more frequently to the north and especially in the gorge of the Red River in Kentucky. In fact, the gorge contains more arches than anyplace else in the eastern United States, with the possible exception of the Big South Fork National River and Recreation Area, which is still being inventoried. The only other rival to Red River Gorge in the United States is Arches National Park in Utah.

Red River Gorge Geological Area

A preserve surrounding the middle portion of the Red River, the Red River Gorge Geological Area is the most intriguing of the special areas in the Daniel Boone National Forest. At this location, the Red River carves a deep canyon as it flows westward to its confluence with the Kentucky River; and the wind and rain have sculpted majestic and delicate rock formations, especially the many stone arches found in the watershed. Hundreds of caves are also in the area, many of them unexplored. Relics and petroglyphs found under rock overhangs show that Indians frequented the area.

In the early 1960s, the Army Corps of Engineers proposed damming the Red River for flood control and recreation and to supply water for nearby Lexington. The dam and reservoir were authorized by Congress in 1962. The proposed project created a storm of controversy, and people marched on the state capitol opposing the dam.

Environmentalists feared the loss of habitat for rare animals and plants, such as the four-toed salamander and the yellow-fringed orchid. The geological area also harbored many northern species of plants that were forced ahead of glaciers as they moved south during the ice ages, including Canadian yew, Canada lily, purple-fringed orchid, wood shamrock, Canadian white violet, spotted wintergreen, and northern swamp thistle. Scenic, archaeological, and geological treasures would have been lost if the dam were built.

In 1969 Governor Louie B. Nunn refused to approve the dam site. The Corps of Engineers then proposed a dam at an alternative site that would less impact the Red River Gorge. However, in 1975 the project was abandoned when studies showed that the benefits of the dam did not offset the cost of building it. The following year the canyon was designated a national geological area in recognition of its unique character. And in 1985 the southeastern half of the geological area was designated the Clifty Wilderness Area, about 11,000 acres to be augmented by another 2,000 acres of private holdings that will become part of the wilderness when they are acquired.

In the 25,662 acres that make up the Red River Gorge Geological Area are more than 200 natural arches, among them perhaps 50 major arches. Arches are still discovered from time to time.

Natural Bridge

Natural Bridge State Resort Park

At nearly the doorstep of the Red River Gorge Geological Area, sits Kentucky's Natural Bridge State Resort Park. The resort facilities were built by the state to provide recreation and accommodations for the many visitors coming to see the Natural Bridge, a large sandstone arch at the top of the mountain, which has a span of 80 feet and a clearance of 65 feet—one of the largest on the Cumberland Plateau. The park was originally established as a resort on the railroad line by the Kentucky Union Railway Company at the turn of the century. The park was donated to the state in 1926 by the L&N Railroad which had acquired the land.

Directions and Services

The **Red River Gorge Geological Area** is near Slade, Kentucky; you approach the region from the east or west along the Bert T. Combs Mountain Parkway, named for a former governor, or along KY15.

You can enter the geological area north from KY15 along KY77 through the Nada Tunnel, which is billed as the entrance to the Red River Gorge. In fact there are two other entrances: south along KY77, a steeply descending mountain road that follows a boulder-strewn, forested stream on the north, and KY715, which heads north from KY15 and joins KY77 to form a loop drive. Along KY715 you'll find the Gladie Creek Historic Site and Information Station. Here you can get maps, brochures, and information on the geological area. The restored two-story log structure at the historic site was built in the late 1800s and was used as a post office and boarding house for loggers.

Camping is permitted anywhere in the geological area except in developed areas such as picnic grounds. The Forest Service also asks that you not camp within 300 feet of a road. Also, do not camp within sight of a trail or under rock overhangs, and camp at least 200 yards away from Grays Arch. When exploring rock overhangs, do not dig for artifacts, which are protected by law.

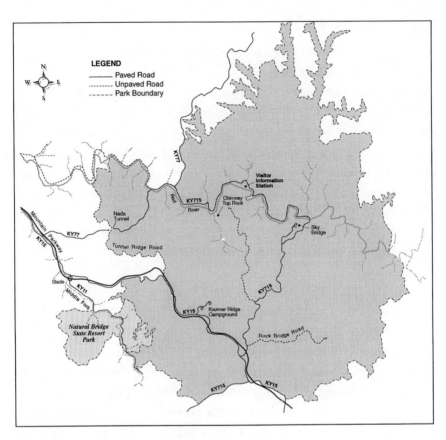

Red River Gorge Geological Area

Hunting is allowed within the geological area boundaries, subject to state laws. The hunting seasons are in the late fall and for a short time in the spring. Fishing is good on the smaller streams.

Koomer Ridge on KY15 is the one developed campground in the geological area. It has 56 campsites for either tents or trailers and a separate section of 14 sites for tents only. The larger area opens around Memorial Day and closes around Labor Day. The tent-only area is open year-round. There are few amenities here; pit toilets, gravel tent pads, and water spigots are about it—no electric hookups and no flush toilets or sinks. But the campsites are well laid out in the forest with plenty of space between most of them.

Canoeing and rafting is permitted on the Red River. The upper part is a Kentucky Wild River and not recommended for inexperienced canoeists because of the numerous boulders in the stream. But if you've got the experience, it's a spectacular ride with rock cliffs and plenty of whitewater. The stretch runs from a concrete bridge on KY746 down to another bridge on KY715. Beginners should stick to the middle portion of the river between the concrete bridge on 715 and the iron bridge on KY77.

You reach **Natural Bridge State Resort Park** by taking KY11 south from KY15 in Slade, Kentucky, or from the Slade exit off the Bert T. Combs Mountain Parkway. The two park campgrounds with 95 sites have electricity and water hookups. They are open April 1 to October 31, and no reservations are accepted. You can also stay at the Hemlock Lodge or in one of the ten cottages. The 35-room lodge has all the amenities, including color television and private balconies. A dining room serves three meals a day. Reservations are accepted for the lodge and cottages.

The park has tennis courts and a swimming pool. Near the pool you'll find an abandoned railroad tunnel through the mountain. You can fish on Mill Creek Lake and on the Middle Fork of the Red River which flows through the state park. In the midst of the river is Hoedown Island, where square dances and clogging demonstrations take place on the weekend evenings.

Loop Tour and Trails

The best introduction to the Red River Gorge is to pass through the Nada Tunnel and drive along the loop formed by KY77, KY715, and KY15—a trip of about 35 miles. As you drive the loop, watch for various trails that lead off to viewpoints and arches. In addition to the **Sheltowee Trace National Recreation Trail,** which passes 22 miles through the geological area, there are 36 miles of trails that combine to form the Red River Gorge National Recreation Trail System.

When you enter the Nada Tunnel, you'll be on a one-lane road over an old railroad bed once used for hauling timber out of the river gorge.

The rail line was built in 1911 by the Dana Lumber Company; the name of the tunnel is simply an anagram of the name "Dana."

Once in the geological area, you'll come to an iron bridge that takes you across the Red River. The river is often quite muddy, which is presumably how it came to be called "Red."

Soon after the bridge, bear to the right on KY715. The road follows the river upstream past the information station at the Gladie Creek Historic Site. Past the information center, watch for the trailhead on the left for the 0.4-mile **Tower Rock Trail.**

Farther down the road, a sign warns that you are approaching a view of Sky Bridge. Unfortunately there is no good place to pull off the road by the time you realize you're there, but you can get a good glimpse if you drive slowly. The arch is at the top of the mountain ridge set against the sky in an impressive display.

The road then winds to the top of the ridge to a turnoff for Sky Bridge on the right. On the way to the arch, you'll pass by overlooks for Devils Canyon and Swift Camp Creek.

From the parking area at the end of the road, the 0.9-mile **Sky Bridge Loop** takes you across the back of the arch, from where you get a panoramic view of the Red River Gorge. Sky Bridge is the most visited of the natural arches, as is obvious from all the names carved in the rock. Completing the loop hike, you'll drop down to the bottom of the arch, which has a length, or span, of about 75 feet and a clearance under the arch of 25 feet. Strictly speaking, "bridge" is an inaccurate word to use for this arch. A natural bridge spans some watercourse, which even if no longer extant, was at least in the distant past the force that cut the bridge. An arch is usually high, away from streams, and was cut by weathering, which includes rain erosion, freezing, and wind; on occasion the intrusion of plant roots can be a factor. Sky Bridge is an arch, most probably formed by two rock shelters, one on each side of the ridge, that deepened through headward erosion until they met, forming a hole.

You can get a good look at Sky Bridge by taking the right turn just before the parking lot. At the end of this side road, you'll find a short trail to the **Sky Bridge Overlook.**

Soon after getting back on KY715 from Sky Bridge Road, a parking area on the right gives access to the 0.3-mile **Whistling Arch Trail.** The small Whistling Arch is a formation that some refer to as a "lighthouse" or "skylight," an intermediate stage between a depression in the rock and a true arch where weathering has expanded and smoothed the opening into a graceful span, such as Sky Bridge.

Farther along the highway, at a large turnout and overlook of the valley, is the trailhead for the 0.3-mile **Angel Windows Trail.** Angel Windows is two small openings; a column, rounded by weathering, separates the two.

Continuing on 715, you'll come to a gravel road on the right to **Chimney Top Rock.** The road is easily negotiated by passenger cars. At the end of the road you'll find a turnaround where you can leave your vehicle and walk the 0.3 mile to the overlook for Chimney Top Rock, the best view of the Red River Gorge; you'll notice a few fields on some private inholdings. To the left is Half Moon Rock.

From the parking area you can also take the 0.2-mile **Princess Arch Trail** to a delicate arch 32 feet long with 8 feet of clearance. The graceful shape of the arch is characteristic of what is referred to as a "finished" arch. Continue along the trail to an overlook of the gorge and Chimney Top Rock.

Continuing down KY715, you'll come upon Rock Bridge Road, a gravel road to the left just before the junction with KY15. At the end of the road, you can hike the 1.3-mile **Rock Bridge Loop.** Rock Bridge with Swift Camp Creek flowing under it is one of the true natural bridges. This arch was formed by a waterfall that once poured over its edge. Finding a weak place in the rock back from the edge, the water scooped out the softer layers beneath, and as the waterfall retreated, it left the span of stone suspended over the creek.

The creek is named for John Swift who was an early explorer of the region, one of the first to write about the Red River Gorge. He claimed to have discovered a deposit of silver that he and his men mined and then buried to retrieve later. While in England trying to raise money to finance an expedition to go back for the silver, Swift was imprisoned when the American Revolution began because he

Princess Arch

had been outspoken about the colonies' independence. While in prison, he became blind. After the war, Swift returned to Kentucky with various companions, only to wander for 14 years searching for the treasure without finding where he had left it. The John Swift silver legend has various renditions and can be heard at other locations in Kentucky: it is said that he buried silver at the Towers in Breaks Interstate Park, and also that his silver was found near Cumberland Falls. In his journals about the Red River Gorge area, Swift referred to a bridge over a stream. Since Rock Bridge is the only such bridge in the area, it is thought to be the site of Swift's base camp, and thus the stream became "Swift Camp Creek."

Along the Rock Bridge Trail, you'll find access to the 6.7-mile **Swift Camp Creek Trail.** In the late 1800s when logging began, Swift Camp Creek was used to bring timber down to the Red River. Splash dams were built at intervals along the creek. The newly cut logs were piled in the water behind the dams, and then each dam in succession

Rock Bridge

was blown with explosives. The released water carried the logs down the creek to the Red River and then on to Clay City to the Broadhead and Garrett Mill, one of the largest sawmills in the eastern United States at the turn of the century. Some of the dams on the creek were revolving dams, which could be used over and over. The remains of these dams can be seen along the trail. You'll also pass Turtle Back Arch and Timmons Arch farther up Swift Camp Creek; both are off trail and you'll have to do some looking.

After getting back on KY715, turn west on KY15 to the Koomer Ridge Campground. From the tent/trailer part of the campground, you can take the 1-mile **Silvermine Arch Trail,** which toward the end, leads down a series of wooden steps to the arch tucked among giant boulders. This arch is a "waterfall step arch," formed by a waterfall that once streamed over the cliff edge. Hitting a hard sandstone layer that was to become the back of the arch, the waterfall first created a shelf. As it retreated, it hit a weak area and was able to scoop out softer layers behind and under the ledge, creating the arch—a process similar to that at Rock Bridge.

From the tent-only part of the campground, the 1-mile **Hidden Arch Trail** leads to a relatively small arch that projects from the rock wall; you'll climb down by way of a wooden stairway. From this area, you can also pick up the 2.2-mile **Koomer Ridge Trail,** which joins the 8.4-mile **Rough Trail** and the 1.5-mile **Buck Trail.**

West of the campground on KY15, Tunnel Ridge Road turns to the north. To the south at this road junction, you'll see the trailhead for the 2-mile **Whittleton Branch Trail** which ends at Natural Bridge State Park; the trail has a short spur that takes you to **Whittleton Arch,** nearly 100 feet in length but not very high. Set in a narrow ravine, this is also a waterfall step arch.

Along Tunnel Ridge Road, you'll come to a turnout for the 0.3-mile **Grays Arch Trail,** which combines with a section of the Rough Trail to lead 0.9 mile to Grays Arch. The arch, with an 80-foot span and a 50-foot clearance, is one of the largest arches; surrounded by steep rock walls, the arch is set within one of the most dramatic landscapes on the Cumberland Plateau. Along the Grays Arch Trail and then the Rough Trail, you can walk the 0.7-mile **D. Boon Hut Trail** to a structure that was first thought to have been one of Daniel Boone's huts. Boone explored the region between 1769 and 1771, often sleeping under rock overhangs. In one rock shelter a small hut was found in 1967 with "D. Boon" carved on one of the boards. Recent studies have determined that this was not one of Boone's huts. Evidence of saltpeter mining is also there; a chain link fence keeps vandals out.

Just before the parking for the Grays Arch Trail, you can also pick up the 1.8-mile **Pinch-Em-Tight Trail,** and 1.0-mile **Rush Ridge Trail,** which connect with the Rough Trail.

As you drive along the ridgetop on Tunnel Ridge Road, you'll pass over the Nada Tunnel at about the halfway point. Then on the right will be a turnout for the 2.4-mile **Courthouse Rock Trail** and 1.1-mile **Auxier Ridge Trail,** to views of Courthouse Rock, Haystack Rock, and Raven Rock. Early settlers thought ravens nested on Raven Rock, but the birds turned out to be buzzards. Courthouse Rock is frequently used

Grays Arch

for climbing. Climbing and rappeling are permitted in the geological area, but because of the number of visitors at Sky Bridge, Grays Arch, and Chimney Top Rock, climbing is not allowed at those locations from April 1 to November 1. The Auxier Ridge Trail provides the best view of Courthouse Rock. The Courthouse Rock Trail links up with the 0.8-mile **Auxier Branch Trail.**

Past the Courthouse Rock turnout on Tunnel Ridge Road you will come to a small turnout for a view of **Star Gap Arch** on the left. You'll need to walk along the path for a short distance and then look across the valley to see this arch, which is 72 feet long with a 13-foot clearance.

At the end of Tunnel Ridge Road you'll find a turnaround and the trailhead for the 1-mile **Double Arch Trail.** The arch is perhaps the most unusual in the geological area, for it is in fact two arches, one on top of the other, although the top one is small. The bottom arch is about 30 feet long with an 11-foot clearance; the top one is 25 feet long with only a 1.5-foot clearance.

At Natural Bridge State Park you can pick up the trail system either from the lodge or from the recreation area along the river. The 0.8-mile **Original Trail** (Trail #1) is the most popular route to the Natural Bridge; once there, if you walk through the arch, you'll find on the other side a fracture in the rock that allows access to the top. If you're not up to climbing the ridge to see the arch, a skylift will bring you to within 600 feet. The skylift is well located; you can hike to the arch and back without ever knowing the lift is nearby.

The 0.8-mile **Balanced Rock Trail** (Trail #2) also leads to the arch. You'll pass by Balanced Rock and climb many zigzagging stone and wooden stairways to eventually emerge onto the back of the arch, a broad rock expanse from which you'll have panoramic views of the valley. You can then descend to the bottom through the fracture on the left.

On top of the arch, you can pick up the 1.3-mile **Battleship Rock Trail** (Trail #3) that leads to the top of the skylift and swings around to Lookout Point for a good view of the Natural Bridge. You can continue out to Lover's Leap and then descend through either Devil's Gulch or the Needle's Eye, both steep stairways, to make connections back to the trailhead.

For long-distance hiking, you can also walk the 8.5-mile **Sand Gap Trail** and the 3.8-mile **Hood's Branch Trail,** which lead from the bottom of the skylift to the Natural Bridge. The 0.3-mile **Hensons Arch Trail** leads from the Whittleton Campground to Hensons Cave Arch, a small, rare, limestone arch.

References

Daniel Boone National Forest. *Recreation on the Daniel Boone National Forest.* Newspaper. Winchester, KY, no date.

Daniel Boone National Forest, Stanton Ranger District. "The Gladie Years." Brochure. Stanton, KY, no date.

Kentucky Dept. of Parks. "Natural Bridge State Resort Park." Brochure. Frankfort, KY, 1989.

———. "Trail Guide, Natural Bridge State Resort Park." Brochure and map. Frankfort, KY, no date.

———. "Visitor's Guide to Natural Bridge State Resort Park." Brochure. Frankfort, KY, no date.

Lander, Arthur B., Jr. *A Guide to the Backpacking and Day-Hiking Trails of Kentucky.* Ann Arbor, MI: Thomas Press, 1979.

Perry, Samuel D. *South Fork Country.* Detroit: Harlo Press, 1983.

Ruchhoft, Robert H. *Kentucky's Land of the Arches: The Red River Gorge.* Cincinnati: Pucelle Press, 1976.

U.S. Dept. of Agriculture, Forest Service. "Red River Gorge Geological Area." Brochure and map. Washington, DC, no date.

Chapter 6

Cumberland Falls

Formed by the confluence of Poor Fork, Clover Fork, and Martins Fork, the Cumberland River meanders westward across the Cumberland Plateau in Kentucky, carving a steep-walled canyon in the surface of the tableland and forming great oxbows in which the river nearly turns back upon itself.

The river had been on maps since at least 1650 and was called the "Shawnee River" until Thomas Walker, on his exploration in 1750, renamed it the "Cumberland" for the Duke of Cumberland. One story has it that Walker, while looking at the river, said the crookedness of the waterway reminded him of the Duke.

In the days when only Indian trails crossed the land, the Cumberland River was one of the easiest routes by which explorers could make their way through the wilderness. In 1780 Zachariah Green and three other longhunters floated down the river in a boat made of the poplar trees which grow throughout the Plateau. On February 12, as the Green party floated with the current, gazing at the rock walls of the river canyon draped with icicles, the group heard the sound of a low rumble. They knew immediately the danger they faced; the rush of the water confirmed they were headed for a waterfall. As the boat accelerated toward a great mist that rose where the water spilled into a deep canyon, the men grabbed their long poles and pushed to shore.

The men could not portage the heavy boat. So one of them took it back into the river and then dove into the cold water and swam for shore, leaving the boat adrift in the current. The men watched as their boat disappeared over the falls in a great splash and spray of water. When they ran to the edge of the pit into which the water spilled, they saw the boat bobbing in the river below the falls, miraculously still in one piece.

Green and his men were among the first white men to encounter Cumberland Falls, a broad waterfall on the Cumberland River, sometimes called "The Niagara of the South." Although the region had been explored on occasion, few apart from the native Indians knew of the Great Falls of the Cumberland until Green's boat sailed off the top of the falls, with the longhunters looking helplessly on.

Cumberland Falls State Resort Park

Cumberland Falls is now the centerpiece for a Kentucky state park surrounded by national forest land, part of the Daniel Boone National Forest.

Lewis and Mary Renfro were the first permanent landowners to live near the waterfall. In 1850, they built a small log cabin beside the falls, which was used as a hospital during the Civil War. Renfro was a Baptist preacher who spent much of his time looking for the John Swift silver mine. Swift, an early explorer, had emerged from the wilderness with silver in his pockets, claiming it could be picked up in handfuls. Some thought he found the silver in Red River Gorge to the north, but Renfro had been convinced by swindlers that the place was near Cumberland Falls. No one ever found silver in either place.

Socrates Owens purchased 400 acres that included the falls from the Renfros in 1875 and built the Cumberland Falls Hotel. The first raft of logs sent down river to construct the hotel was lost over the waterfall. The second raft was successfully floated to the site of the Renfro cabin, where the hotel was built. Hotel guests, at first mostly fishermen, took showers under the falls, which for years was the only way of getting a bath at the hotel.

In 1902, Henry Brunson bought the inn from Owens and renamed it the "Brunson Inn." He enlarged the structure to two stories with 80 guest rooms and a ballroom. It became a popular resort. People came over dirt roads in wagons from Parkers Lake to the west where there was

Cumberland Falls

a train station; the community was then known as "Cumberland Falls Station." There was no established road from the east until one was blazed from Corbin, Kentucky, by the Kiwanis Club and other civic groups in 1927.

In the 1920s, a 50-room hotel was built on the other side of the river from the Brunson Inn and was called the "Cumberland Falls Hotel," as was Owens's inn before its name was changed.

In 1924, the Cumberland River Power Company, owned by Samuel Insull, proposed a diversion dam upstream from the falls; water was to be sent through a tunnel to a power station downstream, bypassing the falls which is in the bend of an oxbow. The company was to provide electric power to Kentucky and parts of Indiana and Ohio.

Controversy arose over the proposed dam, which would divert water from the falls. The opposition consisted of those who did not want the area disturbed because of its scenic value and lumber companies who often sent logs down the river and did not want them stopped by a dam. T. Coleman DuPont, who was then a Delaware state senator living part-time in Louisville and a frequent visitor to Cumberland Falls, offered to buy the falls for the state. It was not until 1930, after DuPont's death, that his offer was accepted; his family donated the funds. The falls, along with 539 surrounding acres, were purchased from Insull's company in 1931, and Cumberland Falls State Park was established. The Brunson Inn was renamed "The Moonbow Inn." Since that time more acreage has been added to the park.

Just 68 feet high, Cumberland Falls is spectacular nonetheless because of the volume of water and its width, which during high water is 125 feet. At flood stage, it can reach 300 feet wide. The width of the falls makes it a rare sight on the Plateau, which usually has slender streams of water falling from great heights.

Several overlooks along a paved trail with wooden rails and walkways that follow the rim of the gorge give several vantage points from which to look at the falls. At one time a wooden walkway built by the Civilian Conservation Corps in the 1930s led behind the falls, but it was swept away in a flood. Apparently there was a walkway behind the falls also during the time of the Brunson Inn.

The trail continues on and leads down to a sandy beach littered with coal and shale along the river bank. The trail passes among the remnants of concrete foundations where a bathhouse once stood. The house was part of the CCC project and was completed in 1934; it burned in 1968, and was never rebuilt. Although arson was suspected in the burning of the bathhouse and also in the burning of the Cumberland Falls Hotel in 1947 and the Moonbow Inn in 1949, no one was charged in any of the incidents.

At the west side of the park the Gatliff bridge crosses the Cumberland River upstream from Cumberland Falls. Before the bridge was built, a ferry carried cars, three at a time, across the river. During flood stage, the ferry could not operate, and people crossed the river in a basket hanging from a cable. On two occasions the ferry broke loose from where it was moored during a flood and was swept over the falls.

The bridge was built in 1953–54 by R. R. Dawson, who traveled to Europe to study the design and construction of bridges on the Rhine River. Therefore, the bridge at Cumberland Falls resembles an Old

World bridge. The steel and concrete construction is faced with native sandstone. The bridge was named for Edward Moss Gatliff, who was Kentucky's Highway Commissioner.

The Moonbow

On a sunny day, a rainbow appears in the mist of Cumberland Falls rising from where the water crashes into the river below. Since the rainbow depends on the force of the water and air currents to carry the mist into the air, the rainbow is not static. One second it may appear truncated; then a billow of mist roils upward, painting the air above the falls with color.

But even more intriguing is the waterfall's ability to produce a "moonbow" on cloudless nights with a full moon shining. The park has claimed that Cumberland Falls is one of only two places in the world where such a phenomenon occurs, the other being at Victoria Falls on the Zambezi River in Zimbabwe. But in fact, moonbows appear anywhere the conditions are right. Niagara Falls' Luna Island is so named for the moonbow that can be seen in the mist of the falls; nearby city lights and lights for the falls now tend to drown the faint luminescence. Lower Yosemite Falls in Yosemite National Park has a moonbow during April and May when the spring melt releases enough water to produce a mist at the bottom of the falls. Moonbows probably occur at many other waterfalls, and it is just that no one has reported seeing them or that no one has yet been there at the right time to have seen them.

But even acknowledging these other moonbows, perhaps it is still accurate to say that Cumberland Falls is one of the few locations where moonbows are easily seen. On many full-moon nights with a clear sky, the Cumberland Falls moonbow appears as the mist rising from the falls refracts the light from the moon. A white light beginning at the base of the falls looms up and arcs downstream. On a chilly night during fall and winter with the moon especially bright, colors may appear in the moonbow, just as in a rainbow.

Several factors must be just right for the moonbow to occur. Of course, there must be a bright moon and a cloudless night, but also enough water must be flowing over the falls to spew mist into the air; the mist is then affected by wind direction and velocity.

Finally, to get a glimpse of the moonbow, a person must be standing in the right location with respect to the position of the moon in the sky and the mist rising into the air. Face the falls, and the moon will rise over the mountain and trees from behind. It seems the best view is with the moon almost directly behind. Take a few steps to the right or left at an angle, and the moonbow begins to fade.

The time of night the moonbow will appear depends on how long it takes for the moon to get high enough in the sky to shine over the mountain and down into the canyon, which is of course where the mist rises as the water crashes to the bottom. In winter the moonbow may appear as early as 8:30 in the evening. In summer it may be as late as 1:00 A.M.

Beaver Creek Wilderness

Daniel Boone National Forest west of Cumberland Falls contains the Beaver Creek Wilderness and Wildlife Management Area. Beaver Creek is the only wilderness area in the southern part of the national forest. It is a land of forest, sandstone cliffs, rock overhangs, and waterfalls.

The Cherokees and Shawnees hunted this land from the spring through the fall. Pieces of pottery and flint found under the rock overhangs are evidence that the rockhouses were used as hunting camps.

In the early 1800s settlers came to the Beaver Creek area, probably by flatboat down the Cumberland River. They came to farm and eventually to cut timber; a large lumber mill was once located on Beaver Creek. In the early 1900s, commercial timbering declined, and the land became virtually deserted. With no more intrusion, the forest was able to renew itself, and the land became wilderness once again. The Beaver Creek Wildlife Management Area was established in 1940, and the 4,791-acre Beaver Creek Wilderness became part of the National Wilderness Preservation System in 1975. Much of the wilderness area

Natural Arch

consists of slopes and stream banks with many small creeks cutting through the plateau surface. Mature forest remains in the coves that were too difficult for logging.

North of Beaver Creek Wilderness a huge cave system underlies Sloans Valley. Sloans Valley Cave is variously reported to have 16 to 19 entrances, some of them narrow shafts that require ropes to go down, and others, large entrances, with at least one big enough to drive a truck through.

Natural Arch

One of the largest natural stone arches on the Plateau stands just west of Cumberland Falls State Resort Park and southwest of Beaver Creek Wilderness. Called "Natural Arch," it can be found in the Natural Arch Scenic Area of the Daniel Boone National Forest.

Natural Arch has a span of 100 feet and a clearance of 60 feet. In few arches is the opening as large with the rock above actually in the shape of a bridge, not a hole through a mountain. Its only rivals are the arch at Natural Bridge State Park and Grays Arch in the Red River Gorge Geological Area to the north and Twin Arches in the Big South Fork National River and Recreation Area to the south.

The Natural Arch Scenic Area also contains Chimney Arch, more like a large cavity, 30 feet high and 25 feet wide, with the back part of the roof caved in to create the arch. Crevices and small compartments in the rock make it an interesting place to explore.

Directions and Services

You can get to **Cumberland Falls State Resort Park** from either the east or west along KY90. If you are coming from I-75, pick up US25W and then turn west at the junction of KY90; a large sign directs you to Cumberland Falls State Resort Park, which is approximately 7 miles

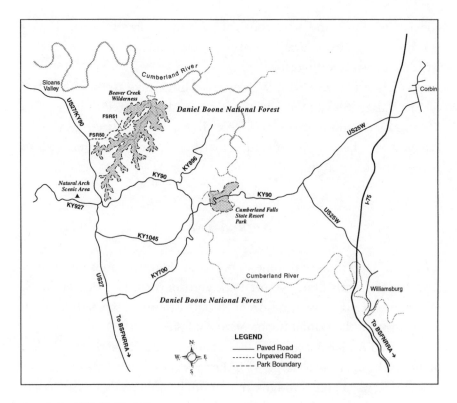

Cumberland Falls Region

from this junction. Along the way you'll pass the Dryland Bridge Overlook that provides views to both sides of the road; the bridge there is called "Dryland" because there is no water under it.

Showers, restrooms, and laundry facilities are available at the campground with 50 sites for tents and trailers. Each site has electric and water hookups. The campground is open April to October. There is no advance registration.

The park contains a swimming pool and a tennis court near the DuPont Lodge, originally built in 1933 by the Civilian Conservation Corps and named for T. Coleman DuPont. After a fire in 1940, the lodge was rebuilt by the Works Progress Administration. It is thought the fire that destroyed the original lodge was the result of a loose rock that fell out of the back wall of the fireplace.

DuPont Lodge

In addition to the original lodge, the CCC built a number of cabins, which are those located near the campground. Also, scattered near the lodge are new duplexes, called the "Woodland Rooms."

The 52-room lodge is open year-round; reservations should be made in advance. A dining room is downstairs. Directly out the back of the lodge is an open patio with a spectacular view of the Cumberland River as it flows toward Cumberland Falls, which is not in sight. Off the lobby you'll find a large sitting room with a huge fireplace. Guests square danced the varnish off the floor of this room at the dedication of the rebuilt lodge in 1942—dancing is now held in a separate square-dance pavilion.

At the end of the sitting room is a door leading to the Robert A. Blair museum, named for a member of the Kiwanis Club team that blazed the first road from Corbin to the falls. The museum is a single room with exhibits explaining the history of the area from the early American Indians to the dedication of the state park.

Until his death in 1981, Blair worked to preserve the falls in its natural state. In the 1920s, he fought to stop the private power interests that wanted to divert water from the river. In 1965 Blair also helped to stop the Army Corps of Engineers from damming the river, and later he helped stop the construction of a chairlift.

Cumberland Falls is 0.75 mile west of the lodge entrance. A gift shop and restaurant stand on the site of the old Moonbow Inn. This stretch of the river, 16.1 miles of the corridor, is designated a Kentucky Wild River.

If you drive out of the far end of the falls parking area and cross the main road, you'll enter a picnic area situated along the river. High rock bluffs make it a secluded place to have lunch and watch the river rolling past.

You can reach the **Beaver Creek Wilderness Area** from Cumberland Falls by heading west on KY90, entering the Daniel Boone National Forest. You'll first pass a turnoff on KY896 for the **Sawyer Recreation Area** on Lake Cumberland, which has a five-unit campground. KY90 then skirts the southern boundary of the wilderness area. The primary road into the wilderness is FSR50 off US27/KY90 north of Parkers Lake. **Sloans Valley** is on US27 about 4 miles north of the FSR50 turnoff for the wilderness area.

To get to the **Natural Arch Scenic Area,** turn south in Parkers Lake on US27; you'll encounter a national forest sign on the right directing you to turn on KY927 to Natural Arch. The natural arch area is about 2 miles along this road. The picnic grounds and the parking area are closed during the winter months, but you can park outside the gate and walk in. Continuing on KY927 past the Natural Arch Scenic Area for another mile, you'll have scenic views at the **Great Gulf Overlook** and the **Straight Creek Overlook.**

Trails

Cumberland Falls State Resort Park contains 18 miles of trails, with the trailheads scattered throughout the area. Although none are long enough for backpacking, the trail system connects with several trails in the national forest.

Trail 2, 7 miles long, begins at the far end of the picnic area and passes along the Cumberland River for a couple of miles before turning north to circle the park and eventually leading back to connect with the wooden walkways at Cumberland Falls. Along the way, Trail 2 connects with the 10-mile **Moonbow Trail,** which crosses national forest land to the Laurel River Lake Recreation Area. The Moonbow Trail is also a section of the **Sheltowee Trace,** the national recreation trail traveling the length of Daniel Boone National Forest. The Trace incorporates the Moonbow Trail and then Trail 2 into the state park and then leaves the park by passing over the Gatliff Bridge and following the Cumberland River upstream.

Trail 4 is a 1-mile nature trail that begins at the DuPont Lodge; you'll find a self-guide brochure at the trailhead. **Trail 6** leads 0.5 mile from the lodge to Cumberland Falls.

If you have time for only one hike, you should take **Trail 9,** which is the only trail that leads to Eagle Falls on the west side of the river downstream from Cumberland Falls where Eagle Creek joins the river. The trailhead is on KY90 west of the Gatliff Bridge just as the road turns away from the river. From here it is 0.75 mile to Eagle Falls. Along the first part of the trail, you'll have great views of Cumberland Falls. **Trail 10** branches off to the left, leading uphill to a shelter and overlook. Farther along you'll cross a small creek, and Trail 10 rejoins 9. Eventually you'll come to a junction with Trail 9 straight ahead, which loops around to join Trail 10, and the Eagle Falls Trail to the right. The trail to the waterfall is steep in places and goes down stairs that can be slippery if wet and covered with leaves. At the bottom you are virtually in the riverbed as you approach Eagle Falls. The 45-foot waterfall is especially notable because it is recessed into a grotto-like depression in the cliff wall; it is said that Eagle Falls was a sacred place for the Cherokees.

Only one short maintained trail exists in the Beaver Creek Wilderness—the **Three Forks of Beaver Creek Overlook Trail.** Turn east on FSR50 off US27 above Parkers Lake; this is the Hammonds Camp Road. In 2 miles turn right on FSR51 and in 1 mile you will come to the trailhead parking lot. The 1-mile trail parallels an old logging road, which it crosses a short distance from the overlook. Go straight ahead to the overlook, 300 feet above the junction of the Freeman, Middle, and Hurricane Forks of Beaver Creek. You can descend to the edge of Beaver Creek by retracing your steps to the logging road and turning right (east) down the ridge for about half a mile.

At the Natural Arch Scenic Area you'll find paved trails leading off to the left and the right—neither is marked. Take the left trail for an overlook of the arch.

At this distance it is hard to get a good idea of the arch's size; so retrace your steps and take the 0.5-mile **Natural Arch Trail** to the right which leads to the arch. The trail is paved all the way and leads out to another overlook before dropping into the canyon by a series of concrete steps.

As you get down into the canyon, you'll intersect with the 5-mile **Buffalo Canyon Loop Trail.** Keep right to complete the trail to the arch. But if you take the loop trail to the left, you'll find Chimney Arch in 1 mile and Cooper Creek in the bottom of Great Gulf in about 2 miles before looping around to the Natural Arch. At the base of Natural Arch, you can pick up the 0.5-mile **Shawnee Nature Trail,** which loops around the ridge and returns through the arch; there is no sign designating the trail.

At the Great Gulf Overlook, you can pick up the 1.2-mile **Gulf Bottom Trail** on the south side of the road, just past the overlook. The trail drops down to pass under the road among high cliffs and loops back to the road; when you emerge on the road, turn left to get back to the overlook parking. A connector along the Gulf Bottom Trail joins with the Buffalo Canyon Trail.

References

Arnow, Harriette Simpson. *Seedtime on the Cumberland.* New York: MacMillan Company, 1960.

Kentucky Dept. of Parks. "Cumberland Falls State Resort Park." Brochure. Frankfort, KY, 1990.

———. "Cumberland Falls State Resort Park Visitor's Guide." Brochure. Frankfort, KY, 1990.

Lander, Arthur B., Jr. *A Guide to the Backpacking and Day-Hiking Trail of Kentucky.* Ann Arbor, MI: Thomas Press, 1979.

McConnell, Jeannie. *The History of Cumberland Falls.* Frankfort, KY: Kentucky Dept. of Parks, 1982.

Perry, Samuel D. *South Fork Country.* Detroit: Harlo Press, 1983.

Chapter 7

Big South Fork

In the northern part of Tennessee on the Cumberland Plateau, just south of the Kentucky-Tennessee dividing line, the Clear Fork and the New River converge to create the Big South Fork of the Cumberland River, originally called the "Flute River" by the Cherokees. As the Big South Fork flows northward into Kentucky, it carves another of the Plateau's deep canyons, reaching depths of 600 feet before joining the Cumberland River far downstream from Cumberland Falls. As it travels west, the Cumberland River dips south into Tennessee and then back north to join the Ohio River not far from where the Tennessee River flows into the Ohio. The waters from the Big South Fork then travel down the Ohio and eventually mingle with the waters of the Mississippi.

The area that the Big South Fork drains is probably one of the most primitive and isolated on the Plateau. Prior to the 18th century, only native Indians had penetrated the region. Longhunters led by Kasper Mansker in 1769 were the first known white men to see the Big South Fork. Later, small, widely scattered farming settlements developed. Then in the early part of the 20th century a population influx was brought on by the extensive mining and logging operations in the watershed; dozens of logging and mining camps grew up, supported by small communities and towns. The largest operation was the Stearns Coal and Lumber Company, founded in 1902, which commanded 30,000 acres of land. In its peak year, the Stearns Company produced 970,000 tons of coal and 18 million board feet of lumber.

With the 1930s depression, the logging and mining industry declined; many camps were deserted and lumber mills and rail lines abandoned. Stearns opened the Blue Heron Mine in 1937, still hoping to bolster its operations. Although the mine continued operation until

1962, the end of the economic boom had already been determined, and eventually the river gorge was left in silence, giving the forest time to heal and grow.

This remote river gorge contains several plant and animal species that the federal government considers endangered: Cumberland rosemary, Cumberland sandwort, Lucy Braun snakeroot, Virginia spirea, spotfin chub, and four species of mussel. There are also several animal species considered rare by the states of Tennessee and Kentucky and many species of plants that the Smithsonian Institution considers threatened. In addition, the river gorge includes habitat for four species on the federal endangered species list: southern bald eagle, Indiana bat, red-cockaded woodpecker, and American peregrine falcon. Some virgin forest remains.

Local conservationists considered the area of prime wilderness value and began pushing for some kind of protected status for the river in the 1960s. That effort eventually led to the establishment of the Big South Fork National River and Recreation Area (BSFNRRA), developed by the Army Corps of Engineers and now managed by the National Park Service (NPS).

Federal involvement with the river dates to 1881, when the Corps of Engineers conducted a study for improving navigation on the river; no action was taken. Then in 1933, the Corps proposed a dam at Devils Jump, a rapids in a narrow part of the river gorge in Kentucky. The dam was originally projected to cost $200 million and would have been almost 500 feet high, the highest dam in the East. Although placed in Kentucky, the dam would have flooded the river gorge and tributary gorges well upstream into Tennessee.

During the 1950s and 1960s, the Devils Jump Dam was authorized several times in the U.S. Senate but never passed the House of Representatives. Over the years, other studies recommended dams at other sites and pump storage facilities.

Tennessee Citizens for Wilderness Planning (TCWP), a local conservation group founded in 1966, set out to stop the dam proposals by having the Big South Fork placed on the impending Tennessee Scenic Rivers Bill. Opposition to the Devils Jump Dam was mounted not only

The Big South Fork

to save a pristine area from being inundated by a lake but also because the dam was economically insupportable—an independent study showed that enough water to generate electricity flowed down the river only during 11 percent of the year. But when the state Scenic Rivers Bill was passed in 1968, the Big South Fork was taken off the list of rivers to be included.

TCWP also succeeded in getting the Big South Fork considered in the draft National Wild and Scenic Rivers Bill. But when this national bill was considered in 1968, the Big South Fork and several other rivers were dropped from the bill before it was passed.

At this point, Congress requested new studies on the Big South Fork—one to examine new dam proposals and a second to study alternatives. The Corps of Engineers, the Bureau of Outdoor Recreation, and the U.S. Forest Service were involved in these studies. At TCWP's urging, the National Park Service was also included among the agencies, and the study area was enlarged to include significant portions of the Big South Fork's tributaries. TCWP then served as an advisor for the alternatives study, which when made public, presented several suggestions, including designating the region as a national recreation area, national forest, national park, or scenic river. The dam study was never published.

During this time, Tennessee Citizens for Wilderness Planning gained strength by forming and heading a union of 21 conservation groups, the Big South Fork Coalition, coordinated by Liane Russell, one of the founders of TCWP. The coalition worked with then-Senator Howard Baker of Tennessee to draft a bill calling for a combination of national river and recreation area. The legislation became part of the 1972 Omnibus Rivers and Harbors Act, which would authorize numerous Corps of Engineers' projects nationwide. The Corps of Engineers would have been given control over the proposed national river and recreation area, but the bill was pocket-vetoed by President Richard Nixon for reasons unrelated to the Big South Fork.

The conservationists, who were a little skeptical about giving the Corps authority to manage the area, took this opportunity to get the bill rewritten so that the National Park Service would take over management after the Corps established the area. The bill was reintroduced as part of the 1974 Water Resources Development Act. Signed into law March 7, this act authorized the Big South Fork National River and Recreation Area.

As it turned out, each delay in the effort to get some kind of protection for the Big South Fork, from exclusion in the Tennessee Scenic Rivers System to the final National River and Recreation Area designation, served to strengthen the protection finally won. If the Big South Fork had been designated only a state scenic river, it would have very little protection today. If the original federal legislation had passed, the Corps of Engineers would be in charge of managing the area instead of the National Park Service, which has more experience and emphasis in preservation activities. In the end, the final resolution provided the best protection.

At one time there were efforts to add further protection by designating as wilderness about 26,000 acres of the BSFNRRA, half in Kentucky and half in Tennessee, referred to as the "Troublesome Creek" or

"Troublesome-No Business" wilderness area. Those efforts have since taken a back seat to the more pressing need to finish acquiring the land within the designated BSFNRRA boundaries.

Purchase of the planned 123,000 acres stalled at around 106,000 acres when 1986 regulations imposed on the Army Corps of Engineers required that federal expenditures be matched with local funds. The counties surrounding the Big South Fork had little money to contribute to the cause. In the meantime, the Corps proceeded with development of trails and recreational facilities, so that eventually both the Corps and the National Park Service decided the time had come for the official transfer of the park to the NPS, which had been managing the park lands in the interim. Legislation authorizing the transfer was passed by Congress in November 1990. On August 25, 1991, the transfer of lands was recognized at the dedication of the new park headquarters; the ceremony was also a symbolic dedication of the recreation area. With the BSFNRRA transferred to the NPS, regulations requiring local matching funds no longer applied, and the way was cleared for purchase of the remaining lands as soon as funds were appropriated. Only a few small tracts remain unpurchased at this writing.

Big South Fork National River and Recreation Area

The BSFNRRA combination of national river and national recreation area is a unique approach to managing federal lands. The park incorporates two management zones. The gorge area is managed essentially as wilderness with few improvements, while the adjacent rim area is the location for established recreation.

This combination of national river and national recreation area may well become a blueprint for future preservation of such places. It is a compromise that settles conflicting arguments between calls for wilderness preservation and the demands that wilderness areas be accessible and useful.

When the BSFNRRA was established, the Corps of Engineers enthusiastically took on its new role as conservationist, although perhaps

Big South Fork River

with too much of a bent toward development. Some funds that went into constructing facilities could have been used to purchase lands within the authorized boundaries that at the time were threatened. At the same time that the Corps acquired lands, it also improved roads, established campgrounds, constructed a visitor center complex and historic exhibits, and created hiking and horse trails. As each piece or section was completed, the National Park Service stepped in to take over interim management of the facilities. The NPS now has complete management responsibility.

Canoeing and rafting are popular pursuits in the park. The Big South Fork is one of the best whitewater streams in the Southeast. The section upstream from Leatherwood Ford is Class III–IV whitewater on a stretch of the river that is pure wilderness; civilization is a long way off if a paddler gets in trouble. Downstream from Leatherwood Ford to Blue Heron Mine is Class I–II with long stretches of calm water, but this river segment also includes a couple of drops, Angel Falls and Devils Jump, that even some experienced paddlers hesitate to run. There are developed portages around these two hazards.

Easier canoeing can be found on lower reaches of the BSF down from Blue Heron and along the river's tributaries. Clear Fork has a 6-mile stretch of Class I–II and 10 miles of Class II–III. White Oak Creek and North White Oak Creek are both Class II. All three are included in the national river area.

The Big South Fork, like most national parks and national recreation areas, has a number of resource and management problems that must be resolved. These problems present special challenges to the park staff and to park supporters.

The primary resource challenge is water quality. Strip mining, timbering, exploring for oil and gas, road construction, and farming in the Big South Fork watershed cause erosion that contributes silt and toxic substances to the river and its tributaries. The New River tributary usually carries a heavy load of sediment because of such activities outside the park. Oil and gas exploration is still permitted under the enabling legislation in the adjacent area within the park boundaries and must be monitored; there are about 300 oil and gas wells in the area.

Acquisition of private lands within the authorized boundaries is not yet complete and awaits Congressional appropriations; in the meantime, landowners have become impatient and are beginning to cut trees and to allow mining on their land. In 1991, the Nature Conservancy optioned 1,200 acres on North White Oak Creek's Laurel Fork to help protect the water quality on this tributary that is critical to Big South Fork system; the land has since been added to the river and recreation area. The Conservancy is looking at other acreage along BSF tributaries. Also, Tennessee's Scott State Forest remains as an inholding; conservationists are urging the state to donate the forest to the park.

In addition, most of the park boundary has not yet been surveyed or marked, a task that will take some time to complete.

Endangered species must be identified and protected; the current inventory of plant resources is inadequate. The reintroduction of native animal species is helping to restore the ecological balance. Otter and turkey have been successfully reintroduced, and black bear reintroduction has recently taken place. Hunting and trapping are still permitted under the enabling legislation and must be monitored.

Archaeological sites of prehistoric Indians and early settlers need to be surveyed and monitored to prevent deterioration and looting. And as in any new park area, trash dumps and junk car piles are periodically found and must be cleaned up.

Except for a few exemptions specified in the enabling legislation, all dirt roads into the gorge have been closed, and the closures must be enforced. The miles of old dirt roads in the adjacent recreation area may remain open, but several have maintenance problems.

Now that the NPS has control, it must manage the new facilities developed by the Corps of Engineers, maintain the historic structures and exhibits, and find resources for any additional development. Included in the plans for possible new facilities are two park lodges which cannot be built until location problems are resolved and funding is found.

A few bridges, such as the Burnt Mill Bridge over the Clear Fork, require costly upkeep and repair. In addition, there is disagreement about the use of the old O&W Bridge over the Big South Fork; some interested in the park are calling for developing it as part of a scenic drive, while conservationists want to preserve the wilderness setting.

Finally, as visitation increases in the Big South Fork, the question of "How much use is too much?" must be answered to protect the natural resources for which the national river and recreation area was established. Coupled with the resolution of this issue should be an educational program to communicate the resource values the park has to offer and the advantages in preserving them.

For most of these management and environmental problems, the park needs additional resources to meet the challenges. But work is underway, not only by the Park Service staff, but by two citizen groups, the Big South Fork Action Network (coordinated by TCWP) and the Friends of the Big South Fork. These groups are working to resolve some of the problems and to support efforts to preserve and manage the park's resources.

Twin Arches

Located in the national river and recreation area, Twin Arches, once also called "Double Arches," is one of the more spectacular geologic formations on the Cumberland Plateau—two large arches aligned nearly end to end. It is remarkable that arches so large are so close together, a stone's throw away from one another.

Formed by headward erosion, these are certainly two of the largest, if not the largest, arches on the Plateau. Twin Arches can only be compared to Natural Arch in the Daniel Boone National Forest, Natural Bridge in Natural Bridge State Park, and Grays Arch in the Red River Gorge Geological Area, all in Kentucky. The Twin Arches complex is so large that there is virtually no vantage point from which to view the entire structure. The south arch has a span of 135 feet and a clearance of 70 feet. The north arch has a span of 93 feet and a clearance of 51 feet.

Small tunnel arches are also part of the Twin Arches complex. At the south end of the south arch, a small tunnel penetrates the base of the arch. This is called "West Tunnel" because it is on the west side of the arch. West Tunnel is 88 feet long. A much smaller East Tunnel, 17 feet long, lies on the east side between the two arches. West Tunnel was caused by the widening of a joint, and East Tunnel was created by water moving through rock. Thus within this one complex, arches were formed by three different processes.

Blue Heron

To the north in Kentucky, just upriver from the Devils Jump rapids, the Blue Heron Mining Community has been restored as a historic exhibit within the national river and recreation area. This is the only extensive development within the river gorge area.

When Blue Heron was built in 1937 by the Stearns Coal and Lumber Company, the largest employer in the area, the mine had state-of-the-art technology. The coal tipple constructed on the east side of the river was a giant machine, which through the use of grids, was able to separate coal into various sizes. A conveyor carried the coal inside the tipple, and coal that was small enough dropped through the vibrating grids. The largest chunks of coal emerged at the end, where pickers were stationed to remove rock and shale. A tram bridge still spans the river on which an electric motor pulled trains loaded with coal from the mines on the west side of the river to the tipple on the east side.

The historic exhibit includes reconstruction of some of the buildings and houses in the Blue Heron community, which was abandoned when the mines closed in 1962; all of the original buildings are gone. The reconstruction consists of "ghost" structures, just a roof mounted on pilings, to give an idea of what the buildings were like. The structures contain exhibits that include the recorded conversations of people who once lived and worked in the Blue Heron community. The tipple has been stabilized, and the tram bridge now serves as a connector between hiking trails on either side of the river.

An upgraded mine road provides access to Blue Heron and to the restored Barthell Coal Mining Camp just outside the park. Also, the Big South Fork Scenic Railway out of Stearns descends into the river gorge to take visitors to Blue Heron and Barthell.

Yahoo Falls

At the northern end of the park, near Alum Ford on the Big South Fork, the Yahoo Falls Scenic Area contains one of the more dramatic waterfalls on the Plateau. The water has cut deeply behind Yahoo Falls, pronounced "Yea-hoe" by some area residents, to create a long rockhouse. A trail leads behind the falls under the massive roof of rock where the slender waterfall drops off the edge 113 feet before splashing into a pool below.

A maze of trails from the parking area leads down to the Big South Fork River and to Yahoo Falls and Yahoo Arch.

Honey Creek

The Honey Creek area lies within the southern boundary of the BSFNRRA. Honey Creek was originally one of the small pocket wilderness areas established by the Southern Division of Bowater, Inc., that are also registered Tennessee state natural areas. The paper company provides maps of their pocket wilderness areas. Honey Creek Pocket Wilderness has since been incorporated into the national river and recreation area.

The Honey Creek scenic area offers broad views of the Big South Fork along a loop trail that drops into the river gorge. Broad rock openings, waterfalls, and small pools wedged under cliff overhangs dot the landscape.

Pickett State Rustic Park

Along the western boundary of the BSFNRRA in Tennessee lies Pickett State Rustic Park and Forest. The Stearns Coal and Lumber Company in 1933 donated 12,000 acres to establish the state forest. The park was developed with help from the Civilian Conservation

Corps and the National Park Service in 1934. In 1994, through the efforts of conservationists, 5,000 acres of adjacent Wolf River canyon country, threatened with development, was acquired and added to Pickett State Forest.

The park contains the 15-acre Pickett Lake, sometimes called "Arch Lake" because Pickett Lake Natural Bridge stands in the lake. This bridge is an incised meander; Thompson Creek, before it was dammed, folded back on itself and eventually wore a hole through the ridge to create the arch. Numerous trails pass by other stone arches and large rockhouses.

Buffalo Arch

To the north of Pickett State Park in the Daniel Boone National Forest in Kentucky, resides yet another of the great natural arches. Buffalo Arch is little known because of the difficulty of finding it and the particularly secluded section of the national forest in which it stands. But the arch is well worth the trouble of getting there—an impressive span that looks like a flying buttress holding up the hillside.

Koger Arch

North of Blue Heron, just outside the western edge of the Big South Fork National River and Recreation Area, stands another of the Plateau's large sandstone arches. Koger Arch is on land within Daniel Boone National Forest southwest of the Yamacraw Bridge over the Big South Fork. The arch is not as large as Natural Arch to the north or Twin Arches to the south, but it is nevertheless an impressive mass of suspended stone.

The arch was apparently once a rockhouse, the back part having caved in or eroded away. The circumstances of the collapse—whether it happened in a sudden crash or over millennia in a slow rain of dust, sand, and stone—are obscured by the weathering of the debris.

Directions and Services

The **Big South Fork National River and Recreation Area** can be reached in Tennessee along TN297 either east or west. From the west, take TN154 off US127 north of Jamestown to the intersection with TN297 and turn east into the national river and recreation area. Jamestown can be reached north on US127 from I-40.

From the east, take TN297 out of Oneida, which is on US27. The highway that is now US27, paralleling the Big South Fork north and south, is essentially the old route of the Great Tellico Trail. This ancient highway, first used by the Indians and then early settlers, traversed the eastern ridge of the Plateau from present-day Burnside, Kentucky, south to Kingston, Tennessee, and beyond into the Sequatchie Valley region.

Oneida can be reached west on TN63 from I-75; at that exit and along TN63, you'll pass through the **Royal Blue Wildlife Management Area,** managed by the Tennessee Wildlife Resources Agency. The Nature Conservancy had a hand in preserving the area. The 43,361-acre WMA was dedicated in October 1991 and will preserve a rare wetland on the eastern edge of the Cumberland Plateau. However, the Tennessee Valley Authority still owns the mineral rights and is leasing sections for the strip mining of coal; the intention of a letter of agreement between TVA and TWRA is to see that the mining is done in a manner compatible with the aims of both agencies.

The Kentucky portion of the BSFNRRA can be reached along KY92, which runs from Monticello on the west to US27 south of Whitley City on the east.

In the Tennessee portion of the park, approaching from the east on TN297, you'll see a park headquarters located on the east side of the river before you begin the descent into the river gorge. Continuing west after you've entered the gorge, you'll cross the river on a bridge at Leatherwood Ford and then climb back out of the river gorge to a turn north to the park visitor center at the Bandy Creek complex. The visitor center has information on backpacking, maps of the area, and a list of outfitters that offer canoe and raft trips on the river.

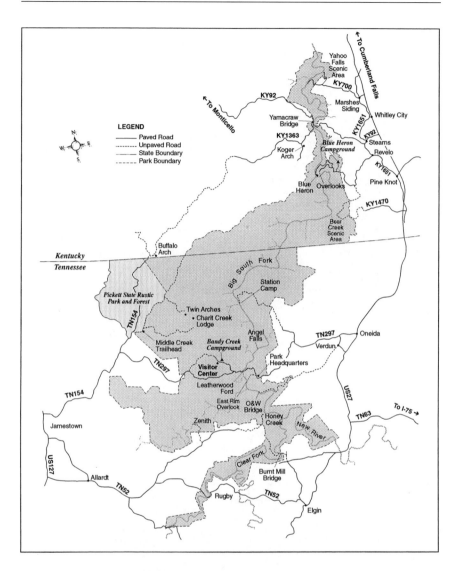

Big South Fork National River and Recreation Area

Bandy Creek also has a horse stable where you can rent a horse or board your own and a campground with 180 campsites, most with hookups; a swimming pool lies near the campground. The nearby Station Camp East area contains a horse camp.

Within the gorge—50 percent of the project area—hunting, fishing, backpacking, canoeing, hiking, bicycling, and horseback riding are the only

Lora E. Blevins House at Bandy Creek

approved activities. Backcountry camping is permitted anywhere in the BSFNRRA at least 25 feet from trails, rock shelters, and major geologic and historic features and at least 100 feet away from roads and parking areas; no permit is required, but it would be a good idea to let a ranger know where you are going. Hunting is subject to federal and state regulations and is permitted only in designated seasons.

Lodges, overlooks, improved roads, and more campgrounds are planned for the rim area. The only lodging currently available, in addition to motels in the surrounding communities and at nearby Historic Rugby and Pickett State Park, is Charit Creek Lodge in the backcountry, which provides cabins and meals; reservations are required.

You can reach **Blue Heron Campground, Barthell,** and **Blue Heron** on KY742 out of Revelo, Kentucky, which is on KY1651. You'll pass a left turn toward the **Bear Creek Scenic Area** with river overlook, a horse camp, and Split Bow Arch. Another left leads to Devils Jumps overlooks. Before Blue Heron, a side road to the right leads to Barthell, which has lodging in rebuilt miner's cabins and a restaurant.

For the Blue Heron/Bear Creek area, an impressive complex of lodge, campground, and recreational facilities is planned and at this time awaits funding. Plans also call for a lodge in the Tennessee portion of the park, perhaps a re-creation of the Tabard Inn at Historic Rugby at the southern end of the park.

You'll find the **Big South Fork Scenic Railway** in Stearns, Kentucky, a company town established by the Stearns Coal and Lumber Company in 1902. The town is located just west of US27 on KY92; the Stearns Visitor Center for the BSFNRRA lies on KY92 east of town. The scenic railway offers trains rides into the river gorge with stops at Barthell and Blue Heron. The railway operates from mid-April to around the end of October; check with the railway for the train schedule. You'll also find in Stearns the **McCreary County Museum** that houses artifacts from the region's past in the old Stearns Office Building constructed in 1907.

To get to **Yahoo Falls Scenic Area,** take KY700 west from US27 just north of Whitley City; you'll cross KY1651 at Marshes Siding and then continue on for a few winding miles until you see

Split Bow Arch

on the right a sign indicating the scenic area. If you continue on KY700, you'll eventually dead-end at the river at Alum Ford, where there is a boat launch and camping. The Sheltowee Trace National Recreation Trail passes through here.

At the Yahoo Falls Scenic Area, turn right on a gravel road. When you make the turn, notice the grave of Jacob Troxel on the right, who as a young man was sent into these western lands during the Revolutionary War to help prevent the Indians from joining the side of the British; he married Cornblossom, the daughter of Cherokee Chief Doublehead, and remained with the Cherokees until his death in 1810. The road into the scenic area, after about a mile, takes you through a picnic area and, at the far end of a loop, to a parking area for the trails that lead to the falls. From here, you can also walk to overlooks of the Big South Fork River; at this point some call it "Lake Cumberland" because the water is backed up from Wolf Creek Dam far downstream on the Cumberland River.

To get to **Pickett State Rustic Park,** take TN154 north from Jamestown. Or if you're crossing the BSFNRRA from the east on TN297, continue to the intersection with TN154, then turn north. The state park accepts reservations for its five chalets, five villas, and ten stone and wood cottages, completely equipped and open year-round. Camping at the park is on 40 sites, most with water and electric hookup; first come, first served. A group camp consists of cabins, bathhouses, and a kitchen and dining lodge. Activities include swimming, fishing, and boating on the lake.

Just north of the intersection of TN297 with TN154, you'll pass **Wildwood Lodge Bed & Breakfast,** offering country breakfasts and a Saturday-night English formal dinner. To the south on TN154 lies **Laurel Creek Travel Park,** which has camping on 50 sites with a swimming pool.

Trails

Many miles of trails and old logging roads crisscross the Big South Fork National River and Recreation Area. Of the 350 miles of trails, 200 miles are hiking trails and 150 miles are horse trails. In addition, you may ride all-terrain bicycles on the roads and horse trails. At this writing, there are two established trails specifically for off-road bicycling; the 5.3-mile **Duncan Hollow Loop** and the 8.3-mile **Collier Ridge Loop;** both begin near the Bandy Creek visitor center. Also from the Bandy Creek area, you can walk the 5.9-mile **John Litton Farm Loop** and the 3.4-mile **Oscar Blevins Farm Loop,** which take you by historic sites.

On the east side of the river, turn west on a gravel road across from the park headquarters, which is on TN297, to get to the **East Rim Overlook.** Along this road, you'll find a trailhead for the 1.3-mile trail to **Sunset Overlook** and the 3.2-mile **Leatherwood Ford Loop,** which drops into the river gorge to Leatherwood Ford before climbing back to the top of the plateau.

Perhaps the most popular trailhead is at the parking area on the east side of the river at Leatherwood Ford where TN297 crosses. This is one of the main put-ins and take-outs for canoeing and rafting the river. From here you can walk the **Angel Falls Trail** 2 miles downstream to Angel Falls, so named by the local people to counterbalance the name "Devils Jump," the rapids to the north in Kentucky. At one time Angel Falls was a low waterfall, but it was blasted in the 1950s to improve passage for fishing boats, with little success. Now what you'll see is a drop in the river, a sluice through which the water rushes on its way downriver.

You can continue along that trail for another 6 miles to Station Camp, another access point that you can reach by going straight ahead on the Station Camp Road 4.8 miles from Oneida instead of continuing on TN297. Along this upgraded gravel road, you can see the Chimney Rocks and take the 1.5-mile trail to the **Dome Rockhouse.**

At the Leatherwood Ford trailhead you also have access to the **John Muir Trail,** a national historic trail that commemorates the 1867 journey through the Cumberlands of the noted conservationist and founder of the Sierra Club. Although Muir became famous wandering the Sierras in California, the Cumberlands were the first mountains he explored. The John Muir Trail connects with the

Sheltowee Trace National Recreation Trail to the north, which descends through Daniel Boone National Forest in Kentucky and passes through the northern part of the BSFNRRA. To the southeast, the John Muir Trail will eventually connect with the Appalachian Trail when construction is complete through Tennessee.

In the Big South Fork, the John Muir Trail is blazed with a blue silhouette of Muir. From Leatherwood Ford you can follow the trail south along the river bank 2.3 miles to the Oneida and Western Railroad Bridge, which was a link in the now-abandoned O&W Railroad that connected Oneida with Jamestown to the west. Many local people would like to see a scenic railroad or a scenic drive established along this old railbed. Conservationists across the state oppose any more transportation into the gorge, which is supposed to be wilderness; they favor using the railbed for a hiking trail or bicycle path.

At Leatherwood Ford, you can also take the John Muir Trail north for views of the river gorge. Cross the river on the bridge and then turn downstream to pick up the trail. You may be able to cross on the old wooden bridge below the highway bridge, but it can be underwater in flood stages, and at times sections are washed away by the river. About 3 miles along the John Muir Trail, after climbing to the top of the river gorge, you'll walk out onto a rock promontory that presents a sweeping view of the river. This is perhaps the best view on the Cumberland Plateau.

The trail you are on at the overlook is part of the **Grand Gap Loop,** which follows the bluff for a few miles and then turns away from the river to link up again with the John Muir Trail.

At the Blue Heron historic area, you can walk the 6.6-mile **Blue Heron Loop** to see Cracks in the Rocks and the Devils Jump rapids. Walking across the tram bridge over the river, you can pick up a trail to the left that follows the old tram road to **Catawba Overlook** and then **Big Spring Falls** in 3.4 miles. The trail continues on to connect with the old Oil Well Road, which leads down from Bald Knob to the site of an abandoned oil well drilled in 1818 by Marcus Huling and Andrew Zimmerman on land leased from Martin Beaty. The well is reported to be the first commercial oil well in the country. The two men were looking for salt, a precious commodity that was used to preserve meat on the old frontier. Oil at the time was relatively useless, but Huling managed to haul barrels of the crude out of the wilderness and sell it for use as an ingredient in liniments and various cure-alls. You may have to tramp around to find the old well if the park staff has not yet erected their planned sign and interpretive display to direct you to the site.

A number of trails loop through the Yahoo Falls Scenic Area. Along the 0.7-mile **Topside Loop,** you'll pass down metal stairs to walk behind the waterfall and pass connecting trails leading to the Sheltowee Trace, which follows the shore of the Big South Fork. Beyond the falls, you'll come to a junction with the 0.2-mile **Cascade Trail,** which branches off to pass Roaring Rocks Cataract and follow the creek along a twisting route through huge boulders before rejoining the maze of trails at the base of the waterfall. You'll also encounter the 0.8-mile **Yahoo Arch Trail** leading to Yahoo Arch, a bare arc of rock with a clearance of 10 feet and a span of 25 feet, nestled against a rock bluff. The trail connects with KY700.

You can get to the 5-mile **Honey Creek Loop** along TN52, just 0.5 mile west from Elgin, Tennessee, or east from Rugby. Turn north just west of Elgin to get to the area. Once you pass through an intersection, you'll be on a dirt road; you'll then bear left and pass over Burnt Mill Bridge on the Clear Fork; you can also reach this area off US27 north of Elgin along the Burnt Mill Bridge access road. The bridge is the main put-in for canoeists and rafters doing the difficult stretch of river down to Leatherwood Ford and also the trailhead for the 4.3-mile **Burnt Mill Bridge Loop** along the Clear Fork. From Burnt Mill Bridge, continue for 3 miles north and turn right at the sign for Honey Creek. Almost immediately on this side road you'll find parking on the left; just down the road on the right is the trailhead for the Honey Creek Loop; the road ahead leads to an overlook of the river. Along the loop trail, you'll pass by Boulder House Falls, which pours through an opening to produce a sheen on the rock floor, and Honey Creek Falls, set in a rock grotto.

For the **Middle Creek Trailhead** in the northwest corner of the Tennessee portion of the national river and recreation area, turn east on a gravel road off TN154 just south of Pickett State Rustic Park. In about half a mile you'll find the pullout for the trailhead from which you can get on a number of trails. If you're just out for a walk, the 3.5-mile **Middle Creek Nature Trail** loops by a number of rockhouses. Other trails of several miles take you past the Indian Rock House and eventually to Bandy Creek Campground to the southeast and the Charit Creek Lodge and Twin Arches to the northeast.

If you don't want to walk several miles to see Twin Arches and then retrace your steps, continue down the gravel road past the Middle Creek Trailhead. You'll pass Fork Ridge Road to the right soon after the Middle Creek Trailhead, and in another three miles you will reach a right turn on the Twin Arches Road that takes you two miles to the beginning of the 0.7-mile **Twin Arches Trail,** which leads to the arches and connects with the 4.6-mile **Twin Arches/Charit Creek Loop,** which can be accessed only by other trails.

You can access other trails by turning on Fork Ridge Road. You will first pass the Sawmill Trailhead on the left. From there, the 3.2-mile **Slave Falls Loop** passes by Needle Arch and Slave Falls and a connector that leads to the Twin Arches/Charit Creek Loop at Jakes Place, the site of the old homestead of Jacob Blevins Jr., and his wife, Viannah, marked only by a stone chimney. The loop also passes the Indian Rock House before circling back to the trailhead.

Continuing on the road past the Sawmill Trailhead, you'll reach a **Y.** If you go to the right, the road dead-ends where a fire tower once stood. Bear to the left and you'll eventually reach a turnout where you can leave your vehicle; the road is blocked just beyond the turnout. Here you'll pick up an 0.8-mile trail that leads to **Charit Creek Lodge,** an old homestead site, possibly that of Jonathan Blevins, Jacob Blevins Jr.'s grandfather, but he may have lived farther down the valley. The lodge that incorporates the old log cabin of the homestead was a hunting lodge before it became a backwoods lodge for overnight stays in the park. The Charit Creek Lodge Trail also connects with the Twin Arches/Charit Creek Loop.

Over 58 miles of hiking trails wander through Pickett State Rustic Park and Forest. The most scenic is the **Hidden Passage Trail,** a 10-mile loop that follows the bluff overlooking Thompson Creek past waterfalls and rockhouses. A section of the 7-mile **Rock Creek Trail** links the Hidden Passage Trail with the Sheltowee Trace, which dead-ends in Pickett State Park.

As you enter the state park from the south on TN154, watch for signs along the road directing you to special geologic formations. You'll first come to the 2.5-mile **Hazard Cave Trail** on your left, a loop that takes you by Hazard Cave, a large rockhouse that may have served as a campsite for Indian hunting parties. Standing at the back of the cave, you'll see a slit of light above the opening that is Hazard Cave Window, revealing that the cave entrance is an arch, caused by erosion and sagging of the lower rock layers at the mouth of the cave.

Directly across the road from the Hazard Cave Trailhead is the 0.25-mile **Indian Rockhouse Trail,** which leads to a long rockhouse in a sweeping rock wall amphitheater.

Farther into the park, you'll pass on your left the turnout for **Natural Bridge,** also called "Highway 154 Natural Bridge." You'll climb down steps to get to the arch, which is almost right beside the road. Likely formed by widening of a joint, the bridge has a span of 86 feet and a clearance of 23 feet. The lintel is extraordinarily thin, less than 2 feet in the middle; a lintel so thin is possible only because it consists of the especially hard and homogeneous Pennsylvania sandstone.

The easiest way to get to the other major arch in the park, Pickett Lake Natural Bridge, is to walk the short trail behind the chalet complex, but you can also follow the 2.5-mile **Lake Trail** loop that takes you down to the dam built by the Civilian Conservation Corps in the 1930s on Thompson Creek and better views of the arch.

A proposed 12-mile **Sgt. Alvin York Trail** will link Pickett State Park with the Pall Mall, Tennessee, homeplace of Sgt. Alvin C. York, the World War I hero. York single-handedly captured 132 German soldiers, killed 28, and neutralized 35 machine-gun bunkers during a skirmish in the Argonne Forest of France, for which he received the Congressional Medal of Honor; a movie was later made of his exploits.

To get to the 0.8-mile **Buffalo Arch Trail,** take TN154 north from Pickett State Park; in five miles you'll cross the Kentucky state line and the road becomes KY167. One-quarter mile past the state line, turn right on 562, a gravel road, and enter Daniel Boone National Forest. In 0.8 mile, take 6305 to the right, and in just a few hundred yards, take the right fork when the road branches. Only 4-wheel drive vehicles can handle this road, so you may want to leave a car at the beginning of 6350 and walk down the road. About half a mile from the fork, you'll pass the **Parker Mountain Trail,** which heads north to the Great Meadows Campground in the national forest. Past the trailhead, the road veers to the left, but continue straight ahead on another dirt road. The Buffalo Arch Trail then leaves the road on the right and heads into the cove where you'll find the arch in 0.25 mile.

To get to the **Koger Arch Trail,** turn west on KY92 off US27 between Oneida, Tennessee, and Whitley City, Kentucky. KY92 will pass through Stearns where you catch the scenic railroad. Stay on 92 and you will eventually descend into the gorge of the Big South Fork and cross the river on the Yamacraw Bridge; the area and the bridge are named for an Indian tribe that once lived there. Immediately after crossing the bridge, turn south on KY1363. Watch for the abandoned **K&T Railroad Bridge** over the river on the left. The road obviously turns southwest away from the river following Rock Creek. At a road to the right, bear left to stay with 1363. You'll cross railroad tracks, pass a drive, and turn left on a dirt road crossing a concrete bridge over Rock Creek. Go about one quarter of a mile. On your left you'll see a place to pull off, a small opening in the forest, and a little creek. A sign says "Koger Arch." The arch is an easy quarter of a mile along the trail; the arch is named for the Koger family, who descended from early settlers in the region. The trail passes through the arch and continues up another quarter mile to the Sheltowee Trace, which, passing through Daniel Boone National Forest, is headed southwest to end at Pickett State Park.

References

Big South Fork National River and Recreation Area staff (Steve Seven, chief of interpretation; William K. Dickinson, superintendent; Ron Wilson, park ranger management assistant; Howard Ray Duncan, park ranger interpreter; and Tom DesJean, NPS archaeologist). Interviews and conversations with author. 1985–91.

Big South Fork Scenic Railway. "Big South Fork Scenic Railway and Historic Stearns." Brochure. Stearns, KY, no date.

Coggins, Allen R. "The Early History of Tennessee's State Parks, 1919–56." *Tennessee Historical Quarterly* 43, no. 3 (Fall 1984): 295–315.

Collins, Robert F. *A History of the Daniel Boone National Forest.* Washington, DC: U.S. Dept. of Agriculture, Forest Service, 1975.

Crogan, James X., and John T. Parks. *Natural Bridges of Tennessee.* Bulletin 80. Nashville: Tennessee Division of Geology, 1979.

Daniel Boone National Forest. "Yahoo Falls Scenic Area." Brochure. Winchester, KY, no date.

Howell, Benita J. *A Survey of Folklife Along the Big South Fork of the Cumberland River.* Knoxville: Univ. of Tennessee, 1981.

Manning, Russ. "Big South Fork." *Tennessee Conservationist,* Sept.–Oct. 1990, 23–25.

———. "The Big South Fork of the Cumberland: A New National River and Recreation Area." *Appalachia,* Dec. 1981, 18–29.

———. "Getting Lost in the Big South Fork." *Outside,* May 1990, 122–23.

———, and Sondra Jamieson. *The Best of the Big South Fork National River and Recreation Area: A Hiker's Guide to Trails and Attractions.* 2d ed. Norris, TN: Laurel Place. 1990.

Perry, Samuel D. *South Fork Country.* Detroit: Harlo Press, 1983.

Russell, Liane B. (TCWP founder, newsletter editor, and Big South Fork Coalition and BSF Action Network coordinator), and William L. Russell (TCWP founder). Interviews and conversations with author. 1977–91.

Sehlinger, Bob, and Bob Lantz. *Streams of Tennessee* 2. Birmingham, AL: Menasha Ridge Press, 1983.

Tennessee Chapter, The Nature Conservancy, "Tennessee Chapter Expedites Acquisition within Public Land Boundaries." *Tenn Notes,* Autumn 1991, 2.

Tennessee Citizens for Wilderness Planning. *TCWP Newsletter.* Oak Ridge, TN, 1968–91.

Tennessee Dept. of Conservation. "Pickett State Rustic Park." Brochure. Nashville, 1977.

———. "Pickett Trails." Map. Nashville, no date.

Tennessee Valley Authority, Mapping Services Branch. "Big South Fork National River and Recreation Area." Map. Knoxville, TN, 1986.

U.S. Army Corps of Engineers. *Big South Fork General Design Memorandum and Final Environmental Impact Statement.* Nashville, 1976.

———. "River Guide." Brochure. Nashville, no date.

U.S. Dept. of the Interior, National Park Service. "Big South Fork." Brochure. Washington, DC, 1982.

———. "Blue Heron Community." Brochure. Washington, DC, no date.

Chapter 8

Rugby

Dearest Lucy,

We came here on the 31st May & arrived at about 7:30 p.m. after a 7 mile drive from Sedgemoor Station, over a rather rough road. We have been in the hotel ever since, but we hope to get into our own house in a few days. I'm sorry to say that Granny is not at all well at present, she has had a very bad attack of gout, but she is getting better now. It was the change of food & water & climate that brought it on I think. The water we drink here has a great deal of iron in it, but the springs are not all alike in Rugby & there are some with scarcely any iron in them. I like the place very much indeed. There are some nice people here, so its not at all dull, in fact I am not likely to be nearly as dull here as I was in London.

ever your loving friend,
Emmy Hughes
July 5th 1881

In the late 1800s, in the virtual wilderness of the Cumberland Plateau, the last English colonization in the United States was taking shape. The dream of Thomas Hughes, noted author of the classic 1857 novel *Tom Brown's School Days*, the Rugby colony was to be a haven for younger sons of English gentry. Due to the practice of primogeniture in England at the time, second sons received no inheritance and, because of social pressure, could make a living only as professionals, such as doctors, lawyers, or clerics. Only by relocating in another country were these sons of the upper class free to earn their way by the work of their hands.

Hughes first looked for a site for colonization in New Zealand and Canada but later became interested in the United States during a trip to America in 1870. Franklin W. Smith, an industrialist who had options on hundreds of thousands of acres in Tennessee on which he had intended to start a colony, brought the Cumberland Plateau to Hughes's attention. Hughes was immediately interested and with his financial backers formed the Board of Aid to Land Ownership, Ltd., which purchased 75,000 acres on the Plateau for the founding of a colony.

At first most of those recruited to settle in the colony were men, but women soon followed, including Hughes's niece, Emmy Hughes who corresponded with her friend Lucy during her years at Rugby, and Hughes's own mother, Margaret E. Hughes, the "Granny" of Emmy's letters.

When Hughes arrived for the dedication of the colony in 1880, he found the church, school, inn, and many residences under construction. Together he and the colonists decided to name the new community "Rugby," after the English school Hughes had attended and which had been the setting for *Tom Brown's School Days.* In his dedicatory address, Hughes said that although at present most of the settlers were English, "our settlement is open to all who like our principles and our ways, and care to come here to make homes for themselves."

The colony was never a financial success; the colonists, who numbered around 400 at one time, were ill-equipped to live the farming life, even with the help of a few local people who joined the colony. They opened a tomato canning factory only to find that no one had planted enough tomatoes to keep the factory operating. Other projects in oil, coal, and manufacturing were also unsuccessful.

The reasons Rugby did not succeed are many—mismanagement and lack of communication between the colony's managers and the London-based Board of Aid, a soil less fertile than expected and which had to be cleared of dense forest, a severe first winter followed by a typhoid epidemic during a drought in the summer, an expected railroad spur to Rugby that was never built, confused land titles that delayed use of the land, and a lack of market for the Rugby products. In addition, the absence of Hughes—the inspiration for the colony, who never came back from England after his mother died in 1887—contributed to the failure. The colonists soon began drifting away, looking for better opportunities. Around the turn of the century, the English investors sold out to American interests.

For decades the community with its Victorian houses and public buildings stood virtually abandoned in the isolation of the Plateau. A few families occupied some of the homes, services were still held at the church, and the library occasionally lent books, but it was far from a thriving community.

Then in the 1960s, Brian L. Stagg, a young man with an intense interest in the local history of East Tennessee, spent much of his time studying the history of Rugby and seeking ways to preserve the buildings that remained. In 1966, Stagg helped form the Rugby Restoration Association, now Historic Rugby, Inc., which after Stagg's untimely death continues the work he began of preserving the historic community. His sister, Barbara Stagg, is now director. A 15-member volunteer board governs the nonprofit organization.

Historic Rugby

Today, Rugby is an unincorporated village on the National Register of Historic Places, with most of the surviving homes still serving as residences. There were once about 65 buildings in Rugby; of the 17 original buildings that remain, several are open to the public and tours are conducted daily from February 1 through December 31, except for major holidays.

At the center of town, several buildings encircle a parking area for visitors. Information and conducted tours are available at the visitor center in the former schoolhouse. This two-story frame building was built in 1907 after the original burned.

Percy Cottage stands nearby. The cottage is a historic reconstruction of the original built on the same location in 1881 by Henry Kimber, a railroad industrialist and chief financial backer of the colony.

Kingstone Lisle

Kingstone Lisle, also adjacent to the parking area, was built as the summer home of Thomas Hughes. It was Hughes's intention to eventually settle in the colony, but his wife's ill health prevented her from moving with him, so Hughes contented himself with extended visits in the summer. Constructed in 1884 in the Queen Anne style, Kingstone Lisle was named by Hughes for the community in Berkshire, England, where he had spent part of his boyhood. It is not known if Hughes ever stayed in the house, for he probably spent his summer visits at Uffington House at the west end of the community, which was the home of his mother and his niece, Emmy. Hughes eventually gave Kingstone Lisle to Christ Church for use as a rectory.

The church, immediately across the road from the parking area, has been continuously used for public worship since its construction as an Episcopal church in 1887. Charles Todd Quintard, Bishop of Tennessee at the time, celebrated Holy Communion at Rugby's opening-day ceremony and gave to the church the stained-glass window in the apse. The window panels are dedicated to Margaret Hughes and Mary Blacklock, mother of the first rector of the church, Joseph Blacklock; the window was made in Germany. The small rosewood reed organ was made in London in 1849 and brought to the colony by the Blacklocks. The hanging lamps, which were originally kerosene and now are connected to electricity, were brought from England by the Gilliat family. The two walnut alms basins, which are still in use, were carved by Henry L. Fry, who also carved one of Queen Victoria's thrones.

Perhaps the most intriguing building in Rugby is the Thomas Hughes Public Library, a 7,000-volume library that opened to the public in 1882; the building stands east of the school. English and American publishers donated most of the books to the colony as a tribute to Hughes. The oldest book was printed in 1687 and the newest in 1899. The building was specially designed to preserve the books, which sat undisturbed for decades: a ceiling vent helps to control the temperature and humidity, and the bookshelves are so situated that the sun can never shine through the windows directly on a book and cause it to fade.

West of Kingstone Lisle are several reconstructed buildings. Although the Harrow Road Cafe is not an original structure, there was a similar establishment by the same name in operation in 1881 in the vicinity of the present building. The Rugby Printing Works, originally located in a structure on the other side of the road, occupies a building that was brought from Deer Lodge, a community south of Rugby that was established around 1890 and was the site of a Polish colonization after 1900. The reconstruction of the Board of Aid office, originally built in 1880 and destroyed by arson in 1977, was completed in 1989; the building now houses the bookstore and archives of the colony. The Commissary houses a craft and gift shop. Plans also call for the reconstruction of the Perrigo Boarding House.

Other buildings in the colony are privately owned, but some are open to the public during the Annual Rugby Pilgrimage held the first weekend in October. Rugby also holds each year a Spring Music and Crafts Festival in May and Christmas at Rugby in December.

Roslyn, built in 1886 by Montgomery Boyle, son of John Boyle who was vice-president of the Board of Aid to Land Ownership, sits at the far

Christ Church, Episcopal

east side of the community. The home was named for Roslyn Castle in Scotland. Across the road, not easily seen through the trees, is another home, Villa Ray, built in 1881 by Charles Kemp, Rugby's physician.

Walton Court, which stood just west of Roslyn, burned in 1988. You'll see only a vacant lot now. The house was built about 1880 by Robert Walton, an Irishman who came from Cincinnati as surveyor-engineer for the Board of Aid and who later served for many years as manager of the colony.

West of the center of town, a dirt road to the north leads to the Laurel Dale Cemetery, where Margaret Hughes was buried in 1887. Along the road sit two reconstructed buildings, Martin's Roost and Oak Lodge. In the field on the left is the site of the Tabard Inn, now marked by only a few foundation stones. The first Tabard Inn, built in 1880, burned in 1884. The second inn, built in 1887, burned in 1899. Historic Rugby, Inc., hopes to reconstruct the inn. One possibility is a new Tabard Inn to serve as a lodge for the Big South Fork National River and Recreation Area which borders the Rugby community; plans for the BSFNRRA call for a lodge on this southern end of the park.

South of the main highway through Rugby, a complex of dirt roads behind the Commissary leads to several homes—Ingleside, built in 1884; The Lindens, with a carriage house in back, also built in 1884; Adena Cottage, built around 1880; and The Wren's Nest, built in 1887. Newbury House, situated beside a small pond, was the Rugby colony's first boarding house. It was first called the "Brown House Hotel," but the name was changed in 1884 to Newbury, after the street by the same name that runs by the house. The house stood vacant from 1950 until Historic Rugby, Inc., restored the building in 1985 and opened it as a year-round bed and breakfast inn. Five upstairs bedrooms are furnished in the Victorian style, as is the large guest parlor downstairs.

At the far west end of town stand Uffington House, which was the home of Margaret Hughes from 1881 to 1887; Ruralia, built in 1884; and Twin Oaks, built about 1884.

Pioneer Cottage, a one-and-a-half-story house available for visitor lodging, also can be found on the west end of town. Constructed in

Thomas Hughes Public Library

1880, it was the first frame house built in Rugby. It was here that new-comers stayed until other housing could be built. Thomas Hughes spent his first night in Rugby in Pioneer Cottage. The next morning, he wrote, "I was roused at five or thereabouts on the morning after our arrival here by a visit from a big dog belonging to a native . . . who seeing my window wide open, jumped in from the verandah, and came to the bed to give me good-morning with tail and muzzle."

After being nuzzled awake, Hughes wrote, "I heard sounds which announced the uprising of the boys, and in a few minutes several appeared in flannel shirts and trousers, bound for one of the two rivers which run close by, in gullies 200 feet, below us. They had heard of a pool 10 feet deep, and found it, too; and a most delicious place it is, surrounded by great rocks, lying in a copse of rhododen-drons, azaleas, and magnolias, which literally form the underwood of the pines and white oak along these gullies. . . . On this occasion, however, I preferred to let them do the exploring, and so went off to breakfast."

"The boys," as Hughes called the single young men staying in Pioneer Cottage, were off to the Gentlemen's Swimming Hole on the Clear Fork, one of the tributaries of the Big South Fork of the Cumberland River.

Allardt

After a visit to Rugby in the winter of 1880–81, John C. Sheppard became convinced that the area a few miles west of Rugby was ideal for colonization. These were lands owned by Cyrus and James N. Clark (father and son) and A. L. Crawford.

Sheppard encouraged M. H. Allardt & Co., which had been involved in colonizations in Michigan, to consider colonization in Tennessee. Allardt and Bruno Gernt, who had also been involved in Michigan colonization, decided on the Clark-Crawford lands for the establishment of a German colony. While the Rugby colony was an eco-

Bruno Gernt House

nomic failure, the Germans who came from Michigan and directly from Germany to settle the town of Allardt were successful in establishing a good financial base. The colony grew to become the present incorporated town, which was named for Allardt, who died just as the settlement began to form.

The remaining historic buildings in the town of Allardt are not as extensive as those in Rugby, which perhaps explains why Rugby is so much better known today, even though Allardt was the more successful of the two colonies. The Bruno Gernt House still remains, built in 1881–82, a large gray farmhouse with brick-red trim that is a good combination of practicality and rural splendor. The house is on the National Register of Historic Places and is open to the public as a bed and breakfast.

Located just east of the main intersection in town, the Gernt Office, a small white building, is where the descendants of Bruno Gernt still manage the family's holdings. The office is also on the National Register.

Colditz Cove

One of the newest Tennessee State Natural Areas, Colditz Cove lies between Rugby and Allardt. In the natural area, Big Branch drops 60 feet into Colditz Cove to form Northrup Falls. The waterfall ranges from a roaring cascade that reportedly shakes the ground in flood season to a whisper in the drier part of summer.

In winter, mist from the falls coats the surrounding vegetation and rapidly freezes, leaving an ice-coated forest. Giant icicles hang from the cliff walls. Large hemlocks stand in the 75 acres of the natural area. In spring and summer, the forest is in bloom with rhododendron, mountain laurel, and pink lady's slipper.

Jamestown

In 1827, John Marshall Clemens came to Fentress County, Tennessee, with his wife, Jane, and son, Orion. Clemens was a lawyer and, as one of the county commissioners, drew the specifications for the courthouse and jail in Jamestown, just west of Allardt and Rugby. The courthouse stood where the present courthouse now stands. The original jail, which no longer exists, operated until 1898 when a new jail was constructed. The 1898 jail, which operated until 1979, now houses the Chamber of Commerce and is on the National Register of Historic Places.

During his 12-year stay in Fentress County, Clemens acquired between 75,000 and 100,000 acres. He thought the area would flourish and so bought as much land as he could with as little public display as possible so as to keep the price of the land low. Some estimates suggest he may have gotten all the land for as little as $500.

When Fentress County did not have the boom Clemens expected, he moved with his family, now including five children, to Missouri. Another child, Pleasant Hannibal, had lived only a few months and is buried in an unmarked grave in the Jamestown cemetery.

In Missouri, Clemens had two more sons, the first of which he named Samuel Langhorne Clemens, who as "Mark Twain" wrote the American classics *The Adventures of Tom Sawyer* and *The Adventures of Huckleberry Finn.* In later years, Twain described his father as "honored and envied as the most opulent citizen of Fentress County." In one of his books, *The Gilded Age,* Twain wrote about his father's move from Jamestown, except in the book it was called Obedstown and the character modeled on his father was Squire Si Hawkins.

Just north of the center of Jamestown, a small park maintained by the Jamestown Garden Club contains the spring from which the Clemens family got their water. The Clemens home, which was described as unusual and elegant, was near the spring, at about the present site of the Jamestown Post Office.

In his autobiography, Twain talks of the 75,000-acre estate his father acquired around Jamestown, which "produced a wild grape of promising sort." Nearly 100 years later, Fay and Kathy Wheeler planted a vineyard and founded Highland Manor Winery south of Jamestown, now operated by O. Irving Martin. Although Highland Manor was established only in 1980, it is the oldest operating winery in Tennessee. Highland Manor has won numerous state, national, and international awards for its wine, including the "International Gold Medal for Quality" in Madrid, Spain, in 1983 and 1984 for a wine made from muscadine grapes, the wild grape referred to by Twain.

Directions and Services

To get to **Rugby** take TN52 7 miles west from Elgin, Tennessee, which is on US27, or 18 miles east from Jamestown, which is on US127. Elgin was originally called "Sedgemoor" and was the nearest train stop through which colonists and supplies arrived for Rugby. A half-mile west of Elgin, you'll pass the road north to the Honey Creek area, part of the Big South Fork National River and Recreation Area.

On weekdays, TN52 is a heavily traveled road, sometimes with

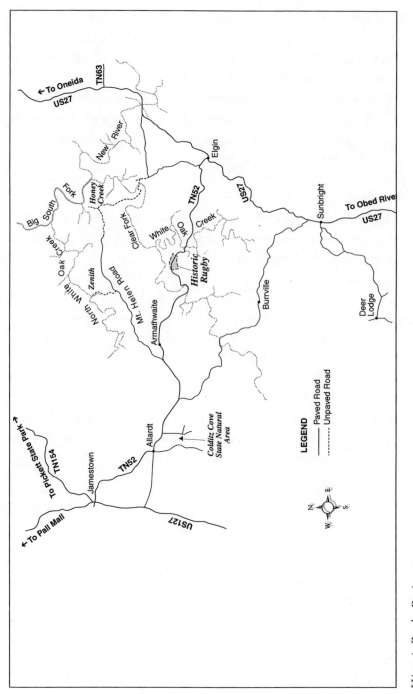

Historic Rugby Region

loaded coal trucks barreling down the highway. The state government now plans to reroute TN52 around Rugby so as to preserve the serenity and historic integrity of the community.

Lodging can be reserved at **Newbury House, Pioneer Cottage, Percy Cottage,** and when those three are full, at some of the private residences that have bedrooms available. Newbury House has a double bed in each of its rooms. Pioneer Cottage is a housekeeping cottage where an entire family or group can set up. The upstairs suite at Percy Cottage contains two bedrooms and a kitchen and parlor for families or small groups. Make reservations at the visitor center.

In addition, on the west end of the community is the **Grey Gables Bed & Breakfast** in a newer English country house about a mile west of the center of the historic district. The house is near the **R. M. Brooks General Store,** constructed in 1930 and proposed for the National Register of Historic Places because it is representative of general stores found throughout rural communities in years past. The Rugby Post Office is located in the store.

The **Harrow Road Cafe** in Rugby is the only restaurant in or near Rugby. It is owned by Historic Rugby, Inc., and is open year-round with limited hours in winter.

Allardt is on TN52 between Jamestown and Rugby. Approaching Allardt from the east, you'll swing into a sharp curve to the left where Base Line Road turns off to the right; just down this road on the right is the **Bruno Gernt House,** which is now open as a bed and breakfast. Make reservations with **East Fork Stables,** which also has rental cabins and a campground six miles south of Jamestown on US127. Several houses on this east end of Allardt that date from the late 1890s and early 1900s have been proposed as the Allardt Historic District for the National Historic Register. The old Allardt schoolhouse built in 1910 in this historic district has since been relocated to a site west of the intersection of 52 and 296 and has been converted into a bed and breakfast. North on TN52 in Allardt, you'll find the Presbyterian Church, built in 1902 and now on the National Register. The community also contains Youngs

Historic District; on the National Register, the district includes two houses with outbuildings on Indiana and Portland Avenues.

To get to **Colditz Cove State Natural Area,** head west 11 miles on TN52 from Rugby to the Crooked Creek Hunting Lodge Road, or east from Allardt, actually before you get out of the town limits. You'll see a small sign to Colditz Cove, but more obvious is the sign directing you to Crooked Creek Lodge. The natural area is about a mile south on the hunting lodge road. Land for the natural area was donated by the Colditz family.

Between Rugby and the Colditz Cove turnoff, you'll pass a turnoff for the **Zenith** area of the Big South Fork National River and Recreation Area on the Mt. Helen Road. At Zenith, you'll find access for canoeing North White Oak Creek and on the north side of the creek the old O&W Railroad bed that's good for off-trail bicycling.

Also on TN52, you'll pass the Sunbright-Burrville Road to the south; it's not marked, but you can spot it easily if you watch for the Pleasant View Church of the Nazarene, which is at the corner. If you take the road as a side excursion, you'll cross the Clear Fork on the Peters Bridge at the southernmost boundary of the Big South Fork National River and Recreation Area. Below the bridge you'll find a popular swimming hole. Continue on the road and you'll pass through Burrville and arrive in Sunbright. Southwest of Sunbright on highway 329, you'll find what remains of **Deer Lodge.** The community was called "Dead Level" until Abner Ross, who had managed the Tabard Inn at Rugby until it burned in 1884, brought the deer he had kept on the inn's grounds to a tract of land he bought in the area; he then promoted Deer Lodge as a health resort.

Jamestown rests at the junction of TN52 and US127. If you take TN52 west out of Jamestown, you'll drop off the plateau along what the local people call "Skyline Drive." Just at the edge of the plateau, a picnic area sits below a rock overhang on your left.

If you travel north 11 miles on US127, you'll reach **Pall Mall,** the home of Sgt. Alvin C. York, the World War I hero whose exploits were made into a movie that brought him national recognition. At the outskirts of Jamestown, you'll pass the York Institute, a school founded by

York for the children of the area. Mark Twain's father, who lived in Pall Mall for a time, established the post office there.

On the way to Pall Mall, you'll drop off the ragged western edge of the Plateau into farm country. Just before entering the community, a sign directs you to turn right to get to the burial site of Sergeant York. The Sergeant York Home, part of what is now a state historic area, stands just before the bridge over the Wolf River. On the other side of the river sits the **Sgt. Alvin C. York Memorial Grist Mill** beside a low dam on the river; York owned and operated the mill. At this writing Alvin York's son, Andrew, gives tours of the mill. In addition to the house and mill, the historic site includes a store and post office once owned by York and a Bible school he built in the community. All are slated for restoration but await funding.

Just west of Pall Mall is the **Cordell Hull Birthplace,** commemorated by a reconstructed log cabin and museum west of TN42 south of Byrdstown on 325W. Born in 1871, Hull was U.S. congressman, senator, and secretary of state and was the author of the "Good Neighbor" policy for the United States. He received the Nobel Peace Prize in 1945.

Highland Manor Winery is 4 miles south of Jamestown on US127. The muscadine wine and also a muscadine champagne are produced in limited quantities because of the scarcity of the muscadine grapes. You can get on the waiting list if you intend to be back that way again. Other wines are sometimes sold out, so call before you drive a long distance to get there. You can tour the winemaking operation and have lunch on the patio.

On a weekend in mid-August each year, US127 south becomes **The World's Longest Outdoor Sale,** a giant yard sale that started in 1986 as a way of getting people off the interstate to explore the backroads of the Cumberland Plateau. Over 3,000 vendors set up along US127 from Covington, Kentucky, through Tennessee to Chattanooga and on into Georgia and Alabama along the Lookout Mountain Parkway to serve more than 100,000 bargain hunters. This stretch of US127 south from Jamestown and on into Sequatchie Valley is one of the most active sections of the yard sale; expect a lot of traffic on this weekend.

Trails

To get to the 0.4-mile **Gentlemen's Swimming Hole Trail** at Rugby, turn north on the Laurel Dale Cemetery Road. The trail to the swimming hole is across from the cemetery at the end of the road. The path drops to cross a small creek; follow it down into the gorge of the Clear Fork, eventually reaching a left path that takes you down to the swimming hole. At the river's edge, a long rock juts into the water, and you can easily picture the Rugby boys taking a quick sprint along the top of the rock and a flying leap into the river.

You can continue straight on the main trail, which is now the **Meeting of the Waters Trail.** In 1 mile you'll reach the confluence of White Oak Creek and the Clear Fork. At the confluence, the trail leads onto a broad slab of rock and then up White Oak Creek a short distance before climbing the bluff and joining a logging road that goes back to the cemetery. The entire loop is about 3 miles.

From the parking area at Colditz Cove State Natural Area, follow an old jeep road, which is now gated, into the area. You'll pass through scrub forest and then walk into a cove of hemlock and rhododendron. Just before you reach the edge of the small canyon, a sign directs you to the left along the mile-long **Colditz Cove Loop Trail,** which brings you back to this point. The trail drops into the canyon and then doubles back along the base of the cliff to pass behind Northrup Falls.

References

Colditz, B. M. *Allardt, A History.* Jamestown, TN: Allardt Homecoming '86 Committee, 1986.

Dickinson, Calvin W. *Morgan County.* Memphis: Memphis State Univ. Press, 1987.

Duncan, Howard Ray. "Sgt. York: The Man, the Hero." In *Tour Guide of Fentress County Tennessee.* Jamestown, TN, no date.

Gernt, Gerald. Conversation with author. Allardt, TN, July 29, 1991.

Historic Rugby, Inc. "A Brief Guide to Rugby Buildings." Brochure. Rugby, TN, no date.

———. "Historic Rugby, English Village in the Tennessee Cumberlands." Brochure. Rugby, TN, no date.

Hughes, Emmy. *Dissipations at Uffington House: The Letters of Emmy Hughes, Rugby, Morgan County, Tennessee, July 5, 1881–July 15, 1887.* Introd. and notes by John R. Debruyn. Memphis: Memphis State Univ., 1975.

Hughes, Thomas. "Rugby, Morgan County, Tennessee, Settlement Founded October 5, 1880 by the Board of Aid to Land Ownership (LTD) of London England." Pamphlet. Cincinnati: Robert Clarke, Printer, 1880.

———. *Rugby Tennessee.* London: Macmillan, 1881. Facsimile ed. Rugbeian Press/Big Sink Books, 1973.

"Mark Twain's Tennessee Heritage." In *Tour Guide of Fentress County Tennessee.* Jamestown, TN, no date.

"The New Rugby." *Harper's Weekly,* Oct. 16, 1880, 665–66; Nov. 6, 1880, 709–10.

"A Pioneer's Dream." Brochure. Allardt, TN: Estate of Bruno Gernt, no date.

Stagg, Brian. *Deer Lodge, Tennessee: Its Little Known History.* Rugby, TN: privately printed, 1964.

———. *The Distant Eden: Tennessee's Rugby Colony.* N.p.: Paylor Publications, 1973.

Chapter 9

Obed River

The Big South Fork of the Cumberland River was not the first conservation effort of the Tennessee Citizens for Wilderness Planning (TCWP). The first issue for the group focused on saving the Obed River in the central part of Tennessee to the south of the Big South Fork.

The Obed has had a long history of dam proposals. In 1932 the Army Corps of Engineers put together a plan for 20 flood-control dams on the river and its tributaries. The Tennessee Valley Authority restudied the need for dams in 1939. In 1946 TVA and the Corps did a joint study, and TVA looked at the river again in 1959. None of the studies showed that dams on the Obed system would be economically justified.

But in later years a new tactic for justification took shape that was used by dam proponents across the nation; they suggested using recreation as an additional benefit from the building of dams. People would surely flock to the lakes formed behind the dams, to fish and race boats, to swim and water ski, bringing with them tourist dollars that would boost the local economies.

So in 1965 TVA began a new study for dams on the Obed River system, recalculating the benefit-cost ratios with recreation thrown in as a benefit.

It was about then that Bill and Liane Russell canoed the Obed for the first time and became enthralled with the wilderness beauty of the Obed River gorge. The Russells are internationally known research geneticists and members of the National Academy of Sciences. They have worked for years in Oak Ridge, a small town that grew up during World War II just off the eastern edge of the Plateau. The federal facilities in Oak Ridge were part of the Manhattan Project, which produced the first atomic bombs; Oak Ridge was responsible for producing the enriched uranium which fueled the bombs. After the war, the research programs at the federal facilities expanded to include a variety of studies in energy and related issues. Oak Ridge is now the site of the American Museum of Science and Energy.

Hearing about TVA's new study of the Obed, the Russells with others formed an organization that would seek to let landowners along the Obed and other citizens interested in preservation of natural resources know about the disastrous consequences of proposed dams on the river. They called their organization "Tennessee Citizens for Wilderness Planning." Dick Lorenz, another researcher in Oak Ridge, was the first president of TCWP; also involved in forming TCWP and serving as the first officers and directors were Ruth Young, Jean Bangham, Rod Davis, Roy McDonald, Elizabeth Peelle, Ernest Dickerman, and Ed Clebsch; Bob Peelle and Hal Smith were also active in the TCWP founding. Other organizations joined with TCWP to oppose the dams, including the Tennessee Scenic Rivers Association and the Sierra Club.

The first dam-fighting strategy used by TCWP was to help write and see through to passage the Tennessee Scenic Rivers Act of 1968, the first such legislation in the country. Unfortunately, dam proponents managed to get the Obed and its tributaries removed from the bill before it was passed by the state legislature.

Soon after, TVA revealed the results of the new study: even with recreation thrown in, the benefit-cost ratio was still unacceptable for dams on the Obed. Although it now seemed that a dam would not soon be built on the Obed, the conservationists still wanted permanent protection for the river.

Not to be thwarted by failure to get the Obed included in state legislation, the Russells and their collaborators turned their attention to the pending National Wild and Scenic Rivers Act. When that bill was passed, also in 1968, TCWP managed to get the Obed and its tributaries included in the study category.

The next step was to get the Bureau of Outdoor Recreation (BOR) moving on the study. TCWP helped to keep the study going by providing data, photographs, and guide service for BOR officials.

The Russells and others also acted as sentries along the river, watching for activity that might hurt the integrity of the river corridor. First, they discovered that a planned Tennessee Valley Authority power line was to cross the area in two places; negotiations resulted in TVA using a helicopter to string cable between two towers well back of the canyon rim so that no vegetation had to be cut near the river.

Then the conservationists found a large strip mine under contract to TVA operating in the Obed gorge; TCWP managed to get TVA officials to have a look at the damage being done, which resulted in the mine being closed and the area reclaimed. Eventually the state was persuaded to deny strip mining permits in the vicinity of the river.

In addition, several conservationists, including the Russells, acted as private nature conservancies, buying small tracts of land along the river to preserve them until the corridor could be protected by legislation.

After many years of study and four public hearings, BOR published its recommendations. The BOR study team had found that about 100 river miles of the system were worthy of inclusion in the National Wild and Scenic Rivers System and that the bulk of the mileage qualified for "wild" status and a small portion for "scenic."

It took a couple of years after completion of the BOR study to get a bill introduced. Local pressure had finally convinced the congressperson through whose district part of the Obed flowed to sponsor a section of a House bill to include the river in the National Wild and Scenic Rivers System. But part of the river system that was in another district, where there was much opposition from strip mining interests and a few private landowners, was not included. So when the U.S. Congress passed the bill in 1976 establishing the Obed National Wild and Scenic River, it included only about half of the recommended 100 river miles.

It had taken ten years of work by conservationists to get the Obed River system designated a national wild and scenic river, and then only half the area was protected—a little over 24 miles of the Obed, 17 miles of Clear Creek, 2 miles of Daddys Creek, and 1 mile of the Emory River. The other half of the recommended river miles remains unprotected at this writing, subject to strip mining, logging, oil exploration, and second-home development. But at least part has been saved, and it is the part that includes the main site for previously proposed dams.

Obed National Wild and Scenic River

The Obed River roars through a deep canyon in the central part of the Cumberland Plateau, gathering water from its many tributaries, including Daddys Creek and Clear Creek, parts of which are included in the Obed National Wild and Scenic River system. A short section of the Emory River, into which the Obed flows, also has wild and scenic status. The walls of the river canyons drop 200 to 400 feet to the river's edge, which is dotted with occasional sandy beaches and house-size boulders.

Ninety percent of the river corridor is forested with mixed hardwood, white pine, and hemlock, some in small pockets of virgin forest. The forest floor is covered with wildflowers and flowering shrubs, including rhododendron, azalea, and laurel. Among the plants are several rare and endangered species.

The Obed gets its name from a man named "Obed" who was reported to have lived with the Indians along the river. The story is told that the name "Daddys Creek" resulted from an argument by a couple traveling through the area in the early years of settlement. The husband won the argument by hitting his wife, and thereafter the creek they were camped near was known as Daddys Creek. Camped along another creek to the southeast the following evening, they got in an argument again. This time, the wife won the argument by hitting her husband with a limb; of course, the creek was then called "Mammys Creek." The Emory River gets its name from James Emory, an early Indian fighter.

Parts of the Obed and of Daddys and Clear Creeks pass through the Catoosa Wildlife Management Area, which will continue to be administered by the Tennessee Wildlife Resources Agency. This 80,000-acre tract of near-primitive land has abundant wildlife typical of the rest of the Obed system: deer, raccoon, quail, rabbit, squirrel, opossum, wild turkey, dove, ruffed grouse, an occasional wildcat, and introduced wild boar.

The Obed's fish population includes rare and endangered species, such as the Cumberland Plateau musky, a sport fish that is the southernmost race of muskellunge. Smallmouth bass, catfish, redeye, bream,

Obed River

and walleye also inhabit the waters. Many reptiles and amphibians, including a rare salamander, live in the gorge. Other endangered species that have habitat in the area include bald and golden eagles, the red-cockaded woodpecker, and the Indiana bat, although these are rarely seen. Otters are being introduced into the river gorge.

At this writing, the National Park Service has acquired 3,400 acres of the proposed 5,100 acres along the 45 miles of river corridor that have wild and scenic status. This acreage is in addition to 4,000 acres already protected within Catoosa Wildlife Management Area and managed by the state. Of the acreage now under the jurisdiction of the NPS, one-third is in conservation easements with the landowners continuing to keep title to the land; the other two-thirds has been purchased by the government. Subtracting some additional acreage owned by the state within the NPS boundaries leaves about 1,600 acres to be acquired by the federal government. Although some funds are already in hand, there is not nearly enough to acquire this acreage, some of which is in danger of being clearcut by the landowners. In 1991 the Senate Subcommittee on Interior Appropriations did not authorize any additional funds for acquisition along the Obed.

Even if appropriations come through soon to purchase this remaining land, the Obed still faces environmental threats. It seems the boundaries are inadequately drawn to protect the water quality from the effects of logging, oil exploration, and building construction. The boundaries could be expanded because the legislation that established the Obed National Wild and Scenic River authorized acquiring up to 14,464 acres.

In addition, the river system could be degraded by developments outside the designated area. A 90-foot-high earthen dam has been constructed on Otter Creek, a major tributary, and another dam has been proposed for Clear Creek, one of the main stems of the Obed; reduction in water flow, sediment, and toxins leached from exposed rock are problems. An environmental study showed a dam on Clear Creek was ill advised, but the study was rejected. At this writing, the dam is on hold while the Corps of Engineers conducts a feasibility study on supplying water to this plateau region.

Local conservation groups, especially TCWP, continue to monitor threats to the river system, to push for appropriations to complete acquisition of the lands along the river and its tributaries, and to urge the National Park Service to restudy the boundaries to see if they can be redrawn to protect the resource more adequately.

Wartburg

Gateway to the Obed System and the Catoosa Wildlife Management area, Wartburg was originally a German colony founded by George F. Gerding. Gerding came from Germany to New York in 1825. After hearing enthusiastic reports of the Cumberland Plateau, he bought a large tract of land in 1842 and helped organize the East Tennessee Colonization Company, which established the colony. Wartburg was named for the castle in Thuringia, Germany, were Martin Luther translated the Bible into German.

The first settlers were 50 people from Mainz, Germany, who arrived in 1845. They were disappointed at the virtual wilderness they found, expecting a farming community when they arrived; some at first stayed at the nearby community of Montgomery. Most of the other German and some Swiss settlers arrived between 1846 and 1855, escaping harsh economic conditions in Europe at the time. Many of the colonists were professionals, including an architect and several physicians.

After dissatisfaction with various agents chosen to manage the colony, Gerding came to Wartburg in 1849 to direct the land company and the colony personally. Vineyards and orchards were planted, and the Germans introduced winemaking to Tennessee. The 1850 census reported 317 foreign-born persons in the area, but some estimates went as high as 2,000. The town was incorporated in 1851. Despite some successes, the colony had continual problems: the settlers' disappointment on arrival, poor crops because of the plateau soil, poor roads. The colonists began to drift away to places like Nashville and Knoxville to make a better start.

Gerding was pro-Confederate during the Civil War but sat out the conflict in Louisville, Kentucky. Upon his return after the war, he found the colony in ruins and decided to sell his land, part of which was eventually purchased by the Board of Aid to Land Ownership, Ltd., for the founding of Rugby, Tennessee. Wartburg remained a community and in 1870 became the seat of Morgan County. By then the town had lost all significance as a German colony; only 98 people in the entire county were German or Swiss.

After leaving the Wartburg colony, Gerding moved to Oliver Springs at the eastern edge of the Plateau, where his family became prominent. The community takes its name from Richard Oliver, who was the first to publicize and develop the mineral springs nearby; he operated a 35-room inn there. Gerding's descendants settled in Colonial Hall, which was built around 1899 in Oliver Springs and is now on the National Register of Historic Places.

Frozen Head State Natural Area

A high mountain capped with snow and frost in winter stands between Wartburg and Oliver Springs. This is Frozen Head Mountain (3,324 feet).

For a time, a forested area that included Frozen Head Mountain was the Morgan County State Forest, which had been carved out of lands on which the Brushy Mountain State Prison had been established in 1894. But through the efforts of a local school teacher, Don Todd, who later got Tennessee Citizens for Wilderness Planning involved, 11,869 acres bounded by Bird Mountain and Little Fork Mountain were set aside by the state of Tennessee as a state park and later designated a state natural area. About 330 of these acres remain with state park designation to contain a visitor center, picnic area, campground, and recreational facilities.

Part of the natural area was originally a piece of a large land grant to

Bletcher Armes in the 1800s. Armes was married to three sisters in succession, from the eldest to the youngest, as each wife died. He had 11 children, and his descendants still live in the area. The story is told of the time Bletcher Armes caught a man butchering one of Armes's sheep and hanged him. The man's family promised that Armes would never die a natural death, but the threat was never carried out; while on his deathbed, nine of Armes's sons carrying rifles stood guard around the house. Armes is buried in the Old Petros Cemetery.

Frozen Head State Natural Area ranks second in the region only to the Great Smoky Mountains for varieties of wildflowers; 120 species of spring wildflowers have been listed thus far. The wildflower program usually held in April is the most popular of the several interpretive programs held at Frozen Head during the year; various experts and guides lead hikes to find and identify the flowers. In this part of the Cumberlands, Frozen Head has one of the few stands of undisturbed hardwood forest and is the only public land that offers a view void of strip-mined mountains.

In what may prove to be a landmark decision, the Tennessee Commissioner of Health and Environment in 1984 ruled 5,200 acres of land bordering the state natural area unsuitable for surface mining under the terms of the federal strip mine law. The basis for the decision was that strip mining would pollute Flat Fork Creek on the northwest boundary of the natural area and that although no mining would take place in the natural area, mining on adjacent mountains would degrade the view from inside, thus reducing the benefit and enjoyment of visitors. The significance of the issue is that this is one of the few instances in which a lands-unsuitable designation has been given to protect the view from inside a park. A similar decision was made concerning mining outside Bryce Canyon National Park in the 1970s.

When jurisdiction for Tennessee mining was transferred from the state to the federal Office of Surface Mining (OSM) in 1984, the lands-unsuitable designation was not recognized by OSM. Conservation groups, including TCWP, filed a petition with OSM to again have the area facing the state park declared unsuitable for strip mining; the effort to preserve Frozen Head was again led by Don Todd, now retired from his teaching position. An Environmental Impact Statement was prepared and hearings held, and in 1990, the OSM reinstated the unsuitable-for-surface-mining designation for the lands in question. A company owning coal reserves in the area appealed the decision, but the appeal was dropped; later, a suit filed in Claims Court was settled out of court. The company has since sold the land, and at this writing, the state hopes to negotiate with the new owner to purchase the land for Frozen Head.

Muddy Pond

Of the many exotic communities that have flourished and floundered on the Plateau, one of the few that has survived is the community of Mennonites near Clarkrange, Tennessee, to the northwest of Wartburg and the Obed River. The people of Muddy Pond live a simple way of life in which automobiles and electricity are shunned by many, though not all.

These are people of a similar religious faith to the Pennsylvania Amish, a strict sect of Mennonites who live in a region often written about in travel magazines. But whereas the Mennonites of Pennsylvania live in picturesque farmland that attracts thousands of tourists each year, these Mennonites of Tennessee enjoy the isolation and solitude of the backwoods of the Cumberland Plateau.

Muddy Pond was formed about 1960 when Mennonite families from Arkansas, Pennsylvania, and Canada came to the hills of the Plateau and cleared land for planting crops. The Mennonite faith originated in the Netherlands about 500 years ago with the teachings of Menno Simms, who preached a simple life and rejection of modern conveniences. The faith of the Mennonites remains grounded in a life of hard work and family values.

The Mennonites of Muddy Pond soon became known for their vegetables and baked bread and sorghum. They invite visitors to their community at certain times of the year to purchase produce. Sorghum making at the end of September and the first of October is the special time of year for visitors.

During the sorghum season, families sell vegetables, breads, cookies, pies, and sorghum. Often girls in long dresses and young boys in overalls tend the tables. This is also a chance to buy potatoes that grow especially well in the Plateau's sandy soil.

Acres of cane sorghum are grown for sorghum making in horse-powered mills. The cane is first cut, stripped of leaves, and hauled to the mill. The workers feed the cane stalks into the mill press as horses, some of them Belgian thoroughbreds, turn the mill by walking in a circle while harnessed to a long pole.

The mill squeezes the sweet juice from the cane. The juice is filtered and collected in barrels. The men then transfer the liquid to evaporation pans heated by wood fires, where the juice is repeatedly strained as it cooks down to the thick molasses called "sorghum." Lighter than molasses found in grocery stores, the sorghum can be used as syrup or in cooking. Someone near the vats will surely be selling shoofly pie.

Monterey and the Standing Stone

West of the Obed River, just at the edge of the Plateau, rests the small community of Monterey. The town was once a noted resort area to which people came, mostly from Nashville, to enjoy the mountain scenery and cooler temperatures in the summer. At one time, seven hotels housed the visitors—the Imperial; the Cumberland; the Dow; the Ramsey; the Ledbetter; the Park; and the oldest, the West Crest, built in the 1890s. Only the Imperial remains, built sometime between 1904 and 1907.

Today, Monterey is notable for the natural arches in the area and the small city park that contains the remnant of the Standing Stone. This fragment of stone, which sits atop a monument in Whittaker Park, is all that remains of the once 12- to 14-foot-high, dog-shaped monolith that once marked the Cherokee Tallonteeskee Trail, which ran east and west across the Plateau. Standing Stone State Park north of Monterey near Livingston, just off the western edge of the Plateau,

Remnant of the Standing Stone

was named for the Standing Stone, although no piece of the stone is located in the state park.

Cherokee legend says that the statue was erected soon after the arrival of the first inhabitants, who were led out of the last world. The god instructed one of the Keetoowah ancestry, an ancient spiritual society, to build a raft and set himself adrift because water was soon to cover and destroy everything. On the day that the ancestor departed, a dog spoke to him from the river bank, asking to go with the man, and said, "When you are in danger of losing your life, let me be the sacrifice." So the man let the dog accompany him.

After 40 days of drifting on the ocean that now covered the earth, the man was near starvation. The dog reminded the man of his purpose for being there, and so the man cast the dog into the water. The dog swam away but returned in seven days with mud on his back, showing that he had found new land. The dog then led the Keetoowah ancestor to the North American continent.

The Keetoowah people that settled the area around Monterey carved a block of sandstone into the shape of a dog in honor of the animal's help in leading the ancestor to the new land. The dog sculpture faced west to signify the god's instruction to the Keetoowah to always travel west until given a sign to stop.

The dog statue reminded the Indians of the supreme law and the supreme power. It was a symbol through which the Indians approached their god. They went to the stone often to replenish their strength and energy and their healing power.

For many generations, the Standing Stone stood at the western edge of the Cumberland Plateau, the hunting grounds of the Cherokees. But then the white man appeared.

Over the years, souvenir hunters chipped off pieces of the rock as they passed where it stood near Monterey. In 1893, what remained of the rock was blasted out of a railroad right-of-way. In 1895, the Cookeville chapter of the Order of the Red Men, a national fraternal organization, sought to preserve the memory of the Cherokees who once inhabited the region. The men wandered beside the railway among the pieces of the sacred stone and selected an 816-pound fragment, which they placed on a tall pedestal in Whittaker Park in Monterey. Soon after, the new town developed into a resort community and the park with its remnant of the Standing Stone became a major attraction.

The city of Monterey has since declared the second Thursday in October as Standing Stone Day; each year on that day, Cherokee groups traditionally congregate at the small park to commemorate their history.

Directions and Services

To explore the **Obed National Wild and Scenic River,** it's best to start at the National Park Service office and visitor center, located in Wartburg at the corner of Court and Maiden. Here you can get information and maps of the area. To get to **Wartburg,** head south from the Big South Fork National River and Recreation Area on US27, or from Oak Ridge take TN62 northwest through **Oliver Springs.** Colonial Hall is at the corner of Main (or Tri-County Boulevard) and Spring Streets in Oliver Springs. In Wartburg, notice the large courthouse built in 1904.

Check at the headquarters to learn which parts of the river corridor are owned by the government at the time of your trip; anywhere else, you'll need permission from the owners to be on their land.

Since the state of Tennessee will retain control of the parts of the Obed, Daddys Creek, and Clear Creek that flow through the Catoosa Wildlife Management Area, the state will be responsible for any development on those sections. Although the river corridor is to be managed as virtual wilderness, a few facilities are necessary to control visitor impact. Plans call for picnic tables, canoe put-ins, and a few campsites at several river access points.

Nemo Bridge on the Emory River is one of the most heavily used access points. A picnic area sits on the east side of the river. Camping is available at Rock Creek Campground on the west side; after crossing Nemo Bridge turn right on a side road to cross a low bridge over Rock Creek to get to the campground.

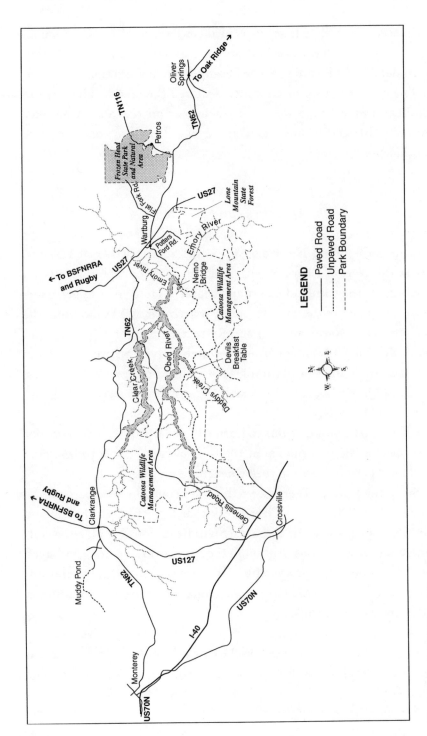

Obed National Wild and Scenic River

Whitewater canoeing and rafting are the most popular uses of the Obed and its tributaries, which—with class II, III, IV, and even V rapids—are primarily for experienced paddlers. The Obed has developed a reputation as one of the best whitewater rivers in the country. Canoes and rafts can put in at the Genesis Road Adams Bridge, Potters Ford, and Obed Junction on the Obed; Barnett Bridge, Jett Bridge, and Lilly Bridge on Clear Creek; and Devils Breakfast Table on Daddys Creek. Nemo Bridge on the Emory River is a take-out point. There is also access on a smaller tributary, White Creek, outside the national river system at Twin Bridge and Lavender Bridge.

Several outfitters with commercial-use permits lead raft and canoe trips on the river; check with the park for a list of those currently operating. Reservations should be made in advance since none are located near the river system. Early spring is usually the only time the rivers are full enough for float trips, but high water is also the time that running the river is dangerous. On the Obed, civilization and rescue are a long way off.

Primitive camping is permitted most anywhere on government lands in the Obed system away from roads and trails. There is no lodging in the area, except in motels in the surrounding communities.

Just south of Wartburg where a backwoods road crosses Crooked Fork Creek you'll find **Potters Falls,** a scenic area not included in the wild and scenic river designation. Out of Wartburg take Kingston Street, which becomes Potters Ford Road. The waterfall consists of an upper falls near the road and a lower falls just downstream. About 3 miles upstream on Crooked Fork Creek from Potters Falls is also Lamance Falls, which can be reached by taking US27 south from Wartburg and then taking a path through the woods to the falls. Check at the visitor center in Wartburg for directions and about getting permission to cross the private land if you want to see the falls. Isaac Laymance had a mill and home on Crooked Fork Creek in the early years.

If you explore the **Catoosa Wildlife Management Area,** you may want to go by the **Devils Breakfast Table,** a large slab of rock lying horizontal atop a pillar of stone to the right of a bridge over Daddys

Lower Potters Falls

Creek; unfortunately, trees have grown up around it and now hide the pillar. To the left of the bridge is also a beautiful pool at the base of a rock bluff. To enter Catoosa, take Church Street, which becomes the Catoosa Road, west off Main Street in Wartburg just north of Maiden where the visitor center is located. In several miles, you'll cross Nemo Bridge on the Emory River and enter the wildlife management area. It's then another 10 miles to Daddys Creek and the stone table; ask for directions at the Obed visitor center. The only times you're allowed to enter Catoosa are during the summer and in spring and fall when there is no hunting. February through March the roads are closed. The name "Catoosa" means "among these hills."

An overlook west of the **Lilly Bridge** crossing of Clear Creek on Ridge Road off TN62 north of Wartburg offers dramatic views. This is just upstream from the confluence of Clear Creek with the Obed.

Frozen Head State Natural Area is located off TN62 between Wartburg and Oliver Springs. You'll see a sign directing your turn north on a paved road that winds past a regional prison and then enters the state natural area. On the right as you enter the park, you'll find a new visitor center facing the mountain outside the park that would have been strip mined if recent regulations had not prevented the mining. The park also has a picnic area with restrooms and a tent camping area with 20 sites plus a group primitive camping area. No reservations can be made for camping.

To get to **Muddy Pond,** head south from Jamestown or north from Crossville on US127 or west from Wartburg on TN62. Take TN62 west in Clarkrange. You can also take TN62 east from Monterey. One mile west of Clarkrange, turn right on the Clarkrange Hunting Lodge Road; during sorghum-making time, a hand-lettered sign indicates the turn toward Muddy Pond. In a mile, cross a paved road and continue straight for another 2 miles into Muddy Pond. The road becomes a dirt road once you are in the community, but passenger cars will have no particular trouble negotiating the route.

Monterey is just off I-40 east of Cookeville and west of Crossville. **Whittaker Park,** where you'll see the remnant of the Standing Stone, is on TN62 on the east side of town. The **Campground Bridge Complex**, one of the natural arches near Monterey, is on the grounds of the **Garden Inn at Bee Rock** bed and breakfast, off US70N south of Monterey and I-40. The complex, to the left of the inn, is two natural bridges that span a narrow crack that is an enlarged joint. The span is 18 feet. The clearance of the front bridge is 41 feet, and the back bridge has a clearance of 25 feet. Bee Rock is behind the inn, where a short trail leads to the promontory, which provides a view of the upper part of the Calfkiller River Valley. You may park outside and walk in; the grounds are open to nonguests 9 A.M.–5 P.M. Mondays through Saturdays and noon-5 P.M. on Sundays and holidays.

Also near Monterey stands **Cracked Bluffs Arch,** sometimes called "The Monterey Window." The arch, although on private land, is a popular place for rock climbing. Just north of I-40 at the west end of Monterey, turn west on a small road off US70N, immediately north of the interstate. To the left, the road travels through a neighborhood and dead-ends at a private home where you must ask permission to see the arch. The top of the arch is to the right of the house. This is the western edge of the plateau, and so the rock bluffs in the area are impressive. Just west of the arch, you can find a difficult and faint trail that works its way down the cliff to the bottom of the arch. Formed by an enlarged joint, Cracked Bluffs Arch has a span of 110 feet and a clearance of about 65 feet. The arch is separated from the cliff by only a few feet.

Trails

The Park Service intends to develop 35 miles of hiking trails that follow the river corridors in the Obed System. At this writing, the 4-mile **Nemo Bridge Trail** has been constructed, starting at the Rock Creek Campground at Nemo Bridge on the Emory River and ending at BreakAway Bluff above the Obed. Take the Catoosa Road out of Wartburg, and just after crossing Nemo Bridge, turn right to get to the campground and trailhead. The trail follows the river corridor to the northwest, climbing out of the river gorge. Eventually the trail will be extended for a total of 12 miles into Catoosa along the Obed and south along Daddys Creek to the Devils Breakfast Table and eventually as far south as I-40. A 2.4-mile **Devils Breakfast Table Trail** has been completed northward from the table; the two trails will eventually meet.

The Nemo Bridge and Devils Breakfast Table Trails will make up a segment of the **Cumberland Trail** that will follow the ridge of the Cumberland Plateau from Cumberland Gap National Park to the Tennessee-Alabama border. The section of the trail along the Obed will have one designated campsite, and along the trail, you will pass the confluence of Clear Creek and the Obed. Before reaching the Obed, the Cumberland Trail will pass through the 3,600-acre Lone Mountain State Forest to the southeast of the Obed. The state forest is located off US27 on Clayton Howard Road, 4 miles southeast of Wartburg. You'll find there the 0.75-mile **Lone Mountain State Forest Nature Trail** and a 12-mile **Horse and Hiking Trail.** Hunting is allowed, so check on the hunting season before you venture on the trails.

The 21.1-mile Whetstone Mountain Section of the Cumberland Trail lies east of Wartburg. With the new effort to revive the trail, this section

Emory Gap Falls

should be repaired soon. It begins in Oliver Springs on Back Valley Road at the intersection of TN61 and 62. The trail follows Walden Ridge southeast and then turns northwest to cross Whetstone Mountain and end on Fairview Road southeast of Lone Mountain State Forest.

About 50 miles of trails wander through the forest and over ridges in Frozen Head State Natural Area, most constructed by the Civilian Conservation Corps in the 1930s. Any overnight camping along the trails requires a permit. Most of the trails range from the main trailhead in the park, which is on the right past the visitor center and the ranger station. But by driving to the end of the road that penetrates the park, you can also pick up the 2.0-mile **Panther Branch Trail,** which is probably the best trail in the park for spring wildflowers. It's a short walk along this trail to Debord Falls. And then, where the trail turns right and crosses Emory Gap Branch on a footbridge, you can continue straight on the 0.3-mile **Emory Gap Trail,** which dead-ends at Emory Gap Falls. From the Emory Gap Branch crossing, the

Panther Branch Trail climbs Old Mac Mountain and joins the 3.6-mile **North Old Mac Mountain Trail,** which leads from the main trailhead to the top of Frozen Head Mountain and a lookout tower. To the right on the North Old Mac Mountain Trail from the junction with the Panther Branch Trail, you'll find in a short walk a side trail that leads to an overlook of North Prong Valley. Other trails, including the 2.8-mile **South Old Mac Mountain Trail,** lead to the top of Frozen Head Mountain, where from the tower on a clear day you can see the Great Smoky Mountains to the east on the Tennessee-North Carolina border, strip-mined Cumberland Mountains to the north, and to the west, the Cumberland Plateau proper.

Immediately below the mountain sits Brushy Mountain State Prison at Petros which was established in 1895; the present building was constructed in 1933–34. James Earl Ray, the convicted slayer of Martin Luther King, Jr., was once imprisoned there. The prison is named for nearby Big Brushy Mountain; the grounds encompass part of the old Bletcher Armes land grant.

The Frozen Head trails also include the 15-mile **Boundary Trail,** which makes a loop with the 5.0-mile **Chimney Top Trail** around the state natural area, passing over Frozen Head Mountain. The 2.5-mile **Spicewood Branch Trail** climbs the mountain to join the Boundary Trail. The 1-mile **Wildflower Trail** leads from the main trailhead and crosses Judge Branch to connect with the South Old Mac Mountain Trail.

References

Avent, Jan Maxwell. "Bridge Dedication Stirs Thoughts of Past in Oliver Springs." *Knoxville News-Sentinel,* Sept. 29, 1985, E1.

———. "Frozen Head State Natural Area Offers Folklore . . . and More." *Knoxville News-Sentinel,* May 26, 1985, S7.

Bullard, Helen, and Joseph Marshall Krechniak. *Cumberland County's First Hundred Years.* Crossville, TN: Centennial Committee, 1956.

"Clarkrange: Historic Land of Mennonites." *Knoxville News-Sentinel,* June 4, 1976, BBB-2.

Coggins, Allen R. "The Early History of Tennessee's State Parks, 1919-1956." *Tennessee Historical Quarterly* 43, no. 3 (Fall 1984): 295–315.

Dickinson, Calvin W. *Morgan County.* Memphis: Memphis State Univ. Press, 1987.

Forester, Donald, site manager of Obed Wild and Scenic River. Interview with author. Nov. 7, 1991.

Jones, James B., Jr. "The Antebellum German-Swiss Settlement of Wartburg, Tennessee." *1990 Morgan County Recreation Guide, Morgan County News,* Mar. 22, 1990, 20-B.

Manning, Russ. "Monterey and the Standing Stone: A Gathering Place." *Tennessee Conservationist,* Sept.–Oct. 1989, 27–29.

————. "The Obed." In *Flowing Free.* Washington, DC: River Conservation Fund, 1977.

"Mennonites Invite Visitors to Molasses Making Days." *Knoxville News-Sentinel,* Sept. 28, 1977, A-9.

Parrott, Paul, former alderman of Monterey, TN. Interview with author. May 3, 1989.

Russell, Liane B. (TCWP founder, newsletter editor), and William L. Russell (TCWP founder). Interviews and conversations with author. 1977–91.

Smith, Crosland, Cherokee medicine man and member of the Keetoowah. Interview with author. Tahlequah, OK, June 22, 1989.

Smith, Monte. *A Paddler's Guide to the Obed/Emory Watershed.* Birmingham, AL: Menasha Ridge Press, 1990.

"Sorghum Jells Old, New for Mennonites." *Knoxville News-Sentinel,* Sept. 1, 1985, B-1.

Tennessee Citizens for Wilderness Planning. *TCWP Newsletter.* Oak Ridge, TN, 1977–91.

Tennessee Dept. of Conservation. "Frozen Head State Natural Area Trails." Map. Nashville, no date.

————. "Frozen Head State Park and Natural Area." Brochure. Nashville, 1989.

Tennessee Division of Geology. *Natural Bridges of Tennessee.* Bulletin 80. Nashville, 1979.

Todd, Don, retired Morgan County teacher. Interview with author. Sept. 23, 1991.

U.S. Dept. of the Interior. *Statement for Management, Obed Wild and Scenic River, Addendum* to the Final Environmental Statement, *Development Plan and Stream Classification.* Washington, DC, 1978.

U.S. Dept. of the Interior, Bureau of Outdoor Recreation. *Obed National Wild and Scenic River Final Environmental Statement.* Washington, DC, 1976.

U.S. Dept. of the Interior, National Park Service. "Obed Wild and Scenic River." Brochure. Washington, DC, no date.

Walker, Opless. "Mysterious Standing Stone Monolith." *Standing Stone Press* 1 (Oct. 11, 1979): 1.

Wyrick, Duane, park manager at Frozen Head State Park and Natural Area. Interview with author. Sept. 19, 1991.

Chapter 10

Cumberland Homesteads

It seems appropriate that the county that is right in the center of the Tennessee portion of the Plateau, that is entirely contained between the tableland's eastern and western edges, and that has seen much of the history of the Plateau because of its location should have the same name. Without much exaggeration, it can be said that Cumberland County is the heart of the Cumberland Plateau.

The old Walton Road, which traversed the Plateau to the settlements along the Cumberland River to the west, passed through Cumberland County. Grassy Cove, in the southeast corner of the county and one of the naturally good farming valleys on the Plateau, was one of the first areas on the Tennessee portion to be settled, around 1800. And the Cumberland Homesteads project, one of President Franklin Roosevelt's New Deal communities that provided work and housing during the Great Depression, is one of the historical showplaces on the Plateau.

Crossville

Located southeast of the Obed and Big South Fork Rivers in the center of Cumberland County, Crossville is one of the few towns on the Plateau that can be called an urban area. The old Walton Road ran by Crossville; the community got its name because it was the junction of several of the roads that crossed the Plateau, including the Burke Road, which connected the Walton Road with the Great Stage Road that ran between Nashville and Knoxville, and the Kentucky Stock Road, used to drive livestock from the Sequatchie Valley south of Crossville north to Kentucky.

Several of the buildings on the main street in Crossville are made with the locally mined Crab Orchard sandstone. The stone occurs in the area of the Plateau between Crossville and Crab Orchard to the east. The fine-grained sandstone is found in thin beds stacked in layers, part of the ancient delta system where the rivers met the sea. The sandstone is multicolored, ranging from tan through gray to blue-gray, with occasional splashes of yellow, brown, mauve, red, or pink forming various swirls, stripes, and figures that sometimes look like leaves or ferns.

Mining the rock has been a large part of the local economy, with much of the sandstone sent outside Tennessee. The sandstone was used in the United Auto Worker's building in Detroit and the U.S. Post Office in Philadelphia, for flagstone in Rockefeller Center in New York, and in the courts and walks around President Roosevelt's swimming pool in Washington, D.C.

The post office and the jail in Crossville are made of the Crab Orchard sandstone. The First National Bank, built around 1905, has the sandstone in several types and colors; slabs in the exterior walls of the bank also demonstrate the results of different methods of cutting and polishing. Directly across the street from the bank sits the old Palace Theater, built in the 1930s using the sandstone in the art deco style.

Across the street from the Chamber of Commerce is a small building constructed entirely of Crab Orchard sandstone, including the roof; also built in the 1930s. Next to the Chamber of Commerce stands one of the oldest buildings in the town; built around 1886, it was originally a courthouse and for a time was a high school; now it is the annex for the county courthouse in the center of town.

Crossville is perhaps most noted in the region for its Cumberland County Playhouse, one of the best regional theaters in the Southeast. The theater was founded by Paul and Mary Crabtree and members of the Crossville community. Before moving to Crossville, the Crabtrees worked in theater and television in New York and California. Soon after settling in Crossville, the local people encouraged them to help with theater in the community. The playhouse opened in 1965 as a nonprofit corporation and immediately established itself as a place for quality theater. The Crabtrees' son, Jim

Crabtree, is now producing director of the theater, and their daughter, Abigail Crabtree, is artistic director.

In addition to established plays, the playhouse produces original
work rooted in the heritage and culture of the region. A Living History
Series included plays about historic Rugby and the Cumberland Homesteads. A Rural America series included a play about Signal Mountain.

The Homesteads

The Cumberland Homesteads project was one of many communities
created across the country during the Depression years by the Federal
Subsistence Homesteads Corporation with money provided by the National Industrial Recovery Act of 1933. By constructing new communities of subsistence farms, the government hoped to give employment
to those out of work and to provide a boost to local economies.

Architects and engineers were brought in to help with the construction of the Cumberland community—many from the newly created
Tennessee Valley Authority, a government-owned utility—but most of
the jobs were given to the local people. Employment reached over 400,
but only 250 families were to receive homes. Those few were selected
from thousands of applicants.

The project plans called for each family to have a house with land
ranging from 3 to over 100 acres of the 10,000 acres set aside for the
project. A barn and other farm buildings were to be built. The community was to have a mill, a store, a coal mine, and other industries for cash
income, plus a school and community center. At first, one-third of the
wages earned were applied as credit toward the purchase of the homes,
but that system created much disagreement. And so it was decided that
each family was to first rent the home and farm for a short period and
then buy them with borrowed money at low interest rates.

The barns were built first, and most of the families lived in these
while the houses were built and the land cleared for cultivation. The
first ten families moved into houses in December 1934.

The project was an opportunity for the people of the Plateau to learn

A Homesteads House

new skills. They set up two sawmills and built a kiln to turn out lumber for construction. They opened quarries to supply the stone for the foundations, fireplaces, and exterior walls. They made shingles and beams by hand, and a blacksmith made some of the hardware. The people planted their gardens as soon as possible.

Various schemes were tried to produce additional income because the subsistence farms were too small to produce cash crops. The community tried a trading post, a gift shop, a cannery, a restaurant, a sorghum plant, a coal mine, and an effort at raising pure-bred hogs. Most of these produced little income. Later, a hosiery mill and a chair factory were attracted to the area, and many of the people found work outside their community.

The Cumberland Homesteads project lasted for 12 years, during which time Eleanor Roosevelt came to visit. It was intended that the families participating in the community would quickly buy the homes and farms using the wages and credit they were given for work on the project and the money they subsequently earned from farming and other endeavors. But because of the distraction of World War II and a degree of mismanagement, few families owned their homes after years of work.

Nationally, the Subsistence Homesteads Project became a problem; no one, it seemed, knew how to make the various communities self-sufficient. Responsibility for the venture was shifted from agency to agency until the Federal Housing Authority took over and negotiated lease-purchase agreements with the homesteaders.

When the Cumberland Homesteads project was terminated in 1945, the families who lived in the community were finally given a chance to buy their homes at reasonable rates. Many of the homes are still owned by the original homesteaders and their children.

Although the project did not succeed in creating a Utopian community, it was one of the more successful of the 102 New Deal communities created across the country during the Depression. Over 200 families acquired homes and subsistence farms, and many more displaced miners and farmers found employment where none had existed.

The sandstone exteriors and the distinctive style of the Homesteads houses, reminiscent of English country cottages, make the homes very easy to spot. The style of the houses is the work of William Macy Stanton, the principal architect of the project, who before coming to the Cumberland Homesteads had worked at another model community, Norris, adjacent to TVA's Norris Dam in East Tennessee. Stanton is responsible for the design of the community, including the dam and mill house at nearby Cumberland Mountain State Park. In addition to the English cottage style and the fact that the outside walls are almost entirely Crab Orchard sandstone, a distinctive feature that helps identify the Homesteads houses is the chimney flanked by windows on both sides in most of the houses.

The solid masonry walls of the Homesteads houses are 12 inches thick. The interior walls are tongue-and-groove paneling, and the floors, hardwood. In those houses that have not been painted sometime during the last 60 years, entire rooms are natural wood, including the ceiling.

The houses had indoor bathrooms when most of the surrounding region still used outside privies. A water-storage tank in the attic provided a water supply; each house had its own well with a hand pump in the kitchen. All the houses were also wired for electricity, even though it was years before power service reached the community.

Cumberland Mountain State Rustic Park

Built as the recreational park for the Cumberland Homesteads and first called "Cumberland Homesteads Park," Cumberland Mountain State Rustic Park still lies within the Homesteads community.

The park includes an old stone dam, which backs up Byrd Lake. The dam was built in the late 1930s by the Civilian Conservation Corps using Crab Orchard sandstone. It is the largest steel-free, masonry structure undertaken by the CCC. The park road crosses the dam; large arches under the road act as spillways.

Just below the dam sits the group lodge, the Old Stone Mill House, one of the original structures in the park. The Mill House was never operated as originally intended; the mill was considered unfair competition for privately owned mills in the area, so project officials decided not to use it. Today, it is the group lodge for the park.

Grassy Cove

Southeast of the Homesteads lies Grassy Cove, a depression in the plateau forming a valley of gracefully rolling fields of corn, soybeans, and grazing land for black angus cattle. Because the cove contains some of the prime farmland on the Plateau, it attracted early settlers searching for a new home. Those who discovered Grassy Cove found a meadow of grass as high as a person's head, land that would easily produce a crop the first year.

John Ford was among the first to see Grassy Cove, around 1801. Traveling the old Walton Road west toward the Cumberland River

Grassy Cove

Valley settlements, Ford or another person in the party of settlers he was leading lost control of his wagon on a steep grade coming through the Crab Orchard Mountains. When the dust settled, the mules that had been pulling the wagon were all dead except one. Unable to continue, Ford and the others looked around for a place to settle and stumbled upon Grassy Cove, where Ford and his family built a log house and secured a land grant, probably in payment for his services during the Revolutionary War.

These early settlers, which included the Lodens, were soon joined by the Dortons, Davenports, and DeRossetts among other families from Virginia and the Carolinas. About 1808 Conrad Kemmer brought his family to the area, apparently from Pennsylvania.

Many of those still living in the cove bear the names of these early settlers. The two general stores along TN68 that traverses the cove are run by Kemmer descendants. Both stores are reminiscent of the old general stores that sold everything a person could want—from hats and bridles to canned goods and produce.

Most everyone that passes through Grassy Cove, which is now a National Natural Landmark, is impressed with the beauty and isolation of the place. Louis L'Amour, the western novelist, became intrigued with the area while driving through, and in his 1985 novel, *Jubal Sackett,* he had the protagonist pass through Grassy Cove and recommend the cove as an excellent place to settle to Sacketts who would follow.

Some have referred to the cove as a giant sinkhole that because of its fertility became a pastoral valley. The soil in the cove is especially rich and productive because the Pennsylvanian sandstone that caps the rest of the Plateau is missing here. The cove was part of the overthrust system that broke the sandstone caprock of this region of the plateau and allowed erosion to sweep out the Sequatchie Valley to the south. Once the sandstone had eroded away and the limestone was exposed in the region of Grassy Cove, numerous sinkholes probably developed which eventually combined to form the cove in the shape of a large sinkhole, called a "uvala" in geologic terms. This is also described as a "karst" area, a limestone region with sinks, underground streams, and caverns.

The cove is 5 miles long, and the width varies from a little over 1,000 feet to 2 miles. The 3,000 acres of the valley floor are surrounded on all sides by mountains rising several hundred feet to form a great bowl—Brady Mountain to the west, Black Mountain to the northeast, and Bear Den Mountain to the south, in somewhat the shape of a triangle.

The cove would be flooded by rainwater if it were not formed of limestone rock that has become perforated with numerous caves. The main drainage, Cove Creek, travels from the southwest corner of Grassy Cove, collecting lesser streams along its way, and finally drains into a cave in the side of Brady Mountain to the west. A grist and sawmill once stood at the mouth of the cave, around 1848, and the cave is now known as the "Old Mill Cave."

Folklore has it that Grassy Cove was once a lake until the water worked its way through the mountain, creating the cave. The creek emerges from Devilstep Hollow Cave on the other side of Brady Mountain, several miles away and several hundred feet lower, forming the headwaters of the Sequatchie River which flows the length

of Sequatchie Valley, the long valley that bisects the southern portion of the Plateau.

For a long time, it was only a folk legend that Cove Creek emerged
as Sequatchie River. In 1961 the Tennessee Valley Authority and the
U.S. Geological Survey decided to find out for sure. They added dye and
painted wood chips to the water in Cove Creek and then waited on the
other side of the mountain. After six days, the dye and chips appeared,
proving the legend true.

Another well-known cave in the cove is Saltpeter Cave. During
the Civil War, Andrew Kemmer (grandson of Conrad) and Richard
Matthews worked the cave for the calcium nitrate used in the production of gunpowder, which the men supplied to the Confederates. Although some of the men of Grassy Cove fought for the Union, most of
the people were for the Confederacy.

Shortly after the Civil War, the body of a Confederate soldier was
found in one of the far reaches of the cave. The body was lying on a
stretcher, a hat covering his face as if he had been laid out to await
burial. The people of the cove speculated he had died of natural causes
and his friends had intended to leave him there only temporarily but
had never returned. Since the body had been left far back in the cave, no
one had noticed it until a group exploring the cave happened upon it.
During the time the soldier lay in the cave, he became petrified; the flesh
was said to be hard as marble and the clothing very stiff.

The soldier's identity was never discovered, and the people buried
him in the Methodist cemetery. It was not long before local wags began
telling ghost stories of the petrified Confederate rising from his grave to
chase anyone passing by the cemetery late at night. The stories so
caught on that children refused to go to their school, which was located
near the church, and some adults refused to travel the road that passed
the cemetery. To put the stories to rest, a group of men exhumed the
body and buried it in a place known only to them. Even as old men years
later, the members of the group refused to divulge the location of the
secret grave because of a "gentlemen's agreement" not to do so for the
good of the community.

Crab Orchard

At the time the first settlers were heading west across the Plateau, crab apple trees grew in profusion at the western foot of the mountains that stand on the eastern edge of the Plateau. The name "Crab Orchard" was given to the mountains, the community that developed there, and eventually the sandstone found in the region.

Crab Orchard was one of the favorite stops along the Walton Road. The meadow where the crab apple trees once proliferated was one of the first places for a pleasant rest after travelers heading west had climbed the eastern escarpment of the Plateau and made their way through the Crab Orchard Mountains that guard the interior. The Cherokees allowed the travelers to hunt within a mile and a half of the road at Crab Orchard, but it was not long before the settlers insisted on having some kind of shelter in the area for their families to rest. Although the request seems not unreasonable, this was the first move in the taking of all of the Tennessee portion of the Plateau from the Cherokees.

Soon there were cabins at Crab Orchard, and an inn was built in 1800. About 1827 a large two-story inn was constructed and was widely known as the "Crab Orchard Inn." The inn stood on a small knoll in town until at least 1933. Though there was talk of restoring the inn, the expense was probably too much, and it was torn down.

On Black Mountain, which stands between Crab Orchard and Grassy Cove, is another registered state natural area. The area contains the Black Mountain Access for the Cumberland Trail. The Black Mountain natural area is owned by the United Methodist Church.

Ozone Falls

Ozone was another of the main stops along the Walton Road after travelers climbed the eastern edge of the Cumberland Plateau. There were inns here in 1806 and 1817. Daniel McNair had a grist mill near the waterfall in the community in 1860, and for a time the place was known as "McNair Falls." It was also called "Mammy" for a while because it is near Mammys Creek. The place was renamed "Ozone" in 1896 for the "stimulating quality of the air." The waterfall became known as Ozone Falls. The area within the community that contains the waterfall is now Ozone Falls State Natural Area.

From the top of the falls it is a sheer drop of 110 feet to the bottom. The water forms a graceful arc into a pool of blue water and then disappears, apparently running under the rocks that surround the pool. The creek emerges farther down the small canyon.

Pomona

Several experimental communities were tried on the Cumberland Plateau. Besides the Homesteads near Crossville and the English and German colonies of Rugby and Allardt to the north, the small community of Pomona in the western part of Cumberland County was founded in the mid-1800s by John M. Dodge, at the time a famous portrait painter. Dodge had 82,000 apple trees planted and named the community for the Roman goddess of fruit and orchards. Many of his friends came to Pomona and built elegant homes.

One of those attracted to the new community was Margaret Bloodgood Peake, a poet who started a philosophical cult that many young people joined. A morning ritual had the young girls rolling naked in the dew-drenched clover fields; the practice was discontinued because of the growing number of young men in the surrounding woods each morning.

During the Civil War, half of the apple trees in Pomona were destroyed. When the inhabitants also learned that the proposed railroad line that was expected to bring prosperity to the community would not be built through the town, their disillusionment was complete. The town was virtually abandoned, but a small community exists there today.

Pioneer Hall

Pleasant Hill

Just west of Pomona lies Pleasant Hill, a community that centers on a complex of buildings that at various times has been a school, a hospital, a sanatorium, and is now a retirement center. Around the end of World War I, May Wharton, a graduate of the University of Michigan School of Medicine, arrived in Pleasant Hill. She came to join her husband who a month before had became the new principal at Pleasant Hill Academy, one of the many schools started in the South by the American Missionary Association. Dr. Wharton began several small clinics in the area that ministered to the needs of the people on the Plateau.

When Dr. Wharton's husband died, the people she had served asked her to stay on as their doctor. She stayed and with the help of Elizabeth Fletcher, art teacher at the Academy, and Alice Adshead, a nurse, founded in 1921 a hospital that came to be known as "Uplands." The hospital began in an old house, called "Sanex," which no longer stands. Uplands then expanded into the Cumberland Mountain Sanatorium, which was devoted to the treatment of tuberculosis and miners' black lung and later became the Cumberland Mountain Hospital.

During these years Dr. Wharton purchased land around Uplands and began giving parcels to people who would come there to retire. She thought that with the facilities located at Uplands, it would be an ideal retirement center. Later she decided the hospital should be located in a more urban area, and she subsequently founded the Cumberland Medical Center in Crossville. The hospital at Pleasant Hill became the Uplands Retirement Center. Today the retirement center is a complex of facilities that includes retirement homes on leased land, apartments, sheltered care, and a nursing home.

Pioneer Hall, constructed in 1887, is the only building that remains of the Pleasant Hill Academy; it served variously as dormitory, library, and lunch room and is now a museum. The building is on the National Register of Historic Places.

Virgin Falls. Photograph by Sondra Jamieson

Virgin Falls Pocket Wilderness

Virgin Falls, at the western edge of the Plateau, is located in another of the pocket wilderness areas set aside by the Southern Division of Bowater, Inc.; these mini-wilderness areas also have state natural area designation. Virgin Falls Pocket Wilderness lies just west of Cumberland County.

The unique features of this area are the waterfalls that plunge from great heights and disappear into the ground. Big Laurel Creek flows over Big Branch Falls and farther downstream washes over Big Laurel Falls before disappearing in an underground cave behind the falls. Farther in the wilderness, a small creek running out of Sheep Cave cascades 50 or 60 feet until it also disappears into a hole in the ground. But the most spectacular is Virgin Falls, which emerges from a cave, runs about 50 feet, drops 110 feet, and disappears into the rocks at the bottom. The water from all these waterfalls apparently runs through the ground, finally draining into the Caney Fork River, which flows through Scott Gulf to the south.

Directions and Services

You'll find **Crossville** south of I-40 at the junction of US127 and US70. The Chamber of Commerce is located in the center of town on US127. **Simonton's Cheese House,** one of the town's better known businesses, has relocated from the town center north to US127 nearer I-40. The store's aged cheddar cheese, among other cheeses, has a national reputation and is ordered from all parts of the country.

On a weekend visit to the community, you might drive out to the **Crossville Flea Market,** one of the largest of its kind, with an incredible display of booths containing everything imaginable, from tools, guns, and small engines to crafts, clothes, books, tires, bowling balls, and in season, fresh produce. The flea market is northwest of town on US70N.

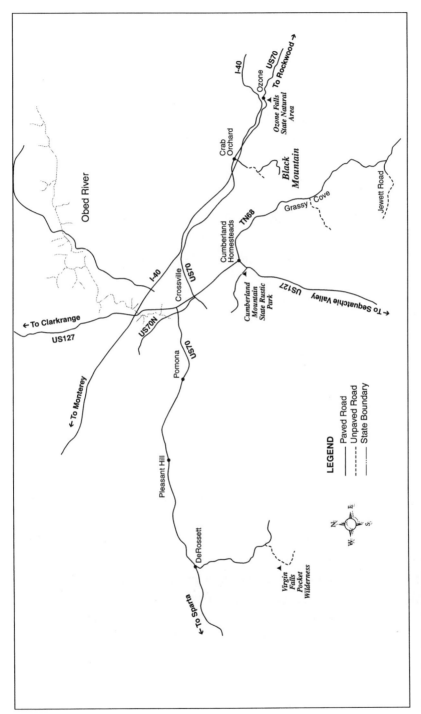

Cumberland Homesteads Region

Across the road from the flea market you'll find the **Plateau Live-stock Exchange,** where cattle and other livestock are auctioned. It's an old-fashioned setup in which the local farmers sit in a semicircular gallery surrounding a pit into which the cattle are driven one at a time and a fast-talking auctioneer rattles off the bids.

To get to the **Cumberland County Playhouse,** take US70 west, the road to Sparta, Tennessee. About 3 miles outside of Crossville, you'll see a sign for the playhouse on the left. The play season runs from mid-March into December. Many of the plays are sold out, so you should make reservations.

For your stay in Cumberland County, motels and restaurants are available in and around Crossville. Also, several resorts are scattered around the county, some of which have lodging for the public, including **Fairfield Glade,** northeast of Crossville and I-40, which has a lodge and villa, and **Holiday Links,** near Cumberland County Playhouse, which has an inn.

But for more of a historical flavor, there's **Cumberland Mountain State Rustic Park,** located 5 miles south of Crossville on US127. You'll turn east on TN419 into the park. The park office and restaurant are just west of the bridge and dam over Byrd Lake. A number of cabins are available for rent at the park, both rustic and modern. One of the cabins, dubbed "Raccoon Hollow," is an original Homesteads house and may be rented on the same basis as the other cabins. The group lodge, the Old Stone Mill House, sleeps 16. The cabins are fully equipped and may be reserved up to one year in advance. Reservations are advisable. There is also a campground with 150 sites, each with hookups, grills, and tables; camping is on a first-come, first-served basis. The Cumberland Mountain restaurant, located in the park, is open for lunch and dinner except during Christmas holidays and the months of January and February. The park also has tennis courts and a swimming pool.

The **Cumberland Homesteads** community surrounds Cumberland Mountain State Park. By driving out the back of the park on the main road on which you entered, you can see several of the original homes built in the late 1930s and early 1940s. The houses are quite

The Homesteads Tower

distinctive; all are at least partially built of the Crab Orchard sandstone. The center of the community is at the intersection of TN68 with US127, and you'll find other homes east along TN68. At the intersection stands the Homesteads Tower, and behind the tower, the school complex. The lower part of the tower, which is four long rooms in the shape of a cross, was once the administration building for the Homesteads project; the tower contains a water-storage tank that once served the school but is no longer used. Now the building is a museum, where for a small donation to help with the preservation, you can climb to the top of the tower for a view of the surrounding countryside. Most of the homestead tracts are within sight of the tower, but the homes are hidden by the trees. The museum is open April through October every day except Wednesdays and Sunday mornings.

Grassy Cove lies 7 miles southeast of the Cumberland Homesteads on TN68. The **Old Mill Cave** in which Cove Creek disappears is directly behind the J. A. Kemmer & Son store on TN68; if the leaves are off the trees, you can spot the cave from the road. The opening is 30 feet wide and 10 feet high. In heavy rains, the cave cannot handle all the water draining out of the cove and the area becomes flooded, at rare times reaching all the way to the back of the Kemmer store. All the land in Grassy Cove is privately owned, so access to the cave is limited. To see the cave, you must ask for permission at the store.

Saltpeter Cave is on private land behind the J. C. Kemmer general store in the southern end of the cove. Turn right on the Kemmer Road beside the store. The road soon becomes gravel. Just after you make the turn, notice the red building on the right, which is one of the old Kemmer stores now used as a warehouse. Along the road you'll pass the Grassy Cove United Methodist Church. A church was built near here in 1803 and was probably the first church in the county; now there is a more modern brick building. Many of the headstones in the cemetery date from the early 19 century; one marks the 1844 grave of John Ford Sr., private in the Sixth Virginia Regiment during the Revolutionary War and the first settler in Grassy Cove. If you continue past the church until you are 2 miles from the highway, you'll be in the vicinity of Saltpeter Cave. You'll need to ask permission from the landowners if you want to gain access.

Crab Orchard, east of Crossville on US70, is just north of I-40. The old rail line between Crossville and Crab Orchard has been proposed for conversion to a trail for hiking, biking, and riding horses; establishment of the trail will depend on the willingness of the Southern Railway to sell the right-of-way and whether the state of Tennessee has the funds to purchase it. When you get to Crab Orchard, you'll notice a large limestone mine in the side of Crab Orchard Mountain. The operation dominates the scene and has bathed the surrounding area in a fine white dust. The limestone is exceptionally pure and is used for mortar and plaster and as chemical limestone in industrial processes. If you turn north off US70 in the middle of the small community, cross the railroad tracks, and then take a right as if you were going to the limestone mine, you'll top the small knoll where the Crab Orchard Inn once stood.

Between Crab Orchard and Crossville, at the Genesis Road exit off I-40, you'll find the **Stonehaus Winery,** the new winery started by Fay and Kathy Wheeler after they left Highland Manor Winery near Jamestown in the mid-1980s. The Genesis Road leads on into the Obed River country.

To get to **Black Mountain** natural area, turn south off US70 in Crab Orchard and cross over the interstate. If a dead-end sign is still there, ignore it, because it's a little premature. Continue to a T; to the left is the dead-end. Turn right and go about a mile and a half along a gravel road until you reach a paved road to the left, which goes to the top of the mountain, entering the natural area along the way. At the top you'll find an air traffic control tower. Before you reach the tower, a small dirt road leads to the left into the woods past an old homeplace; all that remains is the rock chimney and the springhouse. You cannot go far on this road without 4-wheel drive. You'll find in here a maze of large sandstone boulders that's fun to explore. At the springhouse, you can pick up the Cumberland Trail; it's not marked because vandals keep taking the sign down.

Ozone Falls State Natural Area is a drive of about 15 miles from Crossville through Crab Orchard on US70 east. Southeast from Crab Orchard you'll pass the entrance to **Cumberland Gardens Resort,** where lodging is available in condominiums.

Ozone is a community so small that a tiny building serves as both the post office and the library. Just west of Fall Creek in Ozone, you'll find a turnout for the state natural area. It's then just a short walk to the edge of the falls. State natural areas are meant to be places managed in their natural state. Therefore, no handrails are along the top of the falls to prevent people from falling; so hang on to any small children who might go running off into space.

You can also get to the state natural area west from Rockwood, a town just off the eastern edge of the Plateau on US27. Once you've climbed the Plateau headed west, you'll pass **Roosevelt State Forest** to the north.

Six miles west of Crossville past the Cumberland County Playhouse on US70, you'll pass through **Pomona.** Unfortunately, none of the old houses and few apple trees remain. **Pleasant Hill** is 5 miles west of Pomona on US70. In addition to the Uplands Retirement Center, you'll find Pioneer Hall, the museum of the Pleasant Hill Historical Society open Wednesdays and Sunday afternoons.

For **Virgin Falls Pocket Wilderness,** turn south in DeRossett 10 miles west of Pleasant Hill on US70. In 5.9 miles, turn right on a gravel road for 2 miles to the trailhead. **Scott Gulf** adjacent to Virgin Falls was recently donated to the state by Bridgestone/Firestone Corp., as a result of the efforts of the Friends of Scotts Gulf. The area will be managed by the Tennessee Wildlife Resources Agency.

Trails

At Cumberland Mountain State Park, the 5-mile **Pioneer Loop** circles Byrd Lake for a pleasant walk through a hemlock woods among large boulders. The 1-mile **Cumberland Plateau Trail** forms a loop along Byrd Creek downstream from the dam, while the 2.1-mile **Byrd Creek**

Trail forms a longer loop along the creek. There is also the 6-mile **Cumberland Overnight Trail** through second-growth timber.

An 11.7-mile section of the **Cumberland Trail** passes through Cumberland County. This Grassy Cove Section begins at the Black Mountain natural area and descends to cross TN68 north of Grassy Cove and then climbs Brady Mountain to follow the ridgeline, with distant views of Grassy Cove, before ending at Jewett Road to the southwest.

To get to the base of Ozone Falls, take the quarter-mile **Ozone Falls Trail.** From the top of the falls, a short connector trail to the right parallels US70 going west. You'll arrive at a turnout on the road. A sign on a low rock wall indicates the trailhead. Starting here, you descend along the trail to the foot of the falls. Since the water pours off a rock overhang, you can walk behind the falls and peer up the sheer walls of the canyon through a curtain of water.

The **Virgin Falls Trail** in the Virgin Falls Pocket Wilderness is approximately 8 miles round-trip. In addition to the numerous waterfalls along the trail, you'll pass overlooks of the Caney Fork River Valley. A designated backpackers' camping area is located at the end of a side trail near the Caney Fork River.

References

Bowater, Inc., Southern Division. "Bowater Trails." Brochure. Calhoun, TN, no date.

Brookhart, Donald, Cumberland County historian. Interview with author. Aug. 13, 1984.

Bullard, Helen, and Joseph Marshall Krechniak. *Cumberland County's First Hundred Years.* Crossville, TN: Centennial Committee, 1956.

Coleman, Bevley R. *History of State Parks in Tennessee.* Nashville: Tennessee Dept. of Conservation, 1963.

Crabtree, Mary, director of Cumberland County Playhouse. Interview with author. Aug. 23, 1984.

Cumberland Mountain Sanatorium. "History of Uplands, 1920-1946." Pleasant Hill, TN, no date.

Dodge, Emma F. *A History of Pleasant Hill Academy.* Pleasant Hill, TN: Pleasant Hill Historical Society of the Cumberlands, 1938.

Federal Writers' Project. *Tennessee: A Guide to the State.* New York: Hastings House, 1939.

Harvey, Stella Mowbray. *Tales of the Civil War Era.* Crossville, TN: Chronicle Pub. Co., 1963.

Manning, Russ, and Sondra Jamieson. *The South Cumberland and Fall Creek Falls: A Hiker's Guide to Trails and Attractions.* Norris, TN: Laurel Place, 1990.

Mason, Don. "Cumberland County Playhouse a Family Affair." *Knoxville News-Sentinel Showtime,* Mar. 4, 1990, 3.

Raulston, J. Leonard, and James W. Livingood. *Sequatchie: A Story of the Southern Cumberlands.* Knoxville: Univ. of Tennessee Press, 1974.

Stratton, Cora S., and Nettie M. Stratton. *And This Is Grassy Cove.* Crossville, TN: Chronicle Pub. Co., 1938.

Tennessee Dept. of Conservation. "Cumberland Mountain State Park." Brochure. Nashville, no date.

———. "Cumberland Mountain State Rustic Park Trails Map." Nashville, 1982.

Vaden, Emma Jean Pedigo. *Looking Back . . . Cumberland Homesteads Golden Anniversary Album.* Cumberland Homesteads, TN: Vaden, 1984.

Wharton, May Cravath, M.D. *Doctor Woman of the Cumberlands.* Pleasant Hill, TN: Uplands Cumberland Mountain Sanatorium, 1953.

Chapter 11

Sequatchie Valley and Walden Ridge South

When the Cumberland Plateau formed, the rippling effect from the collision of continental plates pushed up a long ridge on the southern portion of the Plateau, of which the Crab Orchard Mountains are the only remaining section. The hard-surfaced sandstone layer along this ridge shattered, allowing erosion to wear down the southern portion in the millions of intervening years.

Along the line of this overthrust system today lies the Sequatchie Valley, which slices through the southern part of the Cumberland Plateau. The finger of plateau that forms the east side of the valley is by convention referred to as "Walden Ridge," and the mass of land that forms the west side is called the "Cumberland Plateau."

Sequatchie Valley

Sequatchie Valley is one of the longest and surely one of the straightest valleys in the world. The valley extends across the state line into Alabama, but only the 70-mile section in Tennessee is referred to as "Sequatchie Valley." The width averages 5 miles.

The valley is one of the few places in the Plateau region that has prime farmland, comparable to the rich soil overlying limestone in Grassy Cove. The Sequatchie River drains Sequatchie Valley, beginning at the river's headwaters at Devilstep Hollow Cave where the waters from Grassy Cove emerge from their subterranean passage; the cave has been proposed for a state natural area. For most of the valley's length, the river gently meanders back and forth but flows generally straight southwest through the center of the valley, eventually emptying into the Tennessee River to the southwest. A highway generally parallels the river, also making a straight shot down the center of the valley through the communities of Pikeville in the north; Dunlap, Whitwell, and Victoria along the way; and Jasper and South Pittsburg in the south.

Pikeville is the eastern access point for Fall Creek Falls State Resort Park, located on top of the Plateau to the west. Dunlap provides an approach to the Savage Gulf Entrance to the Savage Gulf State Natural Area, likewise on the Plateau to the west.

Dunlap is also known for coke ovens, built there in the early 1900s, which are now on the National Historic Register. By 1920 the Chattanooga Iron and Coal Company employed about 350 men at Dunlap for the mining of coal and the production of coke. Coke is produced by heating coal to remove the volatile components. The heating was done in 268 beehive ovens constructed for the coking process. The brick ovens were 12 feet in diameter and 6 feet high with holes in the top for loading the coal. A typical charge was 6 tons of coal, which produced 3 tons of coke. Most of the coke was used in manufacturing centers in the production of pig iron. Now at the Coke Ovens Park historic site in Dunlap, the ruins of the ovens stand in rows in the forest.

The coal for these ovens came from the No. 2 mine located high on the mountain behind the ovens. The cars loaded with coal came down a 3,900-foot incline track from the tipple, where the coal was screened. Since the walk down the mountain was so long, the miners looked for some method of getting down the mountain quickly at the end of the workday. They devised an "incline horse," consisting of a wooden seat with two wheels for riding just one of the rails. A miner would mount his incline horse, balance himself—grasping in each hand a block of wood that he also used for braking—and take off, sometimes exceeding 60 miles an hour in the descent. Obviously it was a dangerous way of leaving work each afternoon, especially when some prankster greased the rails at the bottom.

In the 1870s, the lower portion of Sequatchie Valley experienced an economic boom. An English syndicate purchased 150,000 acres of iron, coal, and timber land and formed the Southern States Coal, Iron, and Land Company, Ltd. The company opened coal mines and began devel-

oping an iron industry. Towns grew up to support the boom—
Whitwell, Kimbal, Victoria, and the model town of South Pittsburg,
with all the connotations of that name (although not spelled like the
name of the Pennsylvania iron city).

Victoria was originally the community of Dadsville, but was renamed for Queen Victoria, who gave a church bell for a community
church. The Bethel United Methodist Church, a white clapboard building now unused, still stands in the community.

East of Victoria on the Sequatchie River remains one of the few water-
powered mills still in operation. Originally built in 1824 by David
Ketner and enlarged in 1867, Ketners Mill is a tall red brick structure
where Clyde Ketner still grinds corn and wheat for meal and flour.

In 1882, the assets of the coal and iron industry in the southern
Sequatchie were acquired by the Tennessee Coal, Iron, and Railroad
Company, which had grown from its start as the Sewanee Mining
Company based at Tracy City on the Plateau to the west. The boom
in this region of the Sequatchie Valley then ended with the 1893
economic depression.

There was some recovery in the region during the first decade after
1900. Several businesses moved into the area, including the Dixie Portland Cement Company, which was founded at Deptford near South
Pittsburg. The community was renamed Richard City in honor of Richard
Hardy, the president and manager of the company. Tom Mix was called
there to be team boss and labor manager for the cement plant in 1908.
Mix, who had been a member of Teddy Roosevelt's Rough Riders, was
also deputy sheriff at nearby Copenhagen before joining a Wild West
show and later becoming one of the first western movie stars.

The year 1913 brought the completion of the Hales Bar Lock
and Dam on the Tennessee River; the dam improved navigation on
the river by flooding the treacherous stretches in the river gorge.
Fifty years later the Hales Bar Dam needed to be replaced, and so in
1964–67, the Tennessee Valley Authority constructed Nickajack
Dam downstream from the old dam. Once the lake was impounded,
the Hales Bar Dam was destroyed.

In the early 1990s, this southern end of Sequatchie Valley was the

Ketners Mill

proposed location for chip mills and associated barge terminals on the Tennessee River. Timber would be harvested from a 42-county region that includes the South Cumberland and then turned into chips and barged down the Tennessee River to the Tennessee-Tombigbee Waterway, which leads to the Gulf of Mexico, with the potential for export. Since the Tennessee Valley Authority must issue a permit for any new river terminal, TVA prepared an Environmental Impact Study that included not only the impact of barge terminals but also the impact to forest and wildlife resources. On the basis of this study, permits for barge terminals to handle wood chips were denied.

Even so, log exports out of the plateau region continue to chip mills in other states, and mills have located where chips can be shipped by rail or truck. A large chip mill operation has located near the Royal Blue area of the northern plateau and is harvesting timber from Campbell and Scott Counties, including the watershed of the New River, one of the two principal tributaries of the Big South Fork. A local group called "TAGER" (Tennesseans/Alabamans/Georgians for Environmental Responsibility) monitors the situation on the South Cumberland and informs the public about the adverse effects of accelerated clearcutting to supply chip mills. The Dogwood Alliance, a network of local organizations, performs the same function for the Southeast as a whole.

Sequatchie Valley was also the proposed location for pumped storage facilities that would have had an environmental impact. Due to the efforts primarily of a local group, Save Our Sequatchie, those proposals were withdrawn, but they could be revived.

Nickajack Cave

One of Tennessee's most famous caves, Nickajack Cave, is located near the Tennessee-Alabama border on the west side of Nickajack Cove on the eastern side of Sequatchie Valley. The cave has one of the largest entrances of any cave in the eastern United States, 140 feet by 50 feet; but now the cave is partially flooded by the waters of Nickajack Lake, the TVA reservoir behind Nickajack Dam.

The cave was once used as a shelter by the Chickamauga Indians, the splinter group of Cherokees who refused to give in to the whites who were taking their land. This region was the general location of two of the Five Lower Towns of the Chickamaugas that were destroyed by Major James Ore in 1794; the Chickamaugas, unable to continue their resistance, soon after rejoined the Cherokee Nation. The site of Running Water Town, the home of the Chickamauga Chief Dragging Canoe, is now under the water of Nickajack Lake, as is probably the burial site of the Chief, who died in 1792.

The cave was mined for saltpeter during the Civil War, and was probably the Confederates' largest saltpeter mining operation in Tennessee. Later the cave was commercialized by Leo Lambert, who promoted several caves in the area, including Lookout Mountain Caverns at Chattanooga.

Today the cave is a wildlife observation area that is part of the Maple View Day Use Area administered by the Tennessee Wildlife Resources Agency and the Tennessee Valley Authority. The cave is a maternity roost for the gray bat and a hibernating site for the Indiana bat, both federally endangered species. To protect the bats, the cave entrance was closed with a fence in 1980.

Russell Cave National Monument

In the early 1950s, members of the Chattanooga Chapter of the Tennessee Archaeological Society began hearing reports of projectile points found in a cave in a part of the Cumberland Plateau in Alabama. The group visited the cave, which is in Doran Cove on the western side of Sequatchie Valley. They found in a drip line at the mouth of the cave flint chips, projectile points, fragments of pottery, animal bones, and shells.

Realizing that the cave may have archaeological significance, four members of the Chattanooga chapter, Paul H. Brown, Charles K. Peacock, LeBaron Pahmeyer, and J. B. Graham, secured a lease from the property owner, Oscar Ridley, and began excavating the cave. Their investigations from 1953 to 1955 convinced them that the site had major significance. They then approached the Smithsonian Institution, which with support from the National Geographic Society, carried out three seasons of excavations. The site was eventually purchased by the National Geographic Society and donated to the country. The cave, known as Russell Cave after Thomas Russell, an early landowner, plus 300 surrounding acres were designated Russell Cave National Monument in 1961. The National Park Service soon after carried out more excavations.

The accumulated evidence, from the tools and weapons found there and the shells and bones of animals, hearth sites, and skeletal remains, showed that this was the site of one of the longest sequences of human habitation in the New World, beginning about 9,000 years ago. The site also provides the earliest evidence of man on the Cumberland Plateau.

Sometime around 7000 B.C., the first inhabitants took shelter in Russell Cave, building a fire on the cave floor to ward off the cold. These were hunters and gathers who lived off the land. For the next 6,500 years, during the time archaeologists call the "Archaic Period," Russell Cave was intermittently inhabited by small bands of extended families, parents with their children and grandchildren. The cave was used especially during the fall and winter, when shelter was necessary for survival. The primary weapon for hunting used by these people was a short spear propelled by an atlatl, a throwing stick. The earliest evidence of these people was found at a depth of 12 feet in the cave floor.

Above the Archaic levels in the cave dirt, the archaeologists found pottery, evidence of the Woodland Indians that existed from about 500 B.C. to 1000 A.D. The smaller projectile points found at this level showed the bow and arrow were used in place of the atlatl. These Indians at times lived in villages, and Russell Cave was probably used only as a hunting campsite.

An even higher level in the cave floor showed evidence of intermittent use as a shelter during the Mississippian Period, after 1000 A.D., a time of the mound builders who had permanent villages and used agriculture to produce their food. In later years the Cherokee Indians who

Upper Piney Falls

inhabited the region made little use of the cave but left a few artifacts found close to the surface of the cave floor on their occasional visits.

Russell Cave National Monument preserves one of the oldest sites of human occupation in the Southeast.

Walden Ridge Natural Areas

Atop Walden Ridge on the east side of Sequatchie Valley lie three natural areas. At Piney Falls State Natural Area near Grandview, the Little Piney Creek drops over Upper Piney Falls about 80 feet into a rock-rimmed pool and then flows on down the creekbed to drop over 40-foot Lower Piney Falls. The natural area encompasses 187 acres.

Just to the west of Piney Falls lies Stinging Fork Pocket Wilderness, owned by the Southern Division of Bowater, Inc., and maintained by the Bowater Southern Division Woodlands. The 104-acre pocket wilderness contains 30-foot-high Stinging Fork Falls on Stinging Fork Creek. As with all the Bowater pocket wilderness areas, Stinging Fork is also a registered state natural area.

A second Bowater pocket wilderness is located on Walden Ridge southwest of Stinging Fork. Laurel-Snow Pocket Wilderness is named for the two waterfalls found there. In the 710-acre registered state natural area, Laurel Creek and Morgan Creek flow into Richland Creek. Laurel Creek drops about 50 feet over Laurel Falls and Morgan Creek, about 30 feet over Snow Falls.

Dayton

The small town of Dayton, Tennessee, in Rhea County is just off the eastern edge of the Cumberland Plateau at the foot of Walden Ridge. The Rhea County Courthouse in Dayton was the site of the Scopes Trial, which brought the theory of evolution to public attention.

In 1925, when Dayton was known as "Monkey Town," John Thomas Scopes stood trial for teaching the theory of evolution, which was a

Laurel Falls

violation of state law. Scopes, a physics and math teacher, had been substituting for the regular biology teacher and purposely taught evolution to challenge the existing law.

The attitude at the time was exemplified by an open letter to teachers published in the *Morgan County Press,* written by A. B. Peters, superintendent of schools and also the publisher of the paper: "We expect you to condemn socialism and bolshevism and evolution as taught by Darwin . . . but do it tactfully."

During the trial, Scopes's attorney, Clarence Darrow, and the prosecution's William Jennings Bryan argued the pros and cons of Scopes's right to teach Charles Darwin's theory in Tennessee public schools. The state won the trial, but Scopes was later released on a technicality. Soon after the trial, while still in Dayton recuperating from the exertion of the court case, Bryan died. *Inherit the Wind,* a play about the trial by Lawrence Jerome and Robert E. Lee, was the basis for several movies of the same title for both theater and television.

The Circuit courtroom that was the scene of the Scopes trial has been restored to its condition in 1925; it is a broad open room of natural wood and large windows—a courtroom typical of the time when court cases were a major entertainment for the town. The room was packed during the famous week, July 11–20.

The basement of the courthouse is now a museum, containing artifacts from the trial, including Darrow's straw hat and Bryan's pith helmet. The courthouse, built in 1891, is a National Historic Landmark.

Directions and Services

You can drive through **Sequatchie Valley** south from Crossville and the Cumberland Homesteads on US127 and then TN28, or north from I-24 and Chattanooga on TN28 and then US127. Approaching the valley south from the Homesteads area, you get the better introduction— arriving at the head of the valley, you have a view of Sequatchie stretching in a straight line southwest.

In **Dunlap** on US127, a sign directs you to turn west on Cherry

Street to get to the Coke Ovens Park; from there, follow the signs. The park has a new two-story museum.

You can rent canoes to float the Sequatchie River at Scott and Ernestine Pilkington's **Canoe the Sequatchie;** stay on US127 south of Dunlap, the highway will bear southeast at the junction with TN28. Just as the road crosses the Sequatchie, you'll see the office located in a houseboat sitting beside the river. The canoeing season lasts from April to October; typically people do a 3- to 9-mile day trip, but there are also longer trips and over-nighters. Maps are available showing river access points for the entire valley.

Victoria lies on TN28 south of Whitwell. Watch for the Bethel United Methodist Church on the west side of the road; the abandoned church stands off the road facing away from the highway. A sign in Victoria directs you to turn east to **Ketners Mill;** just after this side road crosses the Sequatchie River, turn right on a small road that leads to the mill. You can still buy cornmeal, whole wheat flour, and grits ground at the mill.

You can reach **Russell Cave National Monument** on US72 south of I-24. In Bridgeport, Alabama, turn west on county road 91; go straight ahead for 3 miles and turn right on county road 75; you'll reach the monument on the left in another 4 miles. The national monument has a number of exhibits including a display of stratified deposits with artifacts in place in the mouth of the cave. Because the cave is difficult to explore, the inner cave of about 7 miles is closed to the public except by permit. The third Saturday in April, you can attend Indian Day on the grounds of the national monument where you'll see demonstrations of Indian life ways.

Piney Falls State Natural Area is west of TN68 between Grassy Cove and Spring City, which is on US27. At Grandview, turn west on a road beside the school, which becomes gravel; a sign indicates the natural area. In 1.5 miles, you'll see a wooden box sitting on a post beside a jeep road on the right. Park and walk down the jeep road half a mile to enter the natural area. At the end of the gravel road beyond the turnoff to Piney Falls, you'll find a fire tower and a picnic table.

Stinging Fork Pocket Wilderness is on Shut-In Gap Road off

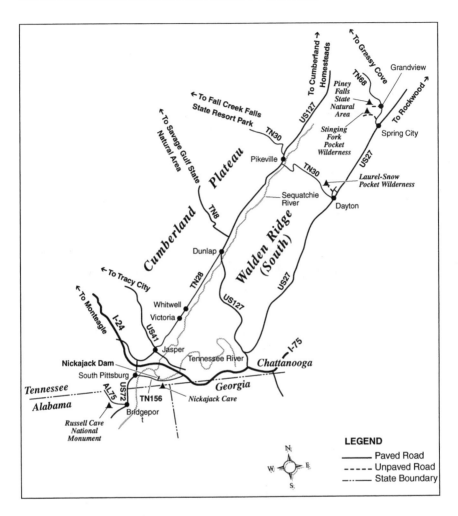

Sequatchie Valley and Walden Ridge South

TN68 just north of Spring City. **Laurel-Snow Pocket Wilderness** can be reached north of Dayton, which is on US27. Turn west on Walnut Grove Road, which is across from the hospital. Along the road a sign directs you left at a Y, and another sign marks the dirt road on the right that leads into the state natural area. At Laurel-Snow, you can find scattered ruins of the coal mining operation once conducted in the region, including rows of overgrown coke ovens south of the parking area.

You can reach **Dayton** south from Spring City or north from Chattanooga on US27. From Pikeville you can travel east to Dayton over Walden Ridge on TN30, part of the state historic route for the Trail of Tears; the actual route was a little to the south of TN30. The route also gives a good view of Sequatchie Valley. Bryan College, established in Dayton in the late 1920s to memorialize William Jennings Bryan, holds a play each July at the Rhea County Courthouse; called "Destiny in Dayton," the play is based on the transcript of the Scopes Trial.

To get to **Nickajack Cave,** take TN156 east from South Pittsburg, which is south of I-24 on US72. You'll pass the access road to Nickajack Dam, and at 5.5 miles from South Pittsburg you'll come to the Maple View Day Use Area. The area is open only during the summer season; there is picnicking and a boat launch but no camping. At the far end of the area, you'll find a gravel path leading to a platform overlook of the cave. At dusk in the summer months, you'll see over 100,000 bats emerge to feed on insects over Nickajack Lake.

Nickajack Dam can be reached also off I-24. On that side of the Tennessee River, you'll find camping available at the **TVA Shellmound Recreation Area.** Camping in the region is also available at the **Marion County Park** 10 miles east of Jasper on US41.

Trails

At Russell Cave National Monument, you'll reach the cave along a short paved trail that branches off a 0.5-mile nature trail. The monument grounds also have a 1.2-mile hiking trail and a 2.5-mile horseback trail leading to the top of Montague Mountain.

At Piney Falls State Natural Area, you'll walk down the jeep road half a mile and then turn right on the 0.7-mile **Upper Piney Falls Trail,** which crosses Little Piney Creek above the waterfall, swings along the edge of the canyon, and then descends to loop behind the waterfall before climbing back out of the canyon and back to your starting point. Just before climbing all the way out of the canyon, you'll see a side trail, at this writing unmaintained, that leads down to Lower Piney Falls. You can also reach the lower falls by following the creek down-

Stinging Fork Falls

stream from the upper falls if the water level is low enough to allow you to rockhop down the creek.

Approaching the Stinging Fork Pocket Wilderness west along Shut-In Gap Road, you'll first pass a picnic area and trailhead for the 10-mile **Piney River Trail,** which crosses Bowater land and ends at the Newby Branch Forest Camp farther up Shut-In Gap Road. From the trailhead you can also walk the 2.5-mile **Twin Rocks Nature Trail.** At the natural area, a 1.5-mile **Stinging Fork Falls Trail** dead-ends at the waterfall.

It has been proposed that the Piney River Trail serve as a section of the **Cumberland Trail** as it makes its way south from Cumberland Gap to the Alabama border; a connecting trail would make Stinging Fork Falls a side excursion. Southwest of Stinging Fork, the Cumberland Trail could also connect with trails in the Laurel-Snow Pocket Wilderness.

The 8-mile **Laurel-Snow Trail** at Laurel-Snow Pocket Wilderness forms a Y. The right branch leads to Laurel Falls and then up on the plateau surface for views at Snake Head Point. The left branch of the trail leads to Snow Falls and Buzzard Point on the plateau. This trail is the first National Recreation Trail in Tennessee and the first in the country on private company land.

References

Bowater, Inc., Southern Division. "Bowater Trails." Brochure. Calhoun, TN, no date.

Camp, Henry R. *Sequatchie County.* Memphis: Memphis State Univ. Press, 1984.

Carter, Reon. "Dayton." *Knoxville News-Sentinel,* Mar. 20, 1988, E1–E2.

Griffin, John W. *Investigations in Russell Cave.* Washington, DC: U.S. Dept. of the Interior, 1974.

Hale, Mrs. Dave, Jr., secretary-treasurer of Bethel United Methodist Church. Conversation with author. Victoria, TN, Sept. 16, 1986.

Ketner, Clyde. Conversation with author. Victoria, TN, Oct. 25, 1991.

Manning, Russ, and Sondra Jamieson. *The South Cumberland and Fall Creek Falls: A* Hiker's Guide to Trails and Attractions. Norris, TN: Laurel Place, 1990.

McDade, Arthur, interpretive park ranger, Russell Cave National Monument. "Beyond the Facts: The Story of Russell Cave NM." *Courier* 35, no. 9 (Sept. 1990): 11 13.

———. Conversation with author. Oct. 30, 1990.

Raulston, J. Leonard, and James W. Livingood. *Sequatchie: A Story of the Southern Cumberlands.* Knoxville: Univ. of Tennessee Press, 1974.

Smith, Marion O. "The C. S. Nitre and Mining Bureau of East Tennessee." *East Tennessee's Historical Society's Publications* 61 (1989): 29–47.

Streetman, Clarence. "Bowater's Pocket Wildernesses." *Tennessee Conservationist,* July–Aug. 1985, 20–21.

Tennessee Valley Authority. "Fact Sheet, Environmental Impact Statement: Chip Mill Terminals on the Tennessee River." Scoping Meeting, South Pittsburg, TN, May 4, 1991. Norris, TN, no date.

U.S. Dept. of the Interior, National Park Service. "8,000 Year Record of Man's Life." Brochure. Bridgeport, AL, no date.

———. "Russell Cave National Monument." Brochure. Washington, DC, 1978.

Chapter 12

Fall Creek Falls

Of all the superlatives that can be used to describe the Cumberland Plateau, one of the most impressive is that it has the tallest waterfall in the eastern United States. Fall Creek wanders among trees and slabs of rock before slipping over a rock ledge and dropping 256 feet, forming Fall Creek Falls.

There are other competitors for the title of tallest waterfall in the East. Buckeye Falls in the Cherokee National Forest north of the Great Smoky Mountains is 500 to 700 feet high, depending on where you decide is the bottom. The problem is, Buckeye Falls is a cascade of water that bounces from rock to rock, freely falling probably no more than a few feet at a time. Also, Amicalola Falls in northern Georgia is several hundred feet of cascade.

In comparison, Fall Creek Falls is a true waterfall, a free-falling column of water for most of its height. So most people are willing to let Fall Creek Falls retain the title of tallest waterfall in the eastern United States. Today, the waterfall is encompassed by a state park.

Fall Creek Falls State Resort Park

In the 1930s, sentiment in the country began to lean toward setting aside special areas to be preserved in their natural state. During this time the federal government acquired 12,000 acres in Tennessee and established the Fall Creek National Recreation Demonstration Area. Much of the acreage had been logged, burned over, and converted to pasture. The plan was to make it into a wildlife sanctuary. Some initial development was done by the Works Progress Administration.

In 1944 the federal government gave the area to the state of Tennessee with the stipulation that the land be preserved; it became Fall Creek Falls State Park and Game Preserve. The state improved roads and visitor facilities. And then from 1969 to 1972 extensive construction took place to make it into a resort park with lodging and recreational facilities, including a golf course, tennis courts, and ball fields. The construction cost $8.5 million, shared equally by the state and the Economic Development Administration.

While the development at Fall Creek Falls State Resort Park might be termed excessive by some, at least, to the credit of park planners, the development is confined to the top of the plateau while the river canyons remain truly wild; some of the coves have been visited seldom, if at all. These wild areas have been given state natural area designation.

Waterfalls

The special attraction of Fall Creek Falls State Park and Natural Area is not only that it contains the highest waterfall in the eastern United States, but that its several waterfalls depict various types of waterfalls on the Cumberland Plateau.

Cane Creek Cascades behind the park nature center took shape in Cane Creek because of the equal hardness of the exposed sandstone. In such places where a creek has not yet eroded to where there is an abrupt interface between hard rock layers above and softer layers below, a cascade forms. In the process, the pour-off ledge erodes upstream so that the lower rocks project out farther than the top and the water bounces down the rock wall in short steps. As long as Cane Creek does not penetrate to softer layers below the sandstone, 45-foot-high Cane Creek Cascades will likely keep slowly wearing away to eventually become simply a steep gradient in the streambed, rather than a true waterfall.

Just downstream from Cane Creek Cascades, Cane Creek drops over Cane Creek Falls, a true waterfall where the water sails off a lip of rock

Cane Creek Cascades

and plunges 85 feet to the pool below. Erosion has proceeded downward into softer layers to create the waterfall. An overlook to the right of the nature center presents an expansive view. Except in dry weather, it is a massive fall of water. Although the softer underlying rock erodes quickly, the high volume of water sweeping down Cane Creek and over the falls has caused the lip of the waterfall to migrate upstream about as fast as the softer layers beneath erode, so there is a straight wall of rock behind the waterfall.

Rockhouse Falls spills into the same massive rock-walled plunge basin as Cane Creek Falls. This slender 110-foot stream of water, practically nonexistent during dry weather, is just to the right of the Cane Creek Falls Overlook.

The plunge basin for Cane Creek Falls and Rockhouse Falls is the beginning of Cane Creek Gorge, the main drainage in the park. All streams flow into Cane Creek, which then passes into the Caney Fork River to the north.

The other waterfalls in the park can be found along a scenic drive that parallels Cane Creek Gorge. The first stop is an overlook for Fall Creek Falls. Depending on whether it has rained much recently, the waterfall can be a graceful trickle or a roaring fall of water that kicks up mist to drench the surrounding rocks and anyone standing at the bottom.

The great height of Fall Creek Falls is due to the lower soft layers eroding away more quickly than the hard sandstone at the top of the falls, and so erosion proceeds downward. Once softer layers are exposed below the pour-off in such places, and where the waterfall is not a high-volume falls such as Cane Creek Falls, the swirling water and mist, with accompanying freezing and thawing, also erode behind and under the ledge. In this way, a space similar in shape to an amphitheater is hollowed out behind the waterfall. Only at certain times of the year, especially spring, does Fall Creek Falls have a high water volume, so erosion has had time to sweep out a large amphitheater behind the falls.

Coon Creek Falls, just to the right of Fall Creek Falls, drops into the same plunge basin. In dry weather, the small waterfall is hardly more than a whisper.

The splashes of orange that tint the rock walls of the Fall Creek Falls plunge basin are accumulations of sulphur and iron oxides. These oxides are being released from rock strata exposed during excavation for the Fall Creek Lake Dam upstream from the waterfall.

Last on the scenic drive is the overlook for Piney Creek Falls. This 85-foot waterfall fits somewhere between Fall Creek Falls and Cane Creek Cascades in its development. The water in Piney Creek drops from a rock shelf for about half the height of the falls and then collides into a rock ledge and splashes down a cascade the remaining distance to the plunge pool below. Half waterfall and half cascade, Piney Creek Falls is in transition and may eventually become a full cascade. This waterfall is eroding faster than other waterfalls in the park because a vertical crack, or joint, occurs in the rock directly in the waterfall.

Fall Creek Falls

Piney

Piney Creek flows through the small community of Piney to the south before entering Fall Creek Falls State Resort Park. Around 1976, the AMAX Coal Company proposed strip mining about 10,000 acres surrounding Piney and adjacent to the state park.

Worried about the effects of this proposed strip mining operation—mostly pollution of the streams that flow through the area and blasting damage to houses and wells—the people of Piney banded together to form Concerned Citizens of Piney. Aided by Save Our Cumberland Mountains, a citizens' group headquartered in Lake City that works to improve the quality of life in the coal-producing lands in East Tennessee, the community waged an information campaign to ensure protection of their community.

After some study of the proposed project, the Division of Water Quality Control of the state government denied AMAX's request for a water discharge permit, which was needed before AMAX could apply for a mining permit. The water discharge permit was withheld on the grounds that the AMAX operation would have been so large it would have been necessary to mine through three streams in the area, including Piney Creek. AMAX appealed the decision to the Water Quality Control Board, which in 1977 upheld the denial of a water discharge permit.

Although AMAX was allowed other appeals, the company decided not to pursue the project. A company spokesman was reported in the Knoxville *News-Sentinel* to have said, "It is apparent the state of Tennessee right now doesn't want our kind of business."

Although the Piney Community had been spared a huge strip mining operation, the people could only take a short rest in their fight to preserve their homes and environment. In 1985 the Tennessee National Guard proposed acquiring 114,000 acres in five counties on the Plateau for a national guard training base, with control of the air space over an additional 60,000 acres where helicopter pilots could fly training missions. The proposed base would have completely encircled the Piney Community, making it an enclave in the midst of military maneuvers. The base would also border Fall Creek Falls State Resort Park on the northeast and Savage Gulf State Natural Area to the southwest.

A new training base on the Plateau was opposed by the people of Piney plus other communities involved, along with conservationists across the state and local legislators. In addition to disturbing the people who lived in and near the area, they argued, the drone of planes and helicopters, the rumble of tanks, and the blasting of artillery would have greatly reduced the wilderness experience for visitors in Fall Creek Falls and Savage Gulf. The training activity would probably also have disturbed the endangered gray and Indiana bats that winter in Hubbard Cave, which underlies the area of the proposed base. Newly discovered Paradox Cave, which borders the proposed training area, might possibly have been damaged by shock waves from the impact of shells and bombs during training. The cave, whose location is not generally revealed in order to protect it, is reported to have a large room with five waterfalls, the largest at 175 feet high.

The headquarters of the National Guard eventually rejected the proposed base, saying another training base was not needed. But a constant vigil seems necessary. Skyline Coal Company, a subsidiary of AMAX, has been strip mining within the 10,000-acre tract proposed for mining by AMAX in the 1970s. At first the smaller operation did not receive the opposition the larger project did; that is, until the mining approached within 100 feet of Fall Creek Falls State Park. In the years since the AMAX fight, concerned people of the region have established a South Cumberland Chapter of Save Our Cumberland Mountains to continue the effort begun by the Concerned Citizens of Piney. The group, along with Tennessee Citizens for Wilderness Planning and several individuals, filed a petition for a lands-unsuitable-for-mining designation of the entire Fall Creek Falls watershed. In its Environmental Impact Statement, the federal Office of Surface Mining selected a preferred alternative of allowing stripmining in the Fall Creek Falls watershed on a case-by-case basis, but that position ignored the cumulative impact of numerous individually permitted strip mines. Conservation groups continue to push for the lands-unsuitable designation.

Big Bone Cave State Natural Area

Big Bone Cave is a snarling labyrinth beneath an outlier off the Cumberland Plateau to the west of Fall Creek Falls State Resort Park. Workmen mining the cave for saltpeter in 1811 discovered the bones of a giant Pleistocene ground sloth, which is how the cave got its name. The bones of *Megalonyx jeffersoni* now reside at the Academy of Natural Sciences in Philadelphia.

Big Bone Cave owes its historical significance not so much to the bones of the giant ground sloth, which were remarkably well-preserved and included the only complete pelvic girdle of this sloth species known to exist, but because the cave was a source of saltpeter during the War of 1812 and the Civil War. Gunpowder is made from a mixture of charcoal, sulfur, and potassium nitrate, the chemical name of saltpeter.

The calcium nitrate found in cave dirt originates in the oxidation of decaying plant and animal matter. The miners would fill a large vat with dirt and pour water through it to dissolve the nitrate; the solution drained out the bottom and was collected. They also poured water over wood ashes and then combined the two solutions to produce a chemical reaction in which potassium was substituted for the calcium to form potassium nitrate; the calcium would precipitate out. Filtering the solution and then boiling it dry, they had saltpeter crystals.

When the bones of the ground sloth were discovered in 1811, in the midst of digging up cave dirt for this process, they were sent to a man named Clifford in Lexington, Kentucky, who at the time was buying the minerals mined in the cave. The sloth bones were traded a number of times before ending up in the Academy of Natural Sciences in Philadelphia. More pieces of the skeleton were discovered in 1884 and 1896 and were added to the collection.

During the Civil War, Ben Randall, a Confederate army captain, was in charge of the mining operations in Big Bone Cave. Various reports claim Big Bone Cave at one time produced saltpeter for one-quarter to two-thirds of the gunpowder used by the Confederacy, but that seems much exaggerated. Whatever percentage came from the cave, the operation was important for the Confederate side.

The Confederates were successful in keeping the location of Big Bone Cave a secret during the war, at least until Union forces occupied Tennessee in 1863. The cave could be kept secret mainly because the area had little strategic importance and as a result few Union soldiers passed through. But at least once, a Union patrol stumbled on the mine while scouting the area. The Confederates ambushed the men and later dynamited the entrance, leaving a single, less-accessible entrance which is the one used today. A cemetery containing the Union soldiers and those who died working the cave rests on a hill overlooking the collapsed entrance.

The historical significance of the cave induced the state of Tennessee in 1976 to designate the cave and the surrounding area the Big Bone Cave State Natural Area. The cave has two main branches: Arch Cave Branch and Bone Cave Branch. About 10 miles of the cave system have been explored.

Several tiers of rock lay over the cave; some of these are layers of sandstone that are practically impermeable to water. The dryness of the cave explains why the skeletons of the giant sloth and other prehistoric creatures found there were so well preserved. The dry environment also preserved the makeshift ladders and the vats used to extract the nitrate; these can still be found in the cave. The vats were made of hand-cut chestnut, held together with pegs and vines. Most of the vats are in the "muster" room in the Arch Cave Branch, a 1,275-foot-long gallery, 30 to 50 feet wide and 12 feet high, where Uriah York once drilled Confederate troops.

Cumberland Caverns

A commercial cave southwest of Big Bone Cave and Fall Creek Falls is one of the largest caves in the United States, with 32 miles of passageways. Cumberland Caverns lie in the southwest side of Cardwell Mountain, an outlier of the Cumberland Plateau.

The caverns contain stalactites, stalagmites, complete columns, and large rooms and galleries. The Hall of the Mountain King (600 feet by 150 feet by 140 feet) is one of the largest cave rooms in the eastern United States. The Waterfall Room contains a 60-foot waterfall, and the Crystal Palace has the best display of selenite crystals of any Tennessee cave. One of the most interesting features of the cave is not on the commercial tour, a 15-foot-high white stalagmite called "Monument Pillar," embedded with calcite crystals, in an eastern stem of the cave system.

The cave was discovered by Aaron Higgenbotham, a surveyor, in 1810, and for a time the cave was called "Higgenbotham Cave." Another part of the cave, called "Henshaw Cave," was the site of saltpeter mining during the War of 1812 and the Civil War. Later exploration in 1953 showed that the two caves were part of the same cave system. The cave was renamed "Cumberland Caverns" in 1955 and is now a National Natural Landmark.

Directions and Services

You can reach the north entrance of **Fall Creek Falls State Resort Park** on TN30 east of Spencer or west from Pikeville, which is on US127. The road from Pikeville takes you up the western wall of Sequatchie Valley, affording views across to Walden Ridge; once on top of the plateau, you'll continue on TN30 into Bledsoe State Forest, where a sign directs you to turn south to get to the north entrance of Fall Creek Falls State Resort Park. The south entrance to

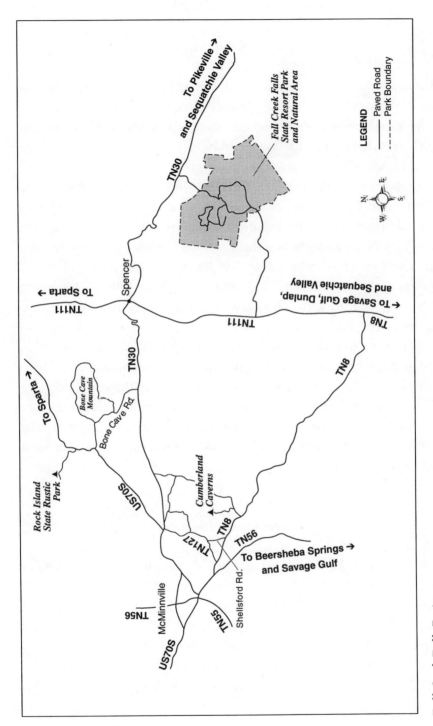

Fall Creek Falls Region

the park lies along TN111 between Spencer and Dunlap. Dunlap also lies in Sequatchie Valley.

The development in Fall Creek Falls State Resort Park surrounds Fall Creek Lake, an artificial lake created by an earthen dam on Fall Creek. You'll find a modern inn, cabins, a boat launch, a cluster of buildings that constitutes a village area with shops and a grocery, and various recreational facilities, including a campground, swimming pool, tennis courts, ball fields, picnic areas, and an 18-hole golf course. On the east side of the park, you can rent horses at a stable. Near the north entrance, you'll find the Betty Dunn Nature Center, with exhibits of the natural and cultural history of the park; the nature center was named for the wife of former Gov. Winfield Dunn, who, like her husband, took an interest in the park and encouraged development of visitor facilities.

Behind the nature center, along Cane Creek, you'll find large symmetrical holes bored into the rock. Wooden piles once stood in these holes, anchored in place by iron spikes, to support mills along the waterway. One of these, the Bickford Mill, stood above Cane Creek Cascades. A log dam diverted water through the mill's high-speed turbine to grind corn. A flood in 1929 washed the mill off its foundation and over the cascade.

In the village you'll find an exhibition room with the paintings of Gilbert Gaul, who at one time owned land that is now included in the state park. He came to the Fall Creek Falls area when he was about 26 years old, inheriting the land from an uncle. He built a studio and during his stay in Tennessee did many of his paintings, including the familiar "The Picket." Gaul used a local bootlegger as the model for the old man standing watch with his gun.

The park inn has 72 rooms along with a restaurant and meeting and banquet rooms for conferences and group gatherings. The 20 two-bedroom cabins are completely furnished, each with a fireplace. Fisherman cabins are located right on the lake so you can throw in your line from your back porch. Reservations should be made well in advance. There are also two group lodges that can handle 104 and 40 people.

The park has 227 campsites in its three campgrounds. All sites have water and electric hookups. There are central bathhouses with hot water and showers. Campsites cannot be reserved.

Between the village and the inn, you'll cross the Fall Creek Lake Dam and then reach the entrance for the scenic drive, which for most of its distance is a one-way loop. In addition to Fall Creek and Piney Falls, the scenic drive takes you by several overlooks of Cane Creek Gorge that afford views into a canyon 800 feet deep. The bottom of the gorge occupies approximately 2,000 acres and contains some old-growth stands of poplar and hemlock.

Millikan's Overlook on the scenic drive offers a panoramic view of Cane Creek Gorge as Cane Creek passes out of the park. The overlook was named for Dr. Glenn A. Millikan, a scientist who often visited the park before falling to his death while on a climbing trip in the park in 1947.

A well-designed bicycle path leads from the inn along the lake and around the scenic drive. Although some of the way is actually on the scenic drive, much of the bicycle trail is separate from the roads, which makes for carefree bicycling through the surrounding woods.

Big Bone Cave State Natural Area is open only on a limited basis because of the accumulation of radon gas in the cave. The radon results from the natural radioactive decay of uranium in the earth and is itself radioactive. The low levels of radon in the cave would have virtually no effect on a visitor; but guides would receive repeated exposure if they conducted tours on a regular basis. The cave could be vented to prevent the accumulation of the gas, but that would also affect the air temperature, pressure, and moisture level in the cave. At present, the state's position is that the geological and archaeological significance of the cave is too important to change the environment in which it has been preserved.

You can only enter the cave by appointment with a guide, preferably with a group. Call ahead to nearby **Rock Island State Rustic Park** to make arrangements. You can reach the park west from Fall Creek Falls State Resort Park along TN30 to near McMinnville and then northeast on US70S. You can also approach the area from Crossville along US70 and then US70S through Sparta. The park is located on US70S at the community of Rock Island, founded in the 1790s, where you'll turn west to get to the state park in about a mile. The Rock Island community and state park are named for a rock island in the midst of the Caney Fork River at the point where the Rocky River flows into the Caney Fork.

Rock Island is not on the Plateau but on the Highland Rim, about 1,000 feet lower than the Cumberland Plateau, and so either along TN30 or US70, you'll descend from the Plateau as you head toward the park. If you approach the park along US70 west from Crossville past the Virgin Falls Pocket Wilderness turnoff in DeRossett, you'll soon drop off the Plateau in an obvious descent. Just at the base of the Plateau, watch for the **Rock House State Shrine** on the left; it's a stone house built about 1840 on the Old Stage Road from Nashville to Knoxville and is now on the National Register of Historic Places.

Entering Rock Island State Park west off US70S, you'll cross the Collins River on a new bridge and pass the abandoned Falls City Cotton Mill, which was built in 1889 beside the Great Falls just below the confluence of the Caney Fork and the Collins Rivers. When the flood of 1902 washed away the mill's waterwheel, which supplied the power, the mill was closed. The building is now on the National Register of Historic Places. Next to the mill is a turnout on the right that leads to an overlook of the Great Falls and the Caney Fork riverbed.

The Tennessee Electric Power Company built the Great Falls Dam near the mill site in 1916, creating the Great Falls Reservoir, with water backed up on both the Collins and the Caney Fork Rivers. With the raising of the water level, the Collins River to the west unexpectedly made its way through subterranean tunnels and now streams down the rock walls as "Twin Falls" to join the Caney Fork below the dam. The power plant in the state park, also built by the Tennessee Electric Power Company, is now operated by the Tennessee Valley Authority.

Camping at the park is available on 50 campsites with electric and

Buzzards Roost on the Scenic Drive

water hookups on a first-come, first-served basis, plus ten campsites for tents. The park also has ten cabins that sleep ten persons each.

Cumberland Caverns lie between TN30 and TN8 south of Rock Island; watch for signs that direct you to the cave. The caverns are open every day from 9 to 5 from June through August, weekends only in May, September, and October, and by appointment November through April. The cave tour takes about 90 minutes. There is a fee. Groups can arrange to camp overnight in the half-mile-long Big Room and have breakfast the next morning in the Volcano Room beneath a crystal chandelier.

Trails

The 0.8-mile **Woodland Trail** at Fall Creek Falls State Resort Park begins at the swinging bridge above Cane Creek Cascades behind the nature center and ends at the overlook for Fall Creek Falls. The 0.7-mile **Cane Creek Gorge Trail** forms a loop with the Woodland Trail and gives you several views of Cane Creek Gorge, including a good view of Rockhouse Falls and Cane Creek Falls. At the Fall Creek Falls overlook, the 0.5-mile **Fall Creek Falls Trail** descends to the foot of the waterfall over a rocky path.

The 4.6-mile **Paw Paw Trail** starts at the nature center and parallels the north entrance road before looping west to overlooks of Fall Creek Falls, Cane Creek Gorge, and Cane Creek Falls and finally returning to the nature center. Near the nature center along this trail, you'll find the junction with the 0.2-mile **Cable Trail,** a difficult descent using a cable that takes you into Cane Creek Gorge to the plunge pool for Cane Creek and Rockhouse Falls.

The 25-mile **Cane Creek Overnight Loops** consist of a 12-mile Lower Loop that descends into Cane Creek Gorge and a 13-mile Upper Loop that stays on the plateau surface. You can pick up both loops at a parking area within a maintenance complex just inside the north entrance to the park. A permit is required for an overnight trip.

Cumberland Caverns is the trailhead for two Tennessee State Trails. The 5-mile **Cardwell Mountain Trail** passes by Balance Rock and Buzzard Bluff, a collection of huge sandstone blocks at the top of Cardwell Mountain, before returning to the starting point. Cardwell Mountain is named for Francis Cardwell, who settled in the area in 1806.

The 2-mile **Collins River Trail** follows a portion of the Trail of Tears, the route taken by the Cherokees under guard of U.S. troops on their forced relocation to Oklahoma in 1838. The Cherokees were moved from the fall of 1838 through 1839. Several detachments stopped at Shellsford on the Collins River for several days to rest, grind corn at a mill there, and care for the sick. The Collins River Trail ends at Shellsford, which was named for James Shell, who operated the gristmill at the river ford. The stone ruins of the mill can still be seen just upstream from the Shellsford Bridge on TN127.

Several graves of Cherokees who died during the overlays at Shellsford are in the cemetery of the Shellsford Baptist Church, which stands just off Shellsford Road that runs between TN8 and 127. The graves are marked with crude unmarked stones, except for the few where family members have returned over the years to re-place the stones with larger gravestones. The church was established in 1810; a modern brick building stands where the original split-log structure once stood. Among the ancient cedars and oaks in the cemetery, you'll also find graves of men killed in the Civil War and World War I.

References

"AMAX Quits Efforts to Strip Coal in Southeast Tennessee." *Knoxville News-Sentinel,* May 25, 1977.

Bayless, Tony. "Bone Cave." In *Van Buren County Historical Record* 2. Van Buren County Library, Sparta, TN, no date.

Brown, Fred. "People of Plateau Ready for Scrap with Guard" and "Plateau Irked by Military Invasion." *Knoxville News-Sentinel,* Sept. 15, 1985, A1 and A6.

Carroll, Stuart, interpretive specialist, Fall Creek Falls State Resort Park. Interview with author. Jan. 26, 1991.

Coggins, Allen R. "The Early History of Tennessee's State Parks, 1919-1956." *Tennessee Historical Quarterly* 43, no. 3 (Fall 1984): 295–315.

Concerned Citizens of Piney and Save Our Cumberland Mountains. "Fact Sheet: AMAX in Tennessee." Brochure. Jacksboro, TN, 1976.

Cumberland Caverns. "Cumberland Caverns." Flier. McMinnville, TN, no date.

———. "Geology, Biology, and Technical Aspects of Cumberland Caverns." Flier. McMinnville, TN, no date.

———. "Trail of Tears, Cardwell Mountain-Shellsford." Flier. McMinnville, TN, no date.

Manning, Russ. "Buckeye Falls vs. Fall Creek Falls." *Tennessee Conservationist,* July–Aug. 1987, 22–23.

———. "A Land of Falling Water." *Tennessee Conservationist,* May–June 1991, 15–18.

———, and Sondra Jamieson. *The South Cumberland and Fall Creek Falls: A Hiker's Guide to Trails and Attractions.* Norris, TN: Laurel Place, 1990.

Raulston, J. Leonard, and James W. Livingood. *Sequatchie: A Story of the Southern Cumberlands.* Knoxville: Univ. of Tennessee Press, 1974.

Smith, Gill, manager of human resources and public information, Skyline Coal Co. Conversation with author. Oct. 29, 1991.

Smith, Marion O. "The C. S. Nitre and Mining Bureau of East Tennessee." *East Tennessee's Historical Society's Publications* 61 (1989): 29–47.

Tennessee Dept. of Conservation. "Day Use Trail Guide, Fall Creek Falls State Park." Nashville, no date.

————. "Fall Creek Falls Self-Guiding Scenic Drive." Pamphlet. Nashville, no date.

————. "Fall Creek Falls State Resort Park." Brochure. Nashville, 1989.

————. "Fall Creek Falls Trails Map." Nashville, 1986.

————. "Rock Island State Park." Brochure. Nashville, no date.

Tretter, Evelyn Kerr. "Rock Island State Park." *Tennessee Conservationist,* Mar. 1987, 9–11.

Chapter 13

Savage Gulf

Most of the southeastern United States was logged in the late 1800s and early 1900s, and so virgin forests are rare these days. But one of the last large stands of virgin mixed-mesophytic forest in the southeastern United States is on the Cumberland Plateau in the depths of a canyon called "Savage Gulf." That the forest remains is due in large part to the Samuel Werner family.

In 1868, Samuel Werner came from Switzerland to the United States and about two years later arrived in Tennessee. In 1885 he established a saw and planing mill in Tracy City on the southern part of the Cumberland Plateau. One of his sons, Sam Werner, took over operation of the business in 1902 after the death of the senior Werner.

With the years and the efforts of the younger Werner, the business expanded into a large enterprise. The Werner lands eventually included 15,000 acres of timberland and several mills. But with the impact of the Great Depression of the 1930s and New Deal reforms, workers leaving to take higher paying jobs, and finally, the additional drain on manpower due to the start of World War II, Werner Lumber was forced to close by 1942. Soon after, with the death of Sam Werner, the family's holdings were left to the grandchildren, Carl E. Werner, Rosalie Werner Boyd, and Samuel Werner. The great-grandson, Samuel Werner, has managed the holdings since the early 1980s.

During all the years in which the Werner business was operating in the region, a strip of land along Savage Creek was never logged. In 1922–26, Sam Werner and his wife, Ellen Young Werner, purchased the 3,400 acres in Savage Gulf that included this

500 acres of virgin forest. The Werners were inclined to leave the gulf forest untouched, although the narrow-gauge railroad the Werner company operated for hauling out timber reached into the area. Eventually the company was not able to renew a lease of land crossed by their railroad, and the tracks had to be taken up, ensuring that the Savage Gulf forest would be left undisturbed. In later years, the Werners' son, Samuel Werner (the grandson of the original Werner), carried on the effort to preserve the old-growth forest by resisting land speculators who tried to encroach on the land and forest by questioning the Werner title.

Through the efforts of the Werner family, the virgin forest of Savage Gulf remains today, now in a state-designated natural area.

Savage Gulf State Natural Area

Because of its size and its ecological importance, the Savage Gulf area became the object of preservation efforts in the 1960s and 1970s. Herman Baggenstoss, chairman of the Grundy County Conservation Board, was instrumental in drawing attention to several areas worthy of preservation in the region. He enlisted the help of planners at the Tennessee Valley Authority to draw up a proposal for the establishment of a South Cumberland Recreation Area that would include Savage Gulf in a state natural area. Local citizens joined to support the proposal by forming the Savage Gulf Preservation League, under the direction of its president, Dr. Wallace Bigbee of McMinnville.

The effort to establish a natural area was mounted to protect the scenic beauty of the Savage Gulf area and to preserve the unlogged stretch along Savage Creek. During the acquisition stage, while the Werners maintained Savage Gulf, the Nature Conservancy stepped in to acquire some of the lands in adjacent canyons, Big Creek and Collins Gulfs. These were purchased from the Huber Lumber Company, which made a significant partial donation by selling at less than appraised value.

Stone Door Overlook

In 1973, with a matching federal grant, the state of Tennessee purchased the two tracts of land from the Nature Conservancy. The state subsequently acquired other areas, including the Savage Gulf tract in 1974 from the Werner family—Carl, Rosalie, and Samuel, the grandchildren of the original Samuel Werner. These areas were combined to create the Savage Gulf State Natural Area, the premier wilderness area on the Cumberland Plateau in Tennessee. The name "Savage" was taken from the gulf that contained the stand of virgin timber; the names "Savage Creek" and "Savage Gulf" had come from an early settler, Samuel Savage. The total acreage in the natural area eventually reached 11,500 acres.

Savage Gulf State Natural Area thus consists of three converging canyons, called "gulfs" by Tennesseans. Savage Creek and Big Creek flow down two side canyons to merge with the Collins River, which has carved the middle canyon. The three 5-mile canyons reach depths of 800 feet.

The 500 acres of virgin forest along Savage Creek includes hemlock, yellow poplar, oak, ash, basewood, beech, maple, and hickory. The trees are not as old or as large as, for example, timber found in the virgin forests of the Great Smoky Mountains National Park to the northeast. The Savage Gulf forest is kept relatively young by the unstable walls of the canyon which periodically send an avalanche of boulders tumbling into the gorge, cutting down the trees as efficiently as a giant scythe. Even so, the forest is impressive. When nominated for the National Natural Landmark status it now holds, the woodland was described as "the best and largest virgin forest left in a mixed mesophytic region of the Eastern deciduous forest."

Beersheba Springs

In 1833 Beersheba Porter Cain was traveling by horseback in the company of her husband, John Cain, southeast from her home in McMinnville toward Chattanooga. Such a journey required crossing the Cumberland Plateau. At the foot of the western escarpment, the Cains stopped to rest at the home of William Dugan. Strolling in the woods surrounding the Dugan house, Beersheba Cain discovered a path that led up the sloping shoulder of the plateau.

Following the path, Cain stumbled upon a spring of iron water and supposedly became the first white person to stoop and take a drink from the chalybeate spring that became known as "Beersheba's Spring." Actually it would have been quite extraordinary if Dugan and his family had not already discovered and used the spring. But because Beersheba Cain was the instigation for the community that grew up around the spring, the story of her discovery is still told today.

Impressed with the high rock bluffs and panoramic views from the top of the plateau, and convinced, as his wife was, that the spring with its iron salts had medicinal value, John Cain purchased land on the plateau and built several log cabins along the edge of the bluff. By 1836 Alfred Paine and George R. Smartt had purchased 1,500 acres and were busy erecting a house to serve as a tavern. In 1839 the Tennessee General Assembly incorporated Beersheba Springs (pronounced "Burr-shah-bah," with accent on the first syllable), and it opened as a summer

The Old Beersheba Springs Hotel

resort under the management of Smartt. By then there was a stagecoach road between McMinnville and Beersheba Springs. In later years, it became a tradition for stagecoach drivers, when at the foot of the mountain, to blow a horn the appropriate number of times to indicate the number of guests they were bringing and for whom the hotel should prepare.

In the 1850s, John Armfield, a former slave trader, with his wife Martha purchased the Smartt tavern, 1,000 acres of land, and a row of guest houses from R. H. Robards, who had purchased the property from Smartt. For his own home, Armfield purchased the William White house which had been built in the early 1840s. Armfield set about immediately to expand the resort and eventually built an additional 20 houses. In 1855 he added a second story and a columned portico to the tavern, which along with the rows of guest cabins, was now being called the "Beersheba Springs Hotel." In 1860 Armfield sold the hotel to the Beersheba Springs Company, set up to operate the resort.

During the summers of 1859 and 1860, the resort reached its height, having on some days as many as 400 guests. Many families came from their southern plantations in horse-drawn carriages followed by retinues of servants. French cooks at the hotel prepared the food, and a French band from New Orleans played dance music. When the hotel overflowed, tents were set up along the bowling alleys to house latecomers.

This idyll was soon interrupted by the Civil War. During the years of fighting, only a handful of people came to Beersheba Springs. Those who lived there year-round were in constant danger from Union soldiers traveling through and bands of thieves that roamed the land. Despite the pillaging of all the cottages and several attempts to burn the hotel, none of the buildings in the community were lost during this period.

Even so, the Beersheba Springs Company was bankrupt after the war, and Armfield repossessed much of the property and sold it at auction from the steps of the county courthouse in Altamont. The hotel changed hands many times in the following years, but no one was able to restore the fame and elegance the resort had known before the Civil War. In 1941 the hotel and guest cottages were purchased by the Tennessee Conference of the United Methodist Church to serve as a retreat.

Today the old hotel, now the Beersheba Springs United Methodist Church Assembly, remains the center of the community. Across the road from the colonnaded hotel entrance, an overlook provides views of the Collins River valley and to the right the Savage Gulf State Natural Area.

About 15 of John Armfield's 20 cottages remain along with some new structures; most are summer homes in the tradition of the old resort. Armfield's house, now the Glasgow Cottage, is west of the hotel along with two of the larger old houses, the Mitchell Cottage and the Turner Cottage.

The Beersheba Springs Historic District, which was placed on the National Register of Historic Places in 1980, contains 220 acres and 55 structures, including the hotel and homes ranging from cottages to multistoried houses.

A drive through the community gives an idea of the refuge the place has afforded over the years—in grandeur before the Civil War, more muted afterward. The enveloping solitude is to be treasured.

Gruetli

Beginning in 1844, Switzerland experienced a major depression, and many people left the country in search of a better life. From 1850 to 1860, about 40,000 Swiss entered the United States; during the next decade, another 22,000 arrived. The feeling in America at the time was that there was yet room in this country for settlement in the sparsely populated regions, and so the Europeans were welcomed with their special skills and industriousness.

In 1867, the Swiss Emigration Society sent E. H. Plumacher to the United States to find a suitable location for a Swiss settlement. Accompanied by John Hitz, consul general for the Swiss Republic, Plumacher came to Tennessee on the recommendation of President Andrew Johnson, who was from Tennessee. While in Nashville, Plumacher and Hitz were enticed by John Armfield to visit the Beersheba Springs resort on the edge of what is now Savage Gulf

State Natural Area. Impressed with this land of deep river canyons and rich forests, and with the plateau's rolling surface that reminded them of Switzerland, Plumacher and Hitz decided this was the location for the Swiss settlement. They chose as the site for their colony the point of land between the Big Creek and Collins Gulfs across the canyon from Beersheba Springs.

They managed to interest a Swiss businessman, Peter Staub, in the proposed settlement. Plumacher built a home in Beersheba Springs, and Staub set about buying land for the colony. Staub, who at the time was living in Knoxville, Tennessee, was later mayor of Knoxville in 1874–75 and 1881–82. Plumacher later was U.S. consul to Venezuela from 1877 until his death in 1910.

The men printed fliers that were circulated over the northern United States and Europe telling of the wonders of the hills of Tennessee. When the first Swiss families arrived in 1869, they expected land ready for farming; instead they encountered a wilderness. But they set to the task of clearing the land and building a community they called "Gruetli," the name of the mountain meadow where the Swiss had declared their independence from Austria in 1291. The name has come to mean "a place of beginning."

The original settlers numbered about 100 families, mostly from the German-speaking cantons of Switzerland. They were joined later by other Swiss families, some of whom settled in the surrounding region; these included the Werners and the Greeters, who entered the lumber business, and John Baggenstoss, who established a bakery in Tracy City. A small community next to Gruetli, called "Laager" after an early Swiss settler, was established in 1920; the two merged in 1980 to become Gruetli-Laager, as it is known today.

In spite of new arrivals, the population of Gruetli gradually declined. Many moved away seeking better opportunity in Nashville, Chattanooga, South Pittsburg, Winchester, and Belvidere; the colony eventually dissolved. Even so, the community today probably still contains as many people of Swiss ancestry as during the colonization. A local Swiss Historical Society currently works to preserve the memory and heritage of the Swiss colony that was once a new beginning.

Hubbard Cave

To the northwest of Savage Gulf and Beersheba Springs, Hubbard Cave opens in a cove on the western wall of the Cumberland Plateau. Owned by the Nature Conservancy, the cave is a registered Tennessee state natural area.

In 1984, the Nature Conservancy purchased the 55 acres that includes Hubbard Cave to protect the 100,000 to 250,000 gray and Indiana bats that hibernate in the cave during the winter; both bats are endangered species.

The cave is named for its discoverer—sort of. Joseph Heberlein found the cave in 1810; his name through the years was corrupted to "Hubbard." The cave is also known as "Bat Cave" for obvious reasons.

The cave has two branches which open in a sinkhole. The entrance to the branch of the cave the bats inhabit during the winter months is blocked by a gate to prevent people from disturbing the bats' hibernation. The other entrance is the one most often used by people exploring the cave; this part of the cave contains a few old wooden troughs, ladders, steps, and bridges, evidence of saltpeter mining during the Civil War.

Directions and Services

Several natural areas on the southern part of the Cumberland Plateau, including **Savage Gulf State Natural Area,** have been combined to form the South Cumberland Recreation Area. The visitor center for the combined natural areas is located east of Monteagle; maps and information are available there as well as at the natural area itself.

Apart from camping, accommodations around Savage Gulf are scarce. You can stay at Fall Creek Falls State Resort Park to the northeast, or there are a few motels in Tracy City and Monteagle to the southwest. There are also a few bed and breakfasts in the area, such as **The Manor** in Altamont on TN56, a historic Federal style home built in

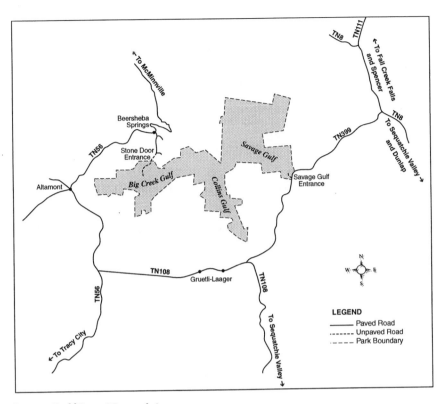

Savage Gulf State Natural Area

1885 that's listed on the National Register of Historic Places; you'll enjoy some time in the 5,000-volume Civil War reading room. Behind the house stands a log home dating from around 1840. On the Manor grounds, there is also a three-bedroom cottage available for overnight stays. Also in Altamont, you'll find the **Woodlee House**, a bed and breakfast on Cumberland Street. Listed on the National Register, the house started as a log cabin built prior to the Civil War; Levi Woodlee came to Altamont in 1890 and bought the cabin, to which he attached a two-story addition in 1895; a kitchen and dining room were added sometime during 1910 to 1920.

Savage Gulf State Natural Area has two entrances—the **Savage Gulf Entrance** and the **Stone Door Entrance**. Each has rangers on site who can give backpacking permits and answer questions. Camping is available at both entrances.

You can reach the Savage Gulf Entrance south from Spencer on TN111 or north from Dunlap on TN8. Turn southwest on TN399 and at 5.5 miles turn right into the natural area. The trails from this end of the natural area provide views of 30-foot Savage Falls and incredible panoramic vistas of Savage Gulf.

The Stone Door Entrance is off TN56 at Beersheba Springs, south of McMinnville and north of Tracy City. In Beersheba Springs, turn east on a side road marked with a Savage Gulf sign; bear right at a Y and then keep straight into the natural area when the road turns left. The Stone Door Entrance is the most popular site in the state natural area because short trails lead to high bluff overlooks of Big Creek Gulf and to the Great Stone Door, a huge crack in the rock bluff that provides access in and out of the canyon. The Great Stone Door was probably used by the Cherokees and Chickamaugas who once dominated the region.

In **Beersheba Springs,** you can get historical information on the community at the small local museum, which is on TN56 on the west end of town next to the post office; TN56 continues southwest to Altamont. The old hotel and many of the houses are on a loop drive that begins at the northeast end of the community across from the turnoff to the Savage Gulf State Natural Area and ends at the museum.

The chalybeate spring that was the focus for the origin of the resort flows no more. When TN56 was built up the mountain following the old Indian trail, the spring dried up. As you climb TN56 to Beersheba Springs from the north, you'll pass on the right a small, rock, arch-shaped enclosure over the place the water once flowed. Here the Chickamaugas knelt to drink from the spring on their way to battle the white men who inevitably would take all their lands on the Cumberland Plateau. It is likely that the trail Beersheba Porter Cain followed to the spring was part of the old Chickamauga Path.

The last weekend in July, the combined community of **Gruetli-Laager** hosts a Swiss Festival at the Swiss Memorial School, which is located north of TN108 on 55th Avenue. Tours are conducted of the

The Old Stage Road House

old homeplaces, only a few of which have the original houses. The old post office, now abandoned, sits at the intersection of 20th Avenue with TN108, west of 55th Avenue. If you turn north on 20th Avenue, you'll pass on the left the road to the Old Stage Road House built in 1870, which sat beside the Chattanooga-Nashville highway that ran through Gruetli. Farther along 20th Avenue, a gravel road to the right leads to the cemetery with gravestones bearing such names as Leitsinger, Suter, Hunziker, Schild, Scholer, and Nussbaum. The road past the cemetery becomes the driveway to the Stampfli home, built in 1870, one of the few original houses that remain; you can see the house from the cemetery.

Hubbard Cave can be found north of Beersheba Springs and south of McMinnville off TN56, near the community of Irving College in the eastern side of the Collins River Valley. Entrances to the cave are in a pit formed by the collapse of the cave roof. Exploring the cave system can be difficult—you must first climb down into the pit, and the cave itself has ledges that must be managed, but experienced cavers use the branch of the cave that is not blocked. The cave area is difficult to get to, and to protect the bats, visitation is not encouraged. However, if you are interested in visiting the cave, you can contact the Tennessee office of the Nature Conservancy in Nashville.

Trails

Hiking is the only way to experience the majestic landscape of Savage Gulf State Natural Area. From the Savage Gulf Entrance, you can walk the 4.2-mile **Savage Day Loop,** which takes you by an overlook of 30-foot Savage Falls and past outstanding views of Savage Gulf, including Rattlesnake Point. The 5.8-mile **South Rim Trail** passes Savage Falls, which stands at the head of Savage Gulf, and then follows the south rim of the gulf; you'll find the Stage Road Campsite along the way. The trail provides panoramic views of Savage Gulf and overlooks of the virgin forest along Savage Creek.

Halfway through the Savage Day Loop, you'll encounter the North Rim/North Plateau Loop. The 6.3-mile **North Rim Trail** leads to the Hobbs Cabin Campsite, which is about 9 miles from the entrance. Along the way, you can see across the canyon to a rock slide that in 1984 took out a section of the virgin forest. In addition to the campsite, Hobbs Cabin itself is also available for overnight stays; it has six bunks for sleeping bags, a fireplace, and a pit toilet. You can get water from a spring in back of the cabin. Hobbs Cabin was originally a shabby, hunters' cabin, which the park replaced with the present log structure when the original burned.

From Hobbs Cabin, the 7.1-mile **North Plateau Trail** loops back east to connect with the Savage Day Loop, passing the Dinky Line Campsite along the way.

The 6.7-mile **Connector Trail** connects the end of the North Rim Trail with the trails in the Collins and Big Creek Gulfs. Hiking this trail you'll cross Savage Creek, Collins River, and Big Creek, all usually dry except during rainy seasons.

The Great Stone Door

Along the Connector Trail, you'll encounter the 1.6-mile **Stage Road Historic Trail,** which follows part of the old 1830 toll road from Nashville through McMinnville to Chattanooga; this section of the old road is now on the National Register of Historic Places. The end of the Stage Road Trail is the junction of the South Rim Trail and the beginning of the 9.9-mile **Collins Gulf Trail.** Along this little-used trail that follows the Collins River, you'll encounter a rugged gorge, waterfalls, sinking creeks, and panoramic views, along with two campsites. The Collins Gulf Trail loops back to join the Connector Trail at the Sawmill Campsite near a short side trail to the Cator Savage Historic Site. The cabin there was built about 1910 by Cator Savage, a descendant of Samuel Savage.

At the end of the Connector Trail, you'll join the 4-mile **Big Creek Gulf Trail,** which continues up Big Creek Gulf and passes by a side trail to 20-foot Ranger Falls, a terminal waterfall where the water disappears into passageways in the rock at the bottom.

From the Stone Door Entrance to the natural area, you can walk the 0.9-mile **Stone Door Trail** to grand overlooks and the Great Stone Door; the Big Creek Gulf Trail begins here by descending through the Great Stone Door into the canyon. You'll likely see rock climbers at the Stone Door Overlook, for this is a favorite place for climbing and rappelling. Rappelling workshops are offered; contact the South Cumberland Recreation Area visitor center in Monteagle for details.

Behind the ranger station at the Stone Door Entrance, you can take the **Laurel Falls Trail** a quarter-mile down the hill to 25-foot Laurel Falls on Laurel Creek. Also from the ranger station, the 2.9-mile **Laurel Trail** passes to the west to Alum Gap and Alum Gap Camp Area to connect with the end of the Big Creek Gulf Trail and the 3.2-mile **Big Creek Rim Trail,** which parallels the canyon bluff back to the Great Stone Door for more views of Big Creek Gulf.

From Alum Gap, you can also take the 1.4-mile **Greeter Trail,** which passes to the west to Greeter Falls—a 50-foot waterfall named for the Greeter family who sold the land to the state to add to the state natural area. Along the way you'll pass Boardtree Falls on Boardtree Creek. You can also get to Greeter Falls from the west through the back end of a new subdivision being developed across from an old sawmill on TN56 between Altamont and Beersheba Springs.

The amphitheater of Greeter Falls has a thick sandstone layer on top of a limestone layer. You can easily see the interface of the two layers; the underlying limestone appears more crumbly. Most waterfalls on the Plateau spill over hard sandstone that caps layers of softer sandstone or shale. The natural area staff has long-range plans to develop trails on both sides of the creek around Greeter Falls and connect them with a suspension bridge.

References

Clayton, David E. "Forgotten Colony." Paper. No place: Gruetli Swiss Historical Society, no date.

Coppinger, Margaret, et al. *Beersheba Springs: A History.* Beersheba Springs, TN: Beersheba Springs Historical Society, 1983.

Hedgepath, Randy, ranger-naturalist, South Cumberland Recreation Area. Interviews and conversations with author. 1986–90.

Jackson, Frances Helen. "The German Swiss Settlement at Gruetli, TN." M.A. thesis, Vanderbilt Univ., 1933.

Livingstone, Terry. "Greeter Falls: A Dose of Wilderness." *Tennessee Conservationist,* July–Aug. 1985, 9–11.

Manning, Russ. "Gruetli: A Place of Beginning." *Tennessee Conservationist,* July–Aug. 1990, 11–13.

———, and Sondra Jamieson. *The South Cumberland and Fall Creek Falls: A Hiker's Guide to Trails and Attractions.* Norris, TN: Laurel Place, 1990.

Nicholson, James L. *Grundy County.* Memphis: Memphis State Univ. Press, 1982.

Nussbaum, Edmund. "The Swiss Colony at Gruetli: History of Its Founding, including the Beersheba Connection." McClung Collection, Lawson-McGhee Library, Univ. of Tennessee, Knoxville, 1980–81.

Prichard, Mack S. "Exploring Savage Gulf—A Last Chance for Wilderness." *Tennessee Conservationist* May–June 1977, 8–11.

Suter, Jake (president, Gruetli Swiss Historical Society), and Rose Stampfli (secretary). Interviews with author. April 10, 1990.

Tennessee Dept. of Conservation. "Savage Gulf and Stone Door Trails Map." Nashville, 1989.

————. "South Cumberland State Recreation Area." Brochure. Nashville, 1984.

Werner, Samuel, great-grandson of the original Samuel Werner. Interview with author. Tracy City, TN, Oct. 24, 1991.

Chapter 14

Fiery Gizzard

In 1850 Leslie Kennedy wandered across the south Cumberland Plateau in search of fortune. Kennedy had come from Ireland two or three years before and settled in Nashville. A new rail line between the cities of Nashville and Chattanooga was being built, and Kennedy wondered what lay along the expected route.

During his wanderings through the Plateau wilderness, Kennedy noticed outcroppings of coal, which perhaps presented the business opportunity for which he had been searching. He carried samples back to Nashville, where he tried to interest investors in his discovery. William N. Bilbo, a lawyer, was the only person who would listen; Bilbo saw the opportunities for profit if enough coal was to be had.

Bilbo accompanied Kennedy back to the Plateau for further exploration, where they came upon Benjamin Wooten digging coal and selling it to blacksmiths in the region. Wooten's son, Tommy, had discovered the coal while trying to rout a groundhog out of its burrow in the area where Tracy City now stands.

Bilbo bought the Wooten property and large tracts of land surrounding the area; some acreage was given to him by landowners who saw no value in the land and hoped to save on their taxes. He then proceeded to New York, where he captured the interest of investors; five accompanied him back to Tennessee, where they became convinced of profitable coal deposits. The businessmen purchased Bilbo's holdings and formed the Sewanee Mining Company with one of them, Samuel F. Tracy, as president. Bilbo returned to Nashville with his profits, while Kennedy seems to have benefited only from getting the job of mine captain.

The first task of the company was to build a railroad spur from the main line of the Nashville and Chattanooga Railroad that by now had been completed through Cowan, Tennessee. From Cowan, the spur climbed the Sewanee Mountain, for which the company had been named, to what is now Midway, Tennessee. "Sewanee" supposedly was an Indian word for "Big Mountain." The rail spur up the mountain was nicknamed "The Mountain Goat" for its steep grade.

The coal mines at Midway proved to be inadequate, and so the Sewanee Mining Company extended the rail line another 10 miles to the location of Tracy City, which grew up around the mining operations and was named for Samuel F. Tracy.

The Sewanee Mining Company soon faced financial problems because of the expense of extending the rail line and the lack of market for the coal. To save some of their capital, the investors and creditors reorganized the company into the Tennessee Coal and Railroad Company.

The Civil War interrupted the mining operations. The Confederate army held the mines and the railroad line at the beginning of the war. But then the Union army occupied the Tracy City area in 1863 and held the mines until the close of the war in 1865. The company resumed operation in 1866.

By the early 1870s, company officials were seeking ways to expand their operation, for they were unable to sell all the coal they could produce. They settled on making coke, which was needed for the production of iron. They proceeded to build 120 ovens, which they used to convert the coal to coke.

To prove that the coke was satisfactory for smelting iron, the company asked its chief engineer, Samuel F. Jones, to build a small test furnace. It was a slapdash affair made of sandstone and odds and ends, including an old stovepipe. On the third day of operation, after producing 15 tons of iron, the stovepipe came crashing down. But the test had been successful; they had proved that the Tracy City coke would smelt iron. The experiment helped launch the Tennessee iron industry, and the company changed its name to the Tennessee Coal, Iron, and Railroad Company, which much later became part of the United States Steel Corporation.

Blue Hole Falls on the Little Fiery Gizzard Creek in Grundy Forest State Natural Area

On the first day of operation of that test furnace, as a white-hot stream of molten iron ran from the billowing smoke and steam, someone in his excitement dubbed the furnace the "Fiery Gizzard." The name is now found throughout this area of the Cumberland Plateau.

An alternative tale says the name originated with Davy Crockett during his time in Tennessee when he burned his tongue on a hot turkey gizzard while camped along a creek in the area, which he named "Fiery Gizzard Creek." Some say it was an Indian that burned his tongue and named the creek. In either case, the iron smelting furnace would have taken on the name of the creek. Another story says that the area got its name from the time an Indian chief threw a gizzard ripped from a freshly killed turkey into a fire to get the attention of whites who had come for a peace talk.

However the name came about, it has clung to this region. The Big and Little Fiery Gizzard Creeks gather in Grundy Forest and flow southeast through Gizzard Cove. Before the Big Fiery Gizzard Creek flows off the plateau to join Battle Creek which heads for the Tennessee River, it is also joined by the Little Gizzard Creek. The Fiery Gizzard Trail of the South Cumberland Recreation Area begins at Grundy Forest, traverses Gizzard Cove along the Big Fiery Gizzard Creek, and ends at 60-foot-high Foster Falls on Little Gizzard Creek.

South Cumberland Recreation Area

Local conservationists quickly recognized the special character of this Fiery Gizzard region of the south Cumberland Plateau. Herman Baggenstoss, Chairman of the Grundy County Conservation Board, approached the state of Tennessee about setting aside several areas of the south Cumberland that had geological and recreational significance. The response was that most were too small to be managed effectively.

Baggenstoss then turned to the Tennessee Valley Authority, the giant federal utility that serves the Tennessee River Valley, to help with shaping the project. TVA helped with surveying the region and assisted in formulating a plan to merge small individual units into one park system.

The state of Tennessee accepted the proposal and in 1978 established the South Cumberland Recreation Area, a combination of several state natural areas and parks managed by the state as one unit. The eight areas that make up the South Cumberland Recreation Area total 12,565 acres and are scattered over a 100-square-mile region. Savage Gulf State Natural Area with its 11,500 acres is the primary unit. The smaller parcels include the 212-acre Grundy Forest State Natural Area and the 175-acre Foster Falls TVA Small Wild Area, which are connected by the Fiery Gizzard Trail. Other components are the 150-acre Grundy Lakes State Park, which is the site of the Lone Rock Coke Ovens; the 1.5-acre Sewanee Natural Bridge State Natural Area, with its 27-foot-high sandstone arch; 140-acre Carter State Natural Area, which contains the Buggytop Trail to Lost Cove Cave; and 250-acre Hawkins Cove State Natural

Area, which preserves the rare Cumberland Rosinweed. The eighth unit is the 136-acre South Cumberland State Park, which contains the visitor center for the recreation area.

The SCRA once included another unit, the Collins State Scenic River. The 40 river miles with scenic status ran from Big Spring in Grundy County, named for Felix Grundy, Tennessee congressman and senator who once owned thousands of acres on the Plateau, to the Great Falls Dam at Rock Island State Rustic Park northeast of McMinnville. But in a peculiar incident, the Tennessee state government voted in 1984 to remove the Collins River from the state scenic river system because of protests from landowners along the river who mistakenly thought private land would be condemned. Land would not have been condemned, but local conservationists were unable to clear up the confusion before the bill excluding the river was passed, over the veto of the governor.

Tracy City

The community of Tracy City lies at the heart of the South Cumberland Recreation Area. On the south part of town, stands the Dutch Maid Bakery established in 1902 by Louise and John Baggenstoss. The Swiss-German Baggenstoss family came to Tennessee in the 1880s from Switzerland, where John Baggenstoss was a master chef. The family was attracted to the area by the Gruetli Swiss colony, which was forming to the north near Savage Gulf.

The bakeshop has been known as the "Baggenstoss Bakery" and is still called that but was incorporated several years ago as "Dutch Maid Bakery." The word "Dutch" is a Tennessee corruption of "Deutsch," which is what the Germans call themselves. Misunderstanding the word "Deutsch," the local people called the Swiss-Germans "Dutch"; the Swiss-Germans who settled in Pennsylvania were similarly called the Pennsylvania "Dutch."

The sons of Louise and John Baggenstoss (John, Robert, Herman, Fritz, Charlie, and Albert) took over the operation of the bakery from their parents, and when they incorporated they adopted the slang name with which they had grown up. The bakery is Tennessee's oldest family bakery, known for its fruit cake, sugar plum cake, and several breads, especially salt-rising bread. Albert Baggenstoss, the baker for many years who welcomed people with his friendly manner, died in 1991; customers often returned to see Albert as much as to buy breads and cookies. Lynn Craig has since become general manager with Herman Lowe as baker. Herman Baggenstoss, known across Tennessee for his conservation work, remained a corporate member of the bakery until his death in 1992. For his efforts in establishing the South Cumberland Recreation Area, Herman's likeness in bronze was placed at the entrance to the SCRA visitor center. All the brothers are gone now, but members of their families remain involved in the operation, including John's son Jack.

The A. M. Shook home—an elegant three-story house with high steep roof lines—is the architectural showpiece of Tracy City and quite remarkable for Cumberland Plateau architecture. The house was built by Col. A. M. Shook, who for a time was general manager of the Tennessee Coal, Iron, and Railroad Company.

Around 1888, Shook donated funds for the building of the James K. Shook School, named in honor of his father. With turret, clocktower, and 500-seat auditorium, the school was as unique in its architecture as the Shook home. Classes began in 1890 with eight grades. The structure, still in use at the time, was destroyed by arson in 1976.

Lone Rock Coke Ovens

The South Cumberland Recreation Area includes the Grundy Lakes State Park southeast of Tracy City. Of the park's four lakes, the Lone Rock Lake dates from the time of the mining operations in the area. The other three lakes were created by dams built by the Civilian Conservation Corps in the 1930s. At the time, Herman Baggenstoss was with the U.S. Forest Service and served as the project supervisor for the CCC crews as they built the dams.

Coke Oven Ruins

The lakes and the surrounding lands that contain the Lone Rock Coke Ovens within the park are on the National Historic Register. The coke ovens were built in 1883 by the Tennessee Coal, Iron, and Railroad Company for the production of coke. The ovens are beehive-shaped, sandstone and brick chambers, covered with a layer of dirt that now is blanketed in grass.

In the process of making coke, coal was brought from the nearby Lone Rock Mine and shoveled into the ovens. The door was then bricked up and sealed with mud. Volatile matter in the coal was usually ignited by the remains of the previous fires, or the fire was started through a small opening at the top. The load was allowed to cook for two or three days, during which combustion gases escaped through the opening at the top. When the process was completed, almost pure carbon remained which could be burned at a high temperature and with little smoke, ideal for smelting iron.

For many years, convicts leased from the state by the Tennessee Coal, Iron, and Railroad Company worked the mines and the coke ovens around Tracy City under cruel conditions. The convicts were beaten if they did not get their work done. Getting enough coal out of the mines to satisfy the bosses often depended on a boy driving the mule cart that hauled out the coal. If the boy was good with the mules and fast at getting the coal out, he was called the convict's "darling." It is not a sweetheart referred to in several convict miner songs—including the one sung at Tracy City called "Lone Rock Song"—that contain the line, "Yonder come my darlin', comin' down the line."

Free miners eventually became disgruntled with the convicts doing most of the work while they stood idle. At one time, 411 convicts, black and white, worked the mines and coke ovens, but only 24 free miners were employed.

A rebellion against the use of convict labor in the coal industry in Tennessee began in the 1890s. Convict workers were first brought to the mines at Tracy City in 1871 and at Coal Creek—present-day Lake City at the eastern edge of the Cumberland Plateau in the northern part of the state—in about 1877. In the subsequent years, their numbers gradually increased. The miners objected, but at the time could do nothing.

The revolt against the convict lease system began in Briceville near Coal Creek in 1891 in what became known as the "Coal Creek Wars." The miners at Oliver Springs, midway along the eastern edge of the Plateau in Tennessee, were also involved. Causes of the "war" included the Tennessee Coal Mining Company at Briceville paying the miners in scrip instead of money and refusing to allow a checkweighman of the miners' choosing to work at the mines to ensure the coal was being weighed and recorded accurately. The company also demanded that the miners sign an agreement relinquishing their right to strike over grievances; the United Mine Workers had formed the year before, and company officials were perhaps afraid the miners would join the union. The miners refused to sign the contract, and so the company locked the miners out and brought in convict laborers to work the mines; previously there had been no convicts in the mines at Briceville.

The miners stormed the stockade where the prisoners were kept at Briceville on July 14th and put the convicts on a train out of the community. The convicts were returned with the aid of the state militia.

A few days later, when the miners stormed the stockade again and for the first time also attacked the stockade in Coal Creek, the convicts were put on a train bound for Knoxville. When the convicts were returned, the miners stormed the stockades once again, burning the stockade at Briceville after releasing the prisoners, this time helping them to escape.

The free miners in Tracy City followed the example of the Briceville and Coal Creek miners and stormed the Lone Rock stockade in August 1892, burned it, and put the convicts on a train to Nashville, the state capital, but the convicts were returned. The convicts themselves mutinied in 1894; a convict and the deputy warden were killed.

The state militia was sent in to put down the insurrections at Briceville, Coal Creek, Oliver Springs, Tracy City, and a few other coal communities. Although resistance continued for a time, the miners eventually gave up their struggle in the face of military pressure. Although the miners' resistance to the use of convict labor appeared to be unsuccessful, the convict lease system was abolished by the state legislature in 1896 when the contracts expired. Soon after, the coal at Lone Rock played out, and the mines and the coke ovens at Tracy City were abandoned.

Although convicts were no longer leased after 1896, the state continued to use convict labor to mine coal. State-run mines were established on the Plateau near Petros, where coal was mined by convicts at Brushy Mountain State Prison until the mid-1950s. The last mine was closed in 1966, sealed with a dynamite blast. In 1969 Brushy Mountain was designated a maximum-security prison.

Monteagle

West of Tracy City lies Monteagle, a small community founded by John Moffat, a Scotsman who arrived in Canada in the early 1800s with his parents. As an adult, Moffat became a leader in the temperance movement and traveled across North America giving lectures and organizing temperance societies.

After retiring from the lecture circuit, he arrived in what is now Monteagle with his family around 1870 and purchased a little over 1,000 acres. His place was originally called "Moffat's Station," but in 1881 Moffat changed the name of the community to "Mont Eagle," and eventually "Monteagle," after Lord Mounteagle, an Englishman who was a friend of Moffat's.

Moffat became concerned about the lack of opportunities for higher education on the Plateau and donated 50 acres to help establish the Fairmount School for Girls. Soong Mei-ling spent one summer at the college; she later became Madame Chiang Kai-shek, wife of the leader of the Nationalist Chinese during World War II who set up a government on the island of Taiwan after fleeing the communist takeover of mainland China. The school operated until 1918; the complex of buildings dominated by Claiborne Hall, which was rebuilt in 1924 after a fire, is now the DuBose Episcopal Conference Center, named for the chaplain of the Fairmont School at its founding, William Porcher DuBose, a theologian who later helped operate the school.

Moffat also donated land to form the Moffat Collegiate and Normal Institute for the training of teachers. Never successful, the school later became the Monteagle Sunday School Assembly for the purpose of the "advancement of science, literary attainment, Sunday School interests, and promotion of the broadest popular culture in the interest of Christianity without regard to sect or denomination." The nondenominational assembly was part of the Chatauqua movement that began at Lake Chatauqua, New York, in 1874, in which summer retreats were established for training Sunday School teachers. At Monteagle, boarding houses were built to house the teachers during the summer sessions, and leaseholders built cottages on the grounds. The first session was held in 1883. In later years the Sunday School Assembly evolved into more of a summer resort of 160 homes, mostly for those who had attended the training sessions and wished to continue coming to the area during the summer. The Assembly, placed on the National Register of Historic Places in 1982 and the only Chatauqua still existing in the South, still has a summer season of activities.

Monteagle and the surrounding area continually flirted with the

Edgeworth Inn at Monteagle Assembly

idea of becoming a training center. At nearby Summerfield, the Highlander School was established in 1932. It was founded as a folk school by Miles Horton, a Tennessean, and Don West, from Georgia. The school took shape with a house and property donated by Dr. Lillian Johnson, a professor at Memphis State Teachers College. The school soon became a training center for labor union organizers and in later years trained organizers for nonviolent demonstrations in the civil rights movement; Martin Luther King Jr. attended sessions at the school.

Although the center was successful, the leftist leanings of the school disturbed the local people. In 1959 the center was raided by local authorities, and some liquor was confiscated. The circuit court judge ruled that Highlander had broken the law by selling beer, violating the existing segregation laws, and using its funds for private gain. Dr. Johnson's deed of the property was set aside, the buildings and grounds confiscated, and the school's charter revoked. The school remained closed while the court case was appealed. Highlander lost the appeal, and the school property was sold at auction. Soon after, the Highlander Center reorganized and, after a time in Knoxville, relocated near New Market in East Tennessee where it continues operation.

Wonder Cave

To the northeast of Monteagle, Wonder Cave opens in a cove at the foot of the plateau. Wonder Cave has commercial tours.

The main entrance to the cave was discovered in 1897 by three Vanderbilt University students wading in the Mystic River that flows from the mouth of the cave and searching for the source of cool air coming from inside the mountain. R. M. Payne opened the cave to tours in 1900. The only entrance was the one from which the river emerged, so Payne had flat-bottomed boats to take people into the cave. Eventually a hole was blasted near the original entrance, so cave tours today are conducted on foot.

Next to the cave entrance stands the J. J. Raulston House, a large log home built during 1920 to 1924. The rockwork around the home, including the stairway from the house to the cave entrance and the rock house at the entrance, adds to the grandeur of the place.

Sewanee

Southwest of Monteagle lies the Domain of the University of the South, an Episcopal school founded in 1857. The school was the idea of Leonidas Polk, Episcopal bishop of Arkansas and Louisiana, who dreamed of founding a school in the South to take a place among the large universities of Europe and North America.

A charter was granted by the state of Tennessee in 1858, and the cornerstone was laid in 1860 on 10,000 acres of land that came to be known as the "Domain." Of this tract, 5,000 acres had been donated by the Sewanee Mining Company along with a million board feet of lumber for construction, 20,000 tons of coal, and free transportation for the building supplies. The Domain remains intact and is probably the largest campus in the world. Much of the land is leased; people can build and own homes on the Domain, but the land remains with the university. The Domain includes a 200-acre stand of old-growth forest in Thumping Dick Cove that has been designated a National Natural Landmark.

During the Civil War, Confederate and Federal forces frequently passed back and forth over the Plateau between Middle Tennessee and Chattanooga. The first few university buildings were destroyed in skirmishes. The most important engagement was the Battle of University Place, as the area was called at the time.

Leonidas Polk, who had become a Lieutenant General in the Confederate army, was killed by a cannonball at Pine Mountain, Georgia, during the war. After the war, Bishop Charles Todd Quintard and George Rainsford Fairbanks reestablished the school, which has since become a respected university, whose cluster of sandstone buildings rests in an idyllic setting. The university is often called "Sewanee," after

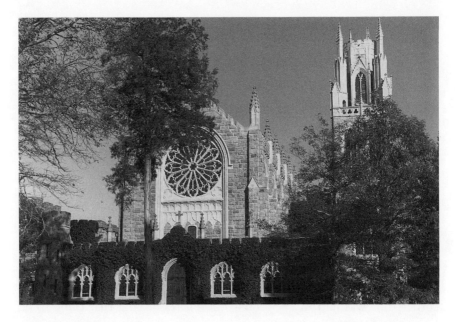

All Saints' Chapel

the Indian name for the area. The history of the university is depicted in stained glass windows in the narthex of All Saints' Chapel on the university grounds.

In 1880, Bishop Quintard attended the dedication ceremony for the Rugby colony to the north and led the Holy Communion. Brian Stagg, founder of the Rugby Restoration Association, attended the University of the South.

Outside of Tennessee, the university is perhaps best known for the *Sewanee Review.* Established in 1892, the *Review* is a nationally recognized journal of literature.

To the east of the university's domain lies St. Andrews School, an Episcopal college-preparatory school which James Agee attended before going to Harvard University. Throughout his writing career at *Time* and *Fortune* and during which he produced his classic books, *A Death in the Family* and *Let Us Now Praise Famous Men*, Agee corresponded with Father James Harold Flye, a teacher at St. Andrews who had been a surrogate parent to Agee during the time he attended the school.

Directions and Services

The **South Cumberland Recreation Area** visitor center is located on US41 between Tracy City and Monteagle. Take US41 east from I-24 and Monteagle, or you can take TN56 south from Beersheba Springs and the Savage Gulf State Natural Area to Tracy City to pick up US41. You can also take US41 northwest from Jasper in the Sequatchie Valley to get to Tracy City.

The visitor center is open seven days a week to provide maps, directions, and other information. The state park that surrounds the visitor center contains tennis courts, picnic areas, nature trails, and a broad expanse of lawn for group activities. There are even showers in the restrooms. Periodic scheduled outings leave from the center. In spring, a waterfall outing takes you to several waterfalls in the area; some, such as Deerlick, Bridal Veil, and Monteagle Falls, are not included in the South Cumberland Recreation Area.

Tracy City stands at the junction of TN56 and US41. You'll find the Dutch Maid Bakery on the southeast end of town on US41. The Shook home stands west off US41 south of the bakery.

Monteagle is located at the junction of I-24 and US41. The **DuBose Conference Center,** at the east end of the community where US41 makes a turn northeast, is available to groups other than those connected with the Episcopal Church; individuals can stay there if space is available. West of the interstate, you'll find **Monteagle Wine Cellars,** which gives tours and tastings of the locally made wine, and the **Smokehouse Lodge and Restaurant.** You can find additional lodging in motels around Monteagle and Tracy City.

The **Monteagle Assembly** is located in the center of Monteagle, north off US41. The 96-acre community of cottages still operates a summer season from mid-June to mid-August in which the general public may enter the community and participate in the activities. The grounds also contain **Edgeworth Inn,** a three-story Victorian inn that is open to the public year-round, and the **North Gate Inn,** a bed-and-breakfast inn also open year-round.

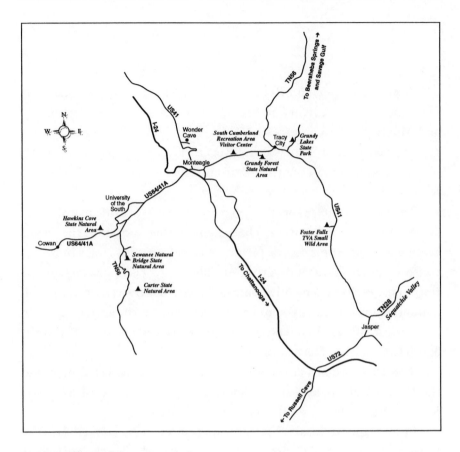

South Cumberland Recreation Area

You'll find the entrance to the 212-acre **Grundy Forest State Natural Area** off US41 a mile west of Tracy City or two miles east of the South Cumberland Recreation Area Visitor Center. You'll see a sign directing you to turn south; follow the signs through two right turns and continue straight into a picnic area where you'll see a picnic shelter built by the Civilian Conservation Corps in the 1930s. Here you'll find the Grundy Forest Day Loop to the right; this is also the northern access for the Fiery Gizzard Trail.

At **Foster Falls TVA Small Wild Area,** scenic trails skirt the rim of the gorge for panoramic views of the falls and the massive rock amphitheater. This small wild area, established by TVA on US41 south of Tracy City, has a campground with running water and hot showers.

There is a fee for camping, which is first come, first served. This is the southern access to the Fiery Gizzard Trail.

East of Tracy City you'll find **Grundy Lakes State Park;** the entrance is off US41 southeast of town before you get to Foster Falls. Swimming, fishing, and boating on the lakes, picnicking and strolling along the shores, and studying the coke ovens are the main activities. There is no camping here.

Although you'll descend the western rim of the Cumberland Plateau as you head northwest along US41 out of Monteagle to get to **Wonder Cave,** the cave is still part of the plateau because it lies in the north side of a cove in the western wall. After you get to the valley floor, signs lead north to the cave and the visitor center. For most of the paid tour, you'll walk along the floodplain of the Mystic River. During the winter, the river overflows and fills much of the lower level of the cave. The original electric lights kept shorting out with the flooding; so today's tours are led with hand-held lanterns. The tour takes you past many well-preserved stalagmites, stalactites, and complete columns; because the cave was commercialized soon after discovery, vandalism was avoided. The adjacent Raulston House is now a bed and breakfast.

The **University of the South** is at Sewanee on US41A/64 east of Monteagle. Maps of the campus are available at various locations around the university. The inns noted on the maps are now dormitories and do not take visitors. And the Sewanee Inn at the eastern edge of the campus is for university use only. All Saints Chapel stands on University Avenue, which turns off US41A/64 to loop through the campus of beautiful stone buildings.

Thumping Dick Cove can be found north of Brakefield Road, which is northwest of the center of the university. The name of the cove came from the constant thumping noise made by a hydraulic ram that ran a sawmill in the cove in the 1870s. The old-growth forest in Thumping Dick Cove is primarily oak, hickory, and sugar maple. An unmarked fire lane into the forest provides access.

The Sewanee campus also contains the **Abbott Cotten Marten**

Ravine Garden, commonly called "Abbo's Alley." Over the years, many flowering plants have been added, so in spring the garden is a special place for a quiet stroll. Turning on South Carolina Avenue off University Avenue in the center of campus, you'll encounter the garden where South Carolina crosses a creek. Trails lead through the garden along the creek to the right all the way to Texas Avenue. To the left, where the road crosses the creek, you can walk through an addition to the garden called "Abbo's Alley Prolongation."

To get to the other units that make up the South Cumberland Recreation Area, head south from Sewanee. **Hawkins Cove State Natural Area** is down the mountain along US41A/64; at this writing, no signs indicate where it is. The Cove was set aside in 1985 to preserve a rare plant, the Cumberland Rosinweed. No trails have yet been built, so the area is inaccessible.

Farther down US41A/64 in the community of Cowan at the western foot of the plateau, you'll find the **Cowan Railroad Museum,** which includes the restored depot that was built in 1904 to replace the original; the depot is now on the National Register of Historic Places. In 1849–52, the Nashville and Chattanooga Railroad constructed a 2,228-foot tunnel through the plateau at Cowan, called the "Cumberland Mountain Tunnel." Cowan was also the junction of the old rail spur built by the Sewanee Mining Company to the coal fields at Tracy City. There is a proposal to transform the old railbed into a bicycle and walking trail; after climbing the mountain, the trail would pass by the University of the South, St. Andrews School, Monteagle, and the South Cumberland Recreation Area visitor center. Once the trail is established, it will become part of the South Cumberland Recreation Area.

Before descending the plateau on US41A/64, you can bear south on TN56 south of Sewanee to get to **Sewanee Natural Bridge State Natural Area.** In about 2 miles, you'll see a sign directing you left to the natural bridge. The area that includes the bridge was donated to the state by the University of the South. Sewanee Bridge has a span of 50 feet and a clearance of 27 feet. The remains of a spring seeps out of the bottom of the rock bluff behind the bridge; the spring was the source of water that carved the formation. Numerous wells that were put down in the area lowered the water table so that now the spring flows only after a good rain. The top of the bridge affords a view of Lost Cove.

Along TN56, you'll pass a right turn to the **St. Mary's Episcopal Retreat and Conference Center.** Perched on the edge of the plateau, the center is open to the public, especially for gatherings and conferences. In addition to a main lodge, the St. Joseph Building has dormitories and a family can stay in the Hermitage, a small stone cabin.

Farther south on TN56 you'll find the parking area for **Carter State Natural Area,** named for Mr. and Mrs. Harry Lee Carter, who donated lands in the area to the state. The natural area contains Lost Cove Cave, which has one of the most impressive cave openings on the Cumberland Plateau. The Buggytop Entrance is in a massive rock wall and measures a 100 feet wide by 80 feet high. A creek emerges from the mouth. The creek enters the cave in a sinkhole to the north in Lost Cove and flows the entire length of the cave. In addition to Buggytop, the cave has three other entrances—the Peter Cave Entrance, where the creek enters, and two unnamed openings. Naturalists from the SCRA visitor center lead tours in the cave.

Another 60,000-acre expanse of forest land south of Carter State Natural Area, which lies in Franklin and Marion counties of Tennessee and extends into Alabama, has attracted the attention of those who would like to see the forest preserved intact. One idea is for the federal government to create a Cumberland Plateau National Forest. The acreage includes the **Walls of Jericho,** a unique narrow canyon of 200-foot limestone walls that stand above a creek with small waterfalls and placid pools; the canyon ends in a deep sinkhole into which the creek flows during wet weather. This area is on private land and at this writing is closed to the public.

Although no longer part of the South Cumberland Recreation Area, the **Collins River** is still used for canoeing and fishing; you can put in at highway rights-of-way where roads cross the river.

Trails

The 12-mile **Fiery Gizzard Trail** is one of the most difficult, yet rewarding trails on the Cumberland Plateau. The trail runs from Grundy Forest State Natural Area to Foster Falls TVA Small Wild Area and has two primitive campsites along the way, the Raven Point Campsite and the TVA Small Wilds Camp Area. If you plan to camp, you need to get a permit at the SCRA visitor center. On the Fiery Gizzard Trail you'll pass Black Canyon, Chimney Rocks, Sycamore Falls, and a 0.4-mile side trail to Raven Point which passes by Raven Point Arch, a span of 27 feet with a clearance of 6 feet. Raven Point is a promontory that thrusts you into the canyon for a panoramic view of Gizzard Cove and, to the south, McAlloyd Cove.

At the Grundy Forest access point for the Fiery Gizzard Trail, the 2-mile **Grundy Forest Day Loop** provides overlooks of waterfalls and cascades and the junction of the Big and Little Fiery Gizzard Creeks. The Fiery Gizzard Trail starts 0.7 mile along the loop.

Along the Fiery Gizzard Trail, you'll pass the junction for the 2.8-mile **Dog Hole Trail,** named for the dog hole mine that is just up the bluff from the trail junction; dog hole mines are low mines that only a dog can stand in upright. The trail rejoins the Fiery Gizzard Trail at its end to form a loop.

The 1.5-mile **Lone Rock Loop** circles Grundy Lake at Grundy Lakes State Park and passes by the remains of the Lone Rock Coke Ovens.

Several trails descend the western wall of the Cumberland Plateau from the campus of the University of the South, affording broad views westward from the trailheads. From the end of Morgan's Steep Road, you can take the **Perimeter Trail** to the right and pick up the 0.8-mile **Bridal Veil Falls Trail,** which descends to the waterfall streaming 50 feet into a sinkhole.

The Perimeter Trail is a 20-mile trail network that encircles the Domain of the university. From Morgan's Steep, you can also go left along the Perimeter Trail to pass through a stone tunnel called "Proctors Hall" and in 1 mile arrive at the war memorial standing at the end of Tennessee Avenue.

The 1.3-mile **Shakerag Hollow Trail,** part of the Perimeter Trail system, is known for wildflowers in the spring. The trail leads from Greens View at the end of Greens View Road down the western bluff of the plateau and then circles back to emerge on US41A/64 near the stone pillars marking the entrance to the University.

The 2-mile **Buggytop Trail** in Carter State Natural Area leads from the parking area on TN56 to the Buggytop Entrance of Lost Cove Cave. A side trail above the cave leads left to the Peter Cave Entrance, the other primary opening for the cave system. You can do a loop by entering the Buggytop Entrance and following the creek upstream that flows through the cave to emerge from the Peter Cave Entrance and then circle back to the main trail. But it's not an easy walk and you must cross the creek a few times; if you try it, take along a couple of flashlights and perhaps a hardhat.

References

Ansley, Fran, and Brenda Bell. "Miners' Insurrections/Convict Labor." *Southern Exposure,* Winter 1974, 144–59.

Ashdown, Paul, ed. *James Agee: Selected Journalism.* Knoxville: Univ. of Tennessee Press, 1985.

Baggenstoss, Herman (chairman, Grundy County Conservation Board, and former owner and publisher, *Grundy County Herald),* and Albert Baggenstoss (Dutch Maid baker). Conversations and interviews with author. 1985–90.

Baker, Lily, et al., eds. *Purple Sewanee.* Sewanee, TN, 1932.

Cameron, Douglas, and James Waring McCrady. *Under the Sun at Sewanee.* Sewanee, TN: Univ. Press, 1978.

DuBose Conference Center. "A Little History of the DuBose Conference Center." Flier. Monteagle, TN, no date.

Dykes, Donna L. "Coke Ovens Are Silent Memorials." *Tennessee Conservationist,* Sept.–Oct. 1983, 2–5.

"Enduring Memorial, A Brief History of the University of the South, Sewanee, Tennessee." Brochure. Sewanee, TN: Univ. Press, 1978.

Green, Archie. *Only a Miner.* Urbana: Univ. of Illinois Press, 1972.

Gregg, Robert. "Origin and Development of the Tennessee Coal, Iron and Railroad Company." Paper. Univ. of the South Library, Sewanee, TN, no date.

"Grundy County, 1844–1976." *Grundy County Herald* (Tracy City, TN), Sept. 2, 1976.

Hedgepath, Randy, ranger-naturalist, South Cumberland Recreation Area. Interviews and conversations with author. 1986–90.

Hutson, A. C., Jr. "The Coal Miners' Insurrections of 1891 in Anderson County, Tennessee." *East Tennessee Historical Society Publications* 7 (1935): 103–21.

Manning, Russ, and Sondra Jamieson. *The South Cumberland and Fall Creek Falls: A Hiker's Guide to Trails and Attractions.* Norris, TN: Laurel Place, 1990.

Nicholson, James L. *Grundy County.* Memphis: Memphis State Univ. Press, 1982.

Reynolds, George. "Sewanee and the Cumberland Plateau in the Civil War." Paper. Univ. of the South Library, Sewannee, TN, no date.

Sehlinger, Bob, and Bob Lantz. 1983. *Streams of Tennessee* 1. Birmingham, AL: Menasha Ridge Press.

Tennessee Dept. of Conservation. "South Cumberland State Recreation Area." Brochure. Nashville, 1984.

———. "Fiery Gizzard & Buggytop Trails Map." Nashville, 1987.

Wonder Cave. "Wonder Cave Offers Underground Exploration." Flier. Pelham, TN, 1989.

York, Stan. "Cowan, A Railroad Town of Yesterday and Today." *Tennessee Conservationist,* July–Aug. 1988, 11–13.

Chapter 15

Lookout Mountain

At one time along highways through the Southeast, it was possible to see—like the ubiquitous Burma Shave signs—barns painted with the message, "See Rock City." About 2,700 birdhouses, painted black and red, carried the same message.

In 1956 at the peak of barn painting, there were 800 "Rock City" barns, ranging as far north as Michigan and as far west as Texas. Now there are only about 90 of the barns left, nearly half in Tennessee; these have been declared Tennessee State Historical Landmarks and are permitted to remain in spite of new legislation that restricts billboards along highways.

The increasing cost of advertising permits and compliance with the National Highway Beautification Act caused the downfall of the Rock City birdhouses. Now they are only sold as souvenirs; originals are sought by collectors.

Although the days of the "See Rock City" barns and birdhouses are nearly gone, Rock City remains atop Lookout Mountain, an outlier that was separated from the Cumberland Plateau as the Tennessee River cut its way westward.

At various places on Lookout Mountain, weathering and erosion have uncovered hard blocks of the sandstone that makes up the surface of the plateau. Some blocks are as large as houses. Where several stand together, their outline suggests a city skyline. These stone fields were often dubbed "Rocktown" or "Rock Village."

Rock City is a 10-acre rock garden that was commercialized in 1932 when Garnet and Frieda Carter decided to open their gardens to the public. Rock City became one of the traditional stops on a typical summer trip through the Southeast. Flagstone pathways wander through the large rock formations, including Fat Man's Squeeze and Needle's Eye. Statues of fairy tale and nursery rhyme characters can be found in underground grottoes in Fairyland Caverns and Mother Goose Village. But the fame of Rock City is in its claim that from Lover's Leap you can see seven states.

It is the panoramic views of the Tennessee River Valley that gave Lookout Mountain its name. The mountain was originally called "Chadonaugsa" or "Chatanuga," a Muskogean word meaning "rock coming to a point." The city of Chattanooga at the foot of Lookout Mountain adopted the Muskogean name. "Chatanuga" is an obvious reference to Point Lookout, a rock promontory that at the northern end of Lookout Mountain overlooks the city of Chattanooga and the Tennessee River where it meanders in the outline of a moccasin, creating Moccasin Bend.

In 1986 the lower 960 acres of Moccasin Bend was named a National Historic Landmark in recognition of its historical and archaeological significance. This bend in the Tennessee River was for thousands of years a trade center for the American Indians that once dominated the region. Spanish artifacts unearthed at Hampton Place, the site of a 16th-century Indian village, indicate that early Spanish explorers, possibly Hernando DeSoto, passed through here. Civil War earthworks also mark the landscape.

Williams Island in the middle of the Tennessee River downstream from Moccasin Bend also has historical significance. The island is littered with archaeological sites, which have yielded Paleo-Indian artifacts dating from the earliest years of human habitation in North America. Indian occupation continued until around 1800 when the Cherokees farmed the island. There are something like 10,000 burials and 26 major archaeological sites on the 450-acre island. Much of the surface has been disturbed by free-lance diggers, but the site of the Indian town of Talimico remains essentially undisturbed. Artifacts indicate the town was also one of the important sites for early European contact in the period 1540 to 1670. Will-

Moccasin Bend

iams Island, named for Samuel Williams who possessed the island prior to the Civil War, is designated a state archaeological site and is on the National Register of Historic Places.

Chickamauga Battlefield

On Lookout Mountain a Civil War battle was fought in the decisive conflict around Chattanooga. Prior to the Battle of Lookout Mountain, the Union and Confederate forces clashed in the Battle of Chickamauga Creek, in which the Union army suffered defeat. That battle took place on the plains just to the south of Chattanooga at the eastern foot of Lookout Mountain, the same general location where Dragging Canoe established the Chickamauga branch of the Cherokees in 1777. The fighting that occurred around Chickamauga Creek was one of the bloodiest battles of the Civil War, with 37,129 casualties in two days of fighting, September 19–20, 1863.

The Battle of Chickamauga was one of the battles to control Chattanooga, which was a strategic location because just west of the city the Tennessee River cut through the Walden Ridge portion of the Cumberland Plateau. The railroads reached for this natural passageway west, and so the city had become the rail center of the South, connecting Charleston, Savannah, Atlanta, and Knoxville with the west.

The stage was set for the Battle of Chickamauga when Union Maj. Gen. William S. Rosecrans outmaneuvered Confederate Gen. Braxton Bragg who was occupying Chattanooga; Bragg had been to Chattanooga—then called "Ross's Landing"—in 1838, when as a young lieutenant he participated in the roundup of the Cherokees. With the Union army almost encircling him, Bragg decided he could not allow his army to be cut off from the rest of the Confederate army and so retreated south from the city. Bragg's retreat enabled the Union troops to take Chattanooga without the loss of a single man. Confident with such an easy capture of the city, Rosecrans sent his troops after Bragg as the Confederate troops made their way toward Atlanta; Rosecrans dreamed of capturing that city too and cutting the communication lines of the Confederacy.

But unknown to Rosecrans, Bragg's army had been reinforced with troops, including Lt. Gen. James Longstreet's corps. Bragg's force had nearly doubled, and Rosecrans was badly outnumbered. Bragg had a couple of opportunities to attack Rosecrans's forward forces, but although he issued orders to attack, his generals inexplicably stalled and the early advantage was lost. Some say the problem was that Bragg had trouble giving clear orders and his generals did not understand what he wanted.

By this time Rosecrans began to recognize that Bragg was no longer in retreat and posed a threat. He ordered a concentration of his forces.

Still hoping to catch Rosecrans at a disadvantage, Bragg finally managed to begin his offensive to recapture Chattanooga. Bragg's forward forces encountered the Union army on the morning of September 19 along Chickamauga Creek. The first day's fighting was indecisive, with brigades encountering each other in the woods. Although

Longstreet's forces had arrived to support Bragg, Longstreet himself did not arrive until that night.

The next day, Bragg gave Longstreet command of his left; and for the right, he assigned Lt. Gen. Leonidas Polk, a bishop and one of the founders of the University of the South at Sewanee. But on the morning of September 20, Bragg once again faced a lack of enthusiasm for carrying out his orders. Polk was to attack at sunrise, but an hour after sunrise, he was found sitting on the porch of a farmhouse 3 miles behind the lines reading a newspaper and waiting for breakfast. Polk finally joined the fighting around 10:00 A.M.; he later placed the blame for the delay on General D. Harvey Hill, who served under Polk and who had been unsuccessfully looking for both Polk and Bragg to receive his orders.

At about 10:30, Rosecrans received a message that there was a hole in the center of the Union line between the divisions of his officers Reynolds and Wood. This was a mistake. Those who reported the gap in the line had not noticed another division deep in the woods that was holding the center. This error was to bring defeat for the Union forces at the Battle of Chickamauga.

Upon hearing of the supposed hole in his line, Rosecrans ordered the division under Brig. Gen. Thomas J. Wood to move to the left to close the gap. When Wood received the order, he protested that there was no gap but felt he had to carry out the order, especially since Rosecrans had earlier reprimanded Wood for slowness in carrying out a directive. When Wood moved his division, he left behind an actual gap a quarter of a mile wide that by coincidence was the exact location where Longstreet launched his Confederate forces. The Confederate troops poured through the gap, severing Rosecrans's army, the right half disintegrating as soldiers scrambled from the field in retreat.

Maj. Gen. George H. Thomas rallied fragments of the Union right wing and made a stand on Snodgrass Hill, holding off Longstreet's forces while the Union army retired from the field. After holding the hill until well into the afternoon, Thomas and his troops finally were forced to retreat. Thomas's actions earned him the title, "The Rock of Chickamauga."

Bragg at first hesitated to pursue Rosecrans's army because of his great loss of horses in the two-day battle. But he was eventually convinced by his generals that they should cross the Tennessee River above Chattanooga, placing the Confederate divisions between Rosecrans in Chattanooga and other Union forces in Knoxville, thus severing communications and forcing both armies to withdraw.

Bragg then received an erroneous message indicating that Rosecrans was already fleeing Chattanooga; so instead of following the plan he and his generals had decided upon, Bragg marched on the city. He found Rosecrans entrenched and realized the message had been wrong. Bragg's decision then was to begin a siege of Chattanooga.

Lookout Mountain and Missionary Ridge Battlegrounds

At the time Rosecrans retreated into Chattanooga, he abandoned Lookout Mountain, which was seized immediately as Bragg surrounded the city. With Lookout in his possession, Bragg had control of the water, rail, and road routes into the city. The only supply route open to the Union troops in Chattanooga was from the rail line at Bridgeport, Alabama, north through Sequatchie Valley and then over Walden Ridge, a difficult passage. Wagon trains carrying supplies to the Union troops along this route were attacked by the Confederates under Maj. Gen. Joseph H. Wheeler, called "Fightin' Joe." In their most famous raid, Wheeler's troops attacked and burned a Union wagon train of about 1,000 wagons.

As the Union troops neared starvation in Chattanooga, President Lincoln gave orders for Gen. Ulysses S. Grant to become commander of the western armies and with forces to go to the aid of the army entrenched in Chattanooga. One of Grant's first acts was to remove Rosecrans as head of the troops and to place in charge Major General Thomas, the hero from the Battle of Chickamauga. Grant asked Thomas to hold the city at all costs.

Grant arrived in Chattanooga on October 23 and immediately put into action a plan to establish a new supply route across Moccasin Bend to a point on the Tennessee River at Browns Ferry, far enough away from the Confederate guns that provisions could be brought in. This was accomplished by capturing the west bank from Confederate troops and then establishing a pontoon bridge across the river. Maj. Gen. Joseph Hooker soon arrived with more reinforcements for Chattanooga and helped by force to hold the Tennessee River crossing.

Bragg ordered Longstreet to dislodge the Federal troops from Browns Ferry, but Longstreet decided instead to attack part of Hooker's army at Wauhatchie, a small rail center to the west of Lookout Mountain. In the night, Longstreet was unable to find the Union rear guard and apparently called off the attack; but a division under Brig. Gen. Micah Jenkins found the Union army, and Jenkins decided to go ahead with the attack. The Union soldiers held their position in the fight, and the Confederates were forced to withdraw; the story is told that the Confederates were routed by stampeding mules from the Union side that ran directly for the Confederate lines, but the mules probably only played a small part in the failure of the Confederate attack.

With Browns Ferry firmly in possession of the Union army, supplies now flowed freely into Chattanooga, while Union Gen. William Tecumseh Sherman was marching from Memphis with additional reinforcements for the beleaguered troops in Chattanooga. It is odd that at a time when the Union army in Chattanooga was growing in number Bragg made the ill-conceived decision to send Longstreet with his troops to Knoxville to attack the Union forces there. Bragg was perhaps overconfident of his supposedly impregnable positions on Lookout Mountain to the south and Missionary Ridge to the east. But the primary reason for the order was that Bragg wanted to be rid of Longstreet, who with other of Bragg's generals had been critical of Bragg's performance; the group had written a letter to President Jefferson Davis, asking that Bragg be replaced. Davis, aware of the conflict between the two, had in fact suggested to Bragg that he send Longstreet to Knoxville. Incredibly, a couple of weeks after Longstreet had left, Bragg sent more troops to reinforce Longstreet's siege of Knoxville, weakening his own defenses further; however, these troops were called back when it became apparent the Union side was about to begin the conflict.

The opening of the battles for Chattanooga occurred on November 23, when on Grant's order, Union troops under Thomas rushed the Confederate defenses on Orchard Knob, a foothill in front of Missionary Ridge. The advance was so unexpected that the Union troops overwhelmed the Confederates, taking the hill and regaining some of the honor they had lost at Chickamauga. The Union troops held the hill in anticipation of an attack on Missionary Ridge, upon which most of Bragg's force was located. But first, Lookout Mountain had to be taken.

On the morning of November 24, rain fell in drizzles and Lookout Mountain was shrouded in mist. The fight that would take place that day was later called "The Battle above the Clouds." At the suggestion of Thomas, Grant ordered Hooker with his three brigades to take Lookout Mountain. Through the fog, the Union troops scrambled up the slope of the mountain while Confederate sharpshooters looked for holes in the mist through which to take aim at the advancing enemy. It was not until the next morning, when the fog had lifted and the armies below could see the United States flag flying from Point Lookout, that it was evident the Union troops had overrun the Confederate defenses and now possessed Lookout Mountain.

During the Battle of Lookout Mountain, Sherman had crossed the Tennessee River from Chattanooga and was now at the northern end of Missionary Ridge. Hooker now advanced from Lookout Mountain toward the southern end of the Confederate defenses. Thomas still held the center at Orchard Knob.

At first the Confederates held against the Union onslaught. Sherman on the left was being rebuffed by Confederate troops under Maj. Gen. Patrick R. Cleburne. Hooker on the right was stuck at the crossing of Chattanooga Creek where the Confederates had burned the bridge. At 3 P.M., Grant gave orders to Thomas in the center to advance on Missionary Ridge.

Bragg's first line of defense was a row of rifle pits at the base of the mountain. Thomas's orders were to take the entrenchments and halt there. The Confederates were not able to stand against the advancing Union troops and so retreated up the slope of Missionary Ridge.

The Union forces captured the line of rifle pits as ordered but soon found it impossible to stay there with the Confederate artillery firing down upon them. The choices were to stand and be slaughtered, retreat, or advance. With some officers ordering their troops up the ridge, and some soldiers simply making their own decisions to advance, the Union troops began climbing the slope of the mountain in pursuit of the Confederates.

Grant, who had joined Thomas on Orchard Knob, was furious, thinking the Union troops had no chance of taking the ridge. He asked who had given the order to advance up the slope. Thomas calmly said he had not. Maj. Gen. Gordon Granger, Thomas's corps commander who relayed orders to the commanders in the field, also denied giving such an order, but added, "When these men get going, all hell can't stop them."

The surging Union troops, vying with each other to be the first to the top, reached the crest of the ridge simultaneously at several locations in the center of the Confederate line. There was furious fighting. But the Confederate defenders were overwhelmed, and those that could retreated down the other side of the ridge. With the center broken, the entire Confederate line disintegrated. Cleburne, who had successfully held off Sherman on the right, now had the task of holding off the pursuing Union troops while the Confederates retreated into Georgia.

The defeat of the Confederates at the Battle of Lookout Mountain on November 24, 1863, and the Union victory in the next day's Battle of Missionary Ridge, so soon after the recent Confederate victory at Chickamauga Battlefield, did much to break the spirit of the Confederate army. The Union army now clearly possessed the rail center of the Confederacy, and the success of the operation led to the promotion of Grant to Commander in Chief of the United States forces. With Chattanooga in their firm grasp, the Union army could

now penetrate the deep South. It was from Chattanooga that
Sherman advanced to Atlanta and launched his "March to the Sea"
that severed the Confederacy. It was at Chattanooga, at the foot of
the Cumberland Plateau, that the Union army ensured its eventual
win of the Civil War.

Years later, two Union veterans of the Chickamauga and Chattanooga battles, Comdrs. Henry V. Boynton and Ferdinand Van
Derveer, saw a need to commemorate these 1863 battles. For years
they gathered support for setting aside a national military park en-
compassing the battlefields upon which the fighting took place. In
1889 a group of Union and Confederate veterans established the
Chickamauga Memorial Association which sponsored reunions at
Chickamauga and promoted the idea of a park. Adolph S. Ochs,
publisher of the *Chattanooga Times*, helped in making arrangements
for the reunions and in supporting the proposed park. In 1890 a bill
establishing the Chickamauga and Chattanooga National Military
Park was passed by Congress and signed by President Benjamin
Harrison; the park was formally dedicated in 1895.

Initially, the military park encompassed the Chickamauga Battlefield, the Orchard Knob reservation from which Grant and Thomas
directed the assault on Missionary Ridge, and on Missionary Ridge
itself, several small reservations including the location of Bragg's headquarters during the assault. The park also included the Signal Point
Reservation on Signal Mountain across the Tennessee River from Lookout Mountain; Signal Point was one of the sites used by the U.S. Signal
Corps during the siege of Chattanooga. The Cherokee name for the area
translates into "mountains looking at each other," a reference to the
facing of Signal Point and Lookout Mountain.

In 1898, Point Lookout and Craven's Terrace, where much of the
fighting took place in the Battle above the Clouds, were added to the
park. Adolph Ochs, by then the publisher of the *New York Times,* led
the movement to have these two areas preserved as part of the park. After these areas were added, Ochs was still concerned about too much
commercial development on Lookout Mountain, and so he along with

Tennessee River Gorge

others slowly acquired 3,700 acres on the sides of Lookout Mountain. In 1935, after Ochs's death, the group gave the land to the federal government to be included in the park.

Tennessee River Gorge

Adjacent to the Signal Point Reservation on Signal Mountain lies Prentice Cooper State Forest, a 26,000-acre woodland only 10 miles from downtown Chattanooga. The forest borders the Grand Canyon of the Tennessee River where the river cuts through Walden Ridge. The 1,200-foot-deep canyon is thought to be the fourth largest in the eastern United States, with steep forested slopes and cliffs. A state survey of the gorge found about 1,000 varieties of plants in the area, including the rare mountain mint, the rose gentian, and the endangered mountain skullcap.

The Tennessee River Gorge Trust, a local land conservation organization, is working to protect the Tennessee River Gorge along a 26-mile stretch of the river. At this writing, 14,037 acres of a proposed 25,000-acre area that includes Williams Island in the river have been given some kind of protection, mostly management agreements with public agencies and a gift of 1,200 acres by the Southern Division of Bowater, Inc. The Trust is working to preserve the biological diversity and the cultural ties to the land by working with private landowners to encourage good land stewardship in the remaining acreage.

The effort to save the Tennessee River Gorge began with a few individuals who recognized the scenic, biological, and cultural values of the region. They enlisted the help of the Nature Conservancy in setting up the Tennessee River Gorge Trust, which has since matured into an independent organization. The Trust was instrumental in preserving Williams Island, now owned by the state and managed by the Trust.

Eastern Escarpment Canyons

Although most of the drainage for the Cumberland Plateau is to the west, occasional creeks have managed to carve through the hard sandstone to flow eastward. Falling Water Creek, North Chickamauga Creek, and Soddy Creek northeast of Chattanooga flow east to drop off the plateau, eventually mingling their waters with the Tennessee River. These three creeks have formed impressive canyons in the eastern escarpment of the plateau and have been the focus of some preservation activities.

Conservationists across Tennessee are familiar with the numerous waterfalls and cascades in Falling Water Canyon. Part of the canyon has been purchased by the state and designated Falling Water Canyon State Natural Area to help preserve it from development and exploitation. Perhaps more of the canyon needs to be set aside.

To the north of Falling Water Canyon, Chickamauga Gulch, through which North Chickamauga Creek flows, has in the past been threatened with strip mining. In addition to its natural and scenic resources, Chickamauga Gulch also has historical significance; the watershed was a supply route for Union troops during the siege of Chattanooga. The Gulch has been set aside as the North Chickamauga Pocket Wilderness, another of the small wilderness areas established and managed by the Woodlands Division of Bowater Incorporated. The area is also a registered state natural area. A trail now enters the Gulch to give access to waterfalls, rock outcrops, and gorge views; along the way the trail passes through a coal mine area with gaping holes in the rock bluff. There are a couple of picnic tables at the creek and a primitive campsite at the end of the 4-mile trail.

Farther north, Soddy Creek has also carved a canyon in the eastern escarpment of the Plateau. Some mining has occurred in the canyon, but there have been recent efforts to reclaim some of the mined area.

Raccoon Mountain

On the south side of the Tennessee River Gorge, across the river from Prentice Cooper State Forest, stands Raccoon Mountain, an outlier of the Cumberland Plateau cut off from the rest of the plateau by the river. The Tennessee Valley Authority has constructed at the top of the mountain the Raccoon Mountain Pumped Storage Plant, one of the few such facilities in the country. When electric power is plentiful, water is pumped to the top of the mountain. When electricity demands increase during peak periods, the water from the storage lake is allowed to fall through generators to produce additional electricity.

On the opposite side of Raccoon Mountain, a cave system opens at the base of the mountain. Originally the cave was known as "Tennessee Caverns." The name was changed to "Crystal City Caves" when it was commercialized and promoted by Leo Lambert, who had commercialized Ruby Falls. Under later owners, the cave became "Crystal Caves" and then "Raccoon Mountain Caverns." Guided tours are offered daily.

Ruby Falls

Lookout Mountain Cave is buried in the heart of Lookout Mountain, running for a length of 1.5 miles through the mountain. The main entrance was closed in 1908 when the Southern Railway with a force of Mexican laborers tunneled through the mountain cutting across the cave opening.

In 1928 a group of men from Gary, Indiana, led by Leo Lambert, decided to drill from above in an attempt to reopen the cave. At 260 feet they unexpectedly hit a cave nearer the surface than the original cave. Lambert went down to explore and emerged 17 hours later with a tale of an underground waterfall. On his second exploration, Lambert took his wife, Ruby, and named the 145-foot waterfall "Ruby Falls."

The cave in which the waterfall was discovered has no natural entrance; the waterfall had been sealed within the mountain until Lambert arrived. The group continued drilling and hit the old cave at 420 feet.

Although Lookout Mountain Cave is now closed, the Ruby Falls Cave, now called "Lookout Mountain Caverns," is open to the public with an admission fee. The visitor center is a small rock castle sitting atop an elevator shaft that takes visitors down to the level of the cave; the castle is now on the National Register of Historic Places.

The Georgia Corner

Covenant College stands on Lookout Mountain a few miles southwest of Chattanooga where the Cumberland Plateau lies across the northwest corner of Georgia. The liberal arts Presbyterian College is housed in the old Lookout Mountain Hotel, which was once called "Castle in the Clouds." The hotel operated only from 1928 to 1930. The towered hotel building can be seen from miles away and is a landmark on this part of Lookout Mountain.

Covenant College

Farther south on the mountain lies Cloudland Canyon State Park, a 2,000-acre Georgia park that surrounds a deep rock-walled canyon in the western side of Lookout Mountain. Overlooks provide expansive views, and a hiking trail leads to waterfalls within the gorge.

Directions and Services

Chattanooga is located in the southeast corner of Tennessee at the junction of interstates 75 and 24. You can get information on the city at the **Chattanooga Visitors Center** downtown on Broad Street next to the Tennessee Aquarium.

The fourth largest city in the state, Chattanooga has plenty of accommodations. The **Read House** opened on Broad Street in 1926 and is on the National Register of Historic Places. **Adam's Hilborne Inn** on Vine Street resides at the edge of the Fort Wood Historic District in an 1889 mayor's mansion. The **Bluff View Inn** stands in the Bluff View Art District at the corner of High and East Second Streets. The **Chattanooga Choo Choo/Holiday Inn,** a 30-acre complex, includes a renovation of the 1909 Southern Railway Terminal Station on Market Street along with restaurants, sleeping quarters in restored train cars as well as traditional rooms, swimming pools, tennis courts, and one of the largest model railroad displays in the world. The terminal building is on the National Register of Historic Places.

If you're a railroad buff, you'll probably also want to see the **Tennessee Valley Railroad Museum,** which has two depots, on Cromwell Road and on North Chamberlain. The two depots are connected by a 6-mile, steam-locomotive train ride that takes you through a tunnel in Missionary Ridge. The museum is one of the largest railroad museums in the country and has working steam and diesel locomotives, rail cars, and other equipment. There is an admission fee. The museum is open daily June through August, and weekends in the fall and spring; large groups can book a train trip in winter. Special trips, called "Dixie Land Excursions," run into the mountains of northwest Georgia.

You'll also find in the city the **Chattanooga Regional History**

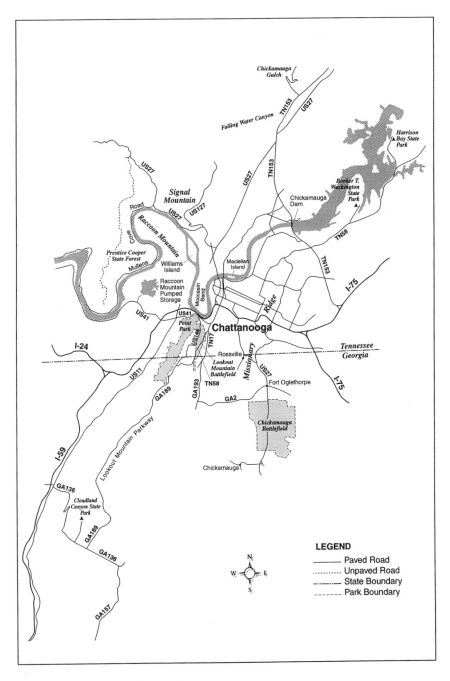

Lookout Mountain North and Chattanooga Vicinity

Museum on Chestnut Street. At the northern end of Chestnut Street, you'll find **Ross's Landing;** the small city park is the approximate location of the landing and ferry established by John Ross about 1816. He sold the landing in 1826 and moved south into Georgia to locate close to the center of what remained of the Cherokee Nation. Though only one-eighth Cherokee at most, Ross was elected the principal chief of the Cherokees and served from 1828 to 1866. Although he objected to the treaties that took the Cherokee lands, his objections were ignored and he was compelled to lead his people to Oklahoma along the Trail of Tears when the Cherokees were rounded up and forced to leave in 1838. In the same year, the community of Ross's Landing was renamed "Chattanooga." The park today contains a boat dock and launch and picnic tables and is the location of the Southern Belle Riverboat, on which you can take sightseeing cruises. The nearby **Tennessee Aquarium** opened in 1992 and is one of the largest freshwater aquariums in the world.

Just upstream from Ross's Landing, you'll see in the river **Maclellan Island,** a woodland preserve that is inaccessible except by boat. The Chattanooga Audubon Society manages the island, where it conducts guided walks and environmental education classes; contact the society if you want to visit. Their office is located at **Audubon Acres,** a 130-acre sanctuary beside South Chickamauga Creek in the East Brainerd Community that the general public can enter with a small admission fee. The society also administers **Audubon Mountain,** a 500-acre preserve along Sale Creek off US27 north of Chattanooga.

The **John Ross House** was built in 1797 by Ross's grandfather, John McDonald, the agent for the British and later for the Spanish who helped supply the Chickamaugas in their resistance to the encroachments of white settlers on their land. Moved a few hundred feet out of the path of commercial development in the 1960s, the house still stands off Chickamauga Avenue behind the John Ross Restaurant in Rossville, Georgia, just south of Chattanooga. The house is open during the summer months in the afternoons, except on Wednesday.

Off Amnicola Highway lies **Tennessee Riverpark** along the Tennessee River. The park includes fishing piers, boat launches, picnicking facilities, and a jogging/walking path. This end of the park is anchored by TVA's Chickamauga Dam, crossed by TN153. The park heads southwest to Ross's Landing and crosses the river on the Walnut Street Pedestrian Bridge; eventually the park will extend westward along the north shore of the river, a total of 22 miles. On the north bank of the river, you'll find the **North Chickamauga Creek Greenway,** where North Chickamauga Creek flows toward the Tennessee River just below the dam. To get to the greenway, take the first exit off TN153 on the north side of the river and go east; then turn left across from the Chickamauga Lock. You'll find here picnic tables, a boat launch, two paved trails for walking and jogging, and a longer trail on a gravel road along North Chickamauga Creek. Adjacent to the greenway, the Tennessee Valley Authority has established on the Chickamauga Dam reservation a 200-acre **Big Ridge Small Wild Area** with a 1.3-mile loop trail through old-growth forest.

Nearby **Booker T. Washington State Park** was originally established as a "Negro Park" on the shores of Chickamauga Reservoir above Chickamauga Dam on lands first leased and then deeded to the state by the Tennessee Valley Authority. The park is north of Chattanooga off TN58 on Champion Road. It has a group camp and group lodge along with swimming, boating, fishing, and picnicking.

Farther north on TN58 you'll also find **Harrison Bay State Park** on the shore of Chickamauga Lake; take the Harrison Bay Road. The park has a campground with 260 sites for tents and trailers, a marina and restaurant, swimming, tennis, and picnicking.

US27 south from Chattanooga takes you just across the state boundary into Georgia and through the Chickamauga Battlefield, part of the **Chickamauga and Chattanooga National Military Park,** the oldest and largest military park in the country. A visitor center at the northern end of the park provides information and an excellent multimedia show.

South of the Chickamauga Battlefield, you can find the historic **Gordon-Lee Mansion** in Chickamauga, Georgia. James Gordon, an early settler and mill owner had the house built in 1840 to 1847. During the Civil War, it served as General Rosecrans's headquarters prior

Gordon-Lee Mansion

to the Battle of Chickamauga and then as a hospital during the fighting. Now on the National Register, the mansion is a bed and breakfast; reservations are recommended. You can also tour the house in the afternoons for a modest fee. South of the battlefield on US27, turn right on Lee/Gordon Mill Road; keep going straight ahead 2.5 miles through several intersections to the Town of Chickamauga; you'll find the mansion on the right. A left turn at the junction of US27 and Lee/Gordon Mill Road will take you by **Lee and Gordon's Mill.** After making the turn, take a sharp right at the next intersection and you'll see the mill on the left sitting beside a creek. The mill is on private property and so must be viewed from the road.

Crest Drive in Chattanooga takes you along **Missionary Ridge,** where the Confederate forces overlooked the city during the siege of Chattanooga. All along the 7.2-mile drive, you'll find monuments and Civil War cannons sitting among large homes crowning the ridgetop. There's not much room to park except at the Bragg and Sherman Reservations, but a long walk along Crest Drive will allow you to stop and read the many plaques.

The **Orchard Knob Reservation** is on Orchard Knob Avenue south of Third Street. It was atop this hill that Grant and Thomas faced the Confederate forces on Missionary Ridge. Southeast of Orchard Knob on Holtzclaw Avenue you'll find the **National Cemetery,** which was established in November 1863 as a place to bury Union soldiers who died in the Civil War battles around Chattanooga.

To get to **Signal Point,** take US127 northwest out of Chattanooga. The highway is a winding road that climbs the escarpment of the plateau. At the top of this road, you are in the vicinity of the girlhood home of Emma Bell Miles, the turn-of-the-century writer who depicted the mountain community and its people in *The Spirit of the Mountains.* Just as you reach the plateautop, turn west off US127 in the town of Signal Mountain and follow the signs to Signal Point Park. You'll turn into the park past the Alexian Brothers Rest Home which incorporates the old Signal Mountain Inn built in 1913. From Signal Point you have a panoramic view of the Tennessee River Gorge as it cuts through the Cumberland Plateau. Before the waters were backed up by TVA's Nickajack Dam downstream, the Tennessee River developed many rapids and whirlpools as it passed through the gorge; one of these whirlpools, the Suck, which was formed as Suck Creek entered the river, sunk many boats as they tried to make their way downstream. As you walk down to the point to view the gorge, you'll find to the right the southern end of the Cumberland Trail. The Cumberland Trail Conference, with the help of volunteer college students, recently renovated this trail head with stairs and ramps to improve access down the bluff.

You can reach **Prentice Cooper State Forest** along TN27 off US127 northwest of Chattanooga. Mullins Cove Road leads west at a junction for a drive through the **Tennessee River Gorge**. From that junction, TN27 climbs the plateau along Suck Creek; in 4 miles turn left toward the state forest. You'll make another left turn in 0.3 mile; the road becomes gravel and enters the state forest. This main road is called Tower Drive because it passes by the forest-fire tower. At road's end in 12 miles, you'll be rewarded with a panoramic view of the Tennessee River Gorge. The forest includes the 350-acre **Hicks Gap State Nature Area,** which protects scenic bluffs and a population of endangered large-flowered skullcap.

Williams Island, managed by the Tennessee River Gorge Trust, is accessible only by boat. A hiking trail system offers wildlife viewing, and a primitive campground has been constructed. You must obtain a permit from the Trust office to visit the island; the staff will facilitate transportation to the island for groups.

You can reach **Falling Water Canyon, Chickamauga Gulch,** and **Soddy Creek Canyon** northwest of Chattanooga on TN153 or US27 toward Soddy-Daisy. At this writing, the state is in the process of constructing a trail into the 100-acre Falling Water Canyon State Natural Area; the trail will start at a parking area on Levi Road and lead to 110-foot Falling Water Falls. Chickamauga Gulch in the North Chickamauga Pocket Wilderness is off Montlake Road, which is just after TN153 crosses North Chickamauga Creek. You'll find Soddy Creek Canyon farther north; where the highway crosses the creek you can look up into the canyon.

To get to **Raccoon Mountain Caverns,** take I-24 east of Chattanooga and get off at the Tiftonia exit on US41 headed west. In 1.3 miles, you'll find the entrance. The cave has a commercial tour of 0.5 mile and a special 4-mile tour for the more adventurous. There's also a campground.

Visitors are welcome at the **TVA Raccoon Mountain Pumped Storage Plant,** which is 1.2 miles farther west on US41 from Raccoon Mountain Caverns. Turn right into the TVA reservation, and you'll travel along the Tennessee River, which at this point is called "Nickajack Lake" because TVA's Nickajack Dam has backed up the waters toward Chattanooga. You'll then ascend Raccoon Mountain to its top where you'll find the man-made lake. At the visitor center, you can take a tour of the facility by descending 1,000 feet in a 17-MPH elevator into the depths of the mountain. You'll see there the most powerful reversible pumps in the world, which pump water to the top of the mountain and then are reversed to become generators when the water is allowed to flow back down to river level.

Thirteen miles farther west on US41 from the pumped storage

plant, you'll find the **Marion County Park** on Nickajack Lake, where you can camp.

Near the base of Lookout Mountain on the western side lies the 300-acre **Reflection Riding** nature preserve and arboretum, with over 1,000 species of native wildflowers, trees, and shrubs. The park has several hiking trails and a 7.3-mile motor nature trail. The **Chattanooga Nature Center** is at the park entrance. There is an admission. To get to Reflection Riding, take Broad Street out of Chattanooga; the street becomes US41 which ascends the shoulder of Lookout Mountain. Continue west on US41 past the junction with TN148 down the west side of the mountain and watch for signs directing you to the park. You'll turn left on TN318 and then right on Garden Road for 1 mile.

To get to **Point Park** on Lookout Mountain, part of the national battlefield, take US41 and turn left on TN148, also called "Lookout Mountain Scenic Highway," and follow the signs as you continue your ascent of Lookout Mountain. If you are coming from the Chickamauga Battlefield, take GA2 west from US27; then turn right on GA193, which joins TN17, which connects with US41 and heads left up the mountain. The drive along 193 and 17 through the Chattanooga Creek Valley affords a good view of the Lookout Mountain escarpment. Or you may want to ride the **Lookout Mountain Incline Railway** on St. Elmo Avenue. This is the steepest passenger incline railway in the world and is on the National Historic Register. Point Park is a short walk from the upper station. The entrance gate to the park was built by the Army Corps of Engineers and resembles the Corps's castle insignia. A visitor center stands near the entrance. The park includes the **Ochs Museum** at Point Lookout, dedicated to Adolph Ochs for his efforts in establishing the national battlefield, and the **Cravens House** on Willingham Road, where the Confederates defending the mountain during the Battle above the Clouds headquartered and where some of the fiercest fighting took place. Robert Cravens built the house in 1856 and rebuilt it in 1866 after it was destroyed during the war.

You may also want to go by **Battles for Chattanooga** on East Brow Road next to the Point Park Visitor Center. The museum houses dioramas of the Chickamauga and Chattanooga battles. It's open daily; there is a fee.

The visitor center for **Ruby Falls** is on TN148 as you come up Lookout Mountain. With an admission fee, you are led on a tour of the cave to the foot of Ruby Falls, an impressive sight that unfortunately has accompanying colored lights and music.

You can reach **Rock City** atop Lookout Mountain by taking TN58 up the mountain beginning on St. Elmo Avenue near the Incline Railway. Or if you have been to Ruby Falls and Point Park, just follow the signs that direct you along the streets atop the mountain to Rock City, which is across the state border in Georgia. With an admission fee, you can tour the gardens, walk out to Lover's Leap, and visit Fairyland Caverns.

South from this northern end of Lookout Mountain, several roads combine to form the **Lookout Mountain Parkway,** which follows the ridge of Lookout Mountain all the way to Gadsden, Alabama. When TN148 crosses the state line into Georgia it becomes GA189, which winds along the ridge of the mountain past **Covenant College.**

Continuing on GA189 to a right on GA136, you'll come to **Cloudland Canyon State Park.** The park has 75 campsites with electric and water hookups and fully equipped cottages. The older cottages sit on the edge of the canyon. The cottages, and even some of the campsites, may be reserved. Tennis and swimming are offered.

The Lookout Mountain Parkway continues south on GA189 and then GA157 until it crosses the state line into Alabama, where it becomes AL117 which leads to Mentone. Here the parkway takes county road 89 south, which is also the DeSoto Parkway.

If you descend the western side of Lookout Mountain from Mentone on AL117, you can then turn north on US11 to **Sequoyah Caverns,** which opens on the eastern side of Sand Mountain, an outlier of the Plateau that runs parallel to Lookout Mountain across Wills Valley to the west. Named for the Cherokee who created the Cherokee language syllabary, Sequoyah is a commercial cave that bills itself as "The Looking Glass Caverns"; it has many pools which reflect the cave ceiling, a unique approach to presenting a cave to visitors. Sequoyah Caverns is about 35 miles southwest of Chattanooga. You can take I-59 south to the Sulphur Springs Road exit and then turn south on US11 until a sign directs you to turn west; or if you are coming from the south, take the Valley Head exit and take US11 north. There is a campground at the cave, and a small herd of buffalo roams the grounds.

Trails

In Chattanooga, you can walk the streets of the city to see several sites listed on the National Register of Historic Places, and otherwise take driving or biking tours of the city and its neighborhoods to visit such places as Ross's Landing, the Read House, the Tennessee Aquarium, and the Chattanooga Choo Choo. Check with the Chattanooga Visitors Center on Broad Street for self-guided tour maps and recommendations on places to visit.

Many trails crisscross the Chickamauga Battlefield, including the 20-mile **Perimeter Trail,** the 6-mile **Confederate Line Trail,** and the 14-mile **Cannon Trail.**

Point Park has several hiking trails around the lip of Lookout Mountain, including the **Bluff Trail** which encircles the northeast end of the mountain and passes by Sunset Rock, and the **Upper** and **Lower Truck Trails** which travel along the northwest flank of the mountain.

On the northwest side of the mountain, on TN318 about 50 yards southeast of the trailhead for the **Skyuka Trail,** you'll find the small **Skyuka Arch,** which is 0.5 mile west on TN318 from its junction with TN148; watch for a "no parking" sign. The arch has a clearance of only 4.5 feet, but it is an interesting arch to see. The arch-shaped rock is sandstone while the surrounding bedrock is siltstone. The most likely explanation is that the arch originated atop the mountain, perhaps as the opening to a cave or spring, but then fell, coming to rest in its present location, forming an arch. Small arches formed by rockfall are common, but because the arch probably took its arch shape in another location before actually becoming an arch, the Skyuka Trail Arch is unique, possibly the only such arch in the world.

A much larger arch is located atop Lookout Mountain. This little-known bridge, the **Lookout Mountain Natural Bridge,** is hidden in a

Cloudland Canyon Waterfall

ravine between the Good Shepherd Episcopal Church and Bragg Avenue off TN148, which is also part of the Lookout Mountain Parkway. TN148 crosses a bridge over the ravine. On Bragg Avenue, you'll find a sign, "Natural Bridge Park," and a footpath that leads down into the ravine where you'll find the arch, 85 feet long with a clearance of 14 feet. There's no parking at the trailhead, but you'll find a pulloff about 50 yards south of the sign. Nearby once stood the Natural Bridge Hotel, which at one time was owned by the Southern Spiritualists' Association. Daily meetings at the hotel in 1885 included seances; later, meetings were held in a separate pavilion. The retreat was abandoned about 1890.

In Prentice Cooper State Forest along the 10.5-mile section of the **Cumberland Trail** that passes through the area, you'll have several overlooks of the Tennessee River Gorge before the trail ends its north-south traverse of Tennessee at Signal Point Park. The state forest contains about 30 miles of hiking trails. In addition to the Cumberland Trail, you can walk the 10-mile **Mullen's Cove Loop Trail** and the 12-mile **Pot Point Loop Trail.** The campsites along the trails are primitive, having only pit toilets and a fire ring. There are also many miles of old forest roads that can be used for horse riding and all-terrain bicycling.

Harrison Bay State Park has a 1-mile **Oak Valley Nature Trail.** Cloudland Canyon State Park has 6 miles of backcountry trail as well as the 4.5-mile **West Rim Loop Trail** and a 0.5-mile **Waterfall Trail,** which branches off the West Rim Trail to take you along a series of wooden stairs and walkways down to two 50-foot waterfalls on Daniel Creek.

References

Coggins, Allen R. "The Early History of Tennessee's State Parks, 1919–1956." *Tennessee Historical Quarterly* 43, no. 3 (Fall 1984): 295–315.

Corgan, James X., and John T. Parks. *Natural Bridges of Tennessee.* Bulletin 80. Nashville: Tennessee Division of Geology, 1979.

Govan, Gilbert E., and James W. Livingood. *The Chattanooga Country, 1540–1976: From Tomahawks to TVA.* Knoxville: Univ. of Tennessee Press, 1977.

Hawks, Graham, Jr., director, Tennessee River Gorge Trust. Interview with author. Oct. 4, 1991.

Homecoming '86 Committee. "Lookout Mountain Trail Map." Brochure. Lookout Mountain, TN, no date.

Lane, James D. "Backpacking in Chattanooga's Backyard: Prentice Cooper State Forest." *Tennessee Conservationist,* May–June 1985, 10–11.

Massey, Barbara, group sales coordinator, Rock City, Lookout Mountain, GA. Conversations with author. June 6, 1986, and Nov. 6, 1991.

McDaniel, Anthonette L. "'Just Watch Us Make Things Hum': Chattanooga, Adolph S. Ochs, and the Memorialization of the Civil War." *East Tennessee Historical Society's Publications* 61 (1989): 3–15.

McDonough, James Lee. *Chattanooga: A Death Grip on the Confederacy.* Knoxville: Univ. of Tennessee Press, 1984.

"Moccasin Bend Area Designated as National Historic Landmark." *Tennes-Sierran,* Oct. 1986, 2.

"North Chickamauga Creek Petition for Lands Unsuitable for Mining." *Tennes-Sierran,* May 1987, 5–7.

Parker, Lin C. "Reconstructing Our Vanishing Heritage (Williams Island)." *Chattanooga News–Free Press,* Dec. 6, 1987. Rpt. *Tennes-Sierran,* Jan. 1988, 4–5, 10.

Patten, Cartter. *Signal Mountain and Walden's Ridge.* Signal Mountain, TN: Cartter Patten, 1962.

Rawlins, Wade. "The Tennessee River Gorge: A Sacred Trust." *Tennessee Conservationist,* Nov.–Dec. 1990, 19–23.

Tucker, Glenn. *The Battle of Chickamauga.* Eastern Acorn Press, 1969.

———. *The Battles for Chattanooga.* Eastern Acorn Press, 1971.

U.S. Dept. of the Interior, National Park Service. "Chickamauga and Chattanooga National Military Park." Brochure. Washington, DC, no date.

———. "Chickamauga Battlefield." Brochure. Washington, DC, June 1973.

———. "Chickamauga Battlefield Trail Guide." Brochure. Washington, DC, no date.

———. "Lookout Mountain." Brochure. Washington, DC, June 1973.

Walker, Robert Sparks. *Lookout: The Story of a Mountain.* Kingsport, TN: Southern Publishers, 1941.

Chapter 16

Little River Canyon

Cotton fields and the flat coastal plain are usually what you think of when Alabama is mentioned. But the Cumberland Plateau adds mountains in the northeastern corner of the state.

Lookout Mountain, an outlier of the Plateau, extends southwest from Chattanooga through the northwestern tip of Georgia into Alabama. Atop the mountain, the Little River, an Alabama Wild and Scenic River and an Alabama Outstanding National Resource Water, flows along the ridgeline for its entire length until it turns east and empties into Weiss Lake on the Coosa River. Along its way, Little River carves a canyon that is one of the deepest and longest narrow canyons east of the Rocky Mountains.

The canyon is characteristic of Plateau canyons, with sheer rock walls of erosion-resistant sandstone dropping to wooded slopes that run down to the river. At its deepest, the river flows 600 to 700 feet below the canyon rim. The depths of the canyon give a sense of a prehistoric place—sandy beaches surrounding massive blocks of sandstone sitting at the river's edge. It's possible to spend the day wandering along the river, going for a swim, and sitting under a rock overhang without seeing another person.

Little River Canyon National Preserve

The scenic and recreational resources of Little River Canyon inevitably attracted national attention. The National Park Service conducted a study, held public hearings, and then recommended the establishment of a new park or recreation area at Little River Canyon. In 1992, Little River Canyon National Preserve was established by an act of the U.S.

Congress. The new preserve consists of 14,000 acres, including Alabama's DeSoto State Park and the adjacent Little River Wildlife Management Area, which is now called the "Special Use Unit," where hunting, ATV riding, camping, and horseback riding take place.

The centerpiece of the park is the Little River Canyon, an 11-mile river gorge, with an additional 5 miles of side canyons, often called the "Grand Canyon of the South." Perhaps the longest narrow river canyon in the eastern United States, Little River Canyon begins below the confluence of the East and West Forks of the Little River at Little River Falls, a 60-foot-high waterfall that at high volume is a thundering mass of water.

The Little River Canyon Rim Parkway, with numerous overlooks, follows the west rim of the canyon. About halfway south, the parkway loops around Bear Creek Canyon, a side canyon that contains Graces High Falls, at 120 feet probably the highest waterfall in Alabama, although it is seasonal with most water in spring and early summer. Since the waterfall is on the south side of Bear Creek Canyon, it can be seen easily only from the north side.

At the southern end of the preserve, the Canyon Mouth Park Unit contains a day-use area with newly renovated bathhouse and picnic tables. This former county park was donated to the preserve by Cherokee County.

DeSoto State Park

When Hernando DeSoto explored what would be the southeastern United States, he traveled through Alabama as far north as Tennessee. Whether he ever saw Little River Canyon is debatable.

But when the Rev. Daniel S. Butrick traveled through northeastern Alabama in 1823, stopping at an impressive waterfall on the West Fork of the Little River, he wrote in his journal of seeing an old fortress. A legend grew claiming that this fortress was built by DeSoto and his band of conquistadors to protect themselves from the natives they encountered. Although most historians and

DeSoto Falls

Little River Canyon

archeologists think the fortress was probably constructed by American Indians living in the area, the legend of DeSoto's visit remains in the name of the waterfall and the 3,600-acre Alabama state park on the West Fork of the Little River, which is now contained within Little River Canyon National Preserve.

DeSoto State Park consists of two segments. The northern-most piece is the area around DeSoto Falls on the West Fork. The 100-foot waterfall spills over a 20-foot ledge and then drops 80 feet into a pool of green water. The falls is just below the A. A. Miller Dam, built in 1925, the first hydroelectric dam in northern Alabama. Visitors to the park use the lake created by the dam for swimming, fishing, and boating.

To the south along the ridge of Lookout Mountain lies the main section of the park with visitor center, lodging, restaurant, and campgrounds. This complex of facilities is crisscrossed with trails, some of which skirt the shore of the West Fork, which flows through the park. Several small waterfalls can be found along these trails.

Noccalula Falls

To the south of the national preserve along Lookout Mountain lie other scenic areas. Yellow Creek Falls spills down the eastern slope of the plateau. Cherokee Rock Village along the crest is a maze of huge stone blocks.

At the southern end of Lookout Mountain, at Gadsden, Alabama, Black Creek plunges 90 feet into a rock gorge, creating Noccalula Falls. The waterfall is named for an Indian woman who, according to the story told in the region, jumped from the rim after her father refused to allow her to marry the man she loved.

Similar legends abound at numerous rock bluffs. Such legends voice the romantic inclination to believe that love is everything and love denied is life not worth living. We name such places "Lovers Leap." The legend at Noccalula Falls is likely no more true than those at any of the other sites.

Directions and Services

To get to **Little River Canyon National Preserve** and **DeSoto State Park,** take the Hammondville/Valley Head exit east off I-59. You'll be on AL117, which leads eventually to Mentone.

I-59 travels down Wills Valley, named for a Cherokee chief,

Noccalula Falls

Red-Headed Will. Wills Town was located in this vicinity, the town where Sequoyah lived and for a time worked on the syllabary that gave the Cherokees a written language. The nearby city of **Fort Payne** on US11 was originally a fort used in the roundup of the Cherokees in preparation for the march along the Trail of Tears. Today Fort Payne is known as the home of the country music band Alabama. The headquarters of the national preserve is located in Fort Payne on Gault Avenue; here you can get information for visiting the preserve and the surrounding area.

As you climb the plateau on AL117, you'll make a sharp right to enter the state park and then reach the top of the plateau at the **DeSoto Parkway**, which is county road 89 and also a segment of the Lookout Mountain Parkway that follows the ridge of Lookout Mountain south from Chattanooga to Gadsden. At this junction, Mentone lies 2 miles to the north; to the south you'll find the state park information center in 7 miles; and straight across the parkway, DeSoto Falls Road leads 1 mile to **DeSoto Falls.**

Or if you are coming from the south on I-59, you can take AL35 east through Fort Payne and climb the plateau to get to the southern end of the DeSoto Parkway; to the left in 5 miles you'll find the state park information center. Continue 5 miles farther east on AL35 and you'll reach the northern end of the **Little River Canyon Rim Parkway.**

Starting at the northern end of the DeSoto Parkway, you'll find lodging in Mentone, a small community dominated by the 1884 Victorian **Mentone Springs Hotel/Bed & Breakfast,** which also contains Caldwell's Restaurant. The hotel is on the National Register of Historic Places. A path leads down through the woods below the hotel to the springs for which the community was named. There's also the **Mentone Inn Bed & Breakfast**, a quaint inn built in 1927 and on the Alabama Register of Landmarks and Heritage.

Then south along the Parkway, you'll reach the turn on DeSoto Falls Road to DeSoto Falls. Continuing south, you'll pass **Cloudmont Ski & Golf Resort**, which has rental chalets, and its Shady Grove Dude Ranch has group lodging and horseback riding. You'll also pass the **Cragsmere Manna Restaurant** on the right, open Friday and Saturday

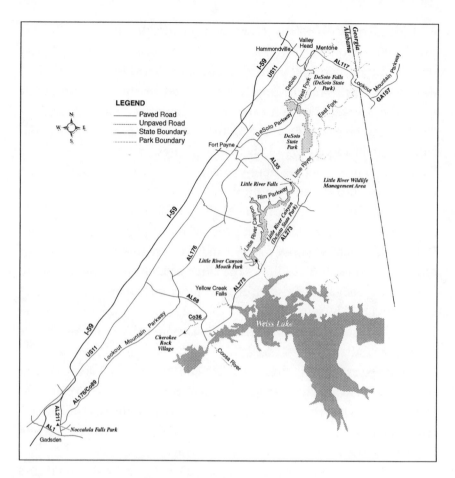

Little River Canyon and Lookout Mountain South

evenings. And then on your left, you'll see the **Comer Boy Scout Reservation.**

The Parkway makes a turn left and then right. If you do not make the right turn, you'll find just beyond the junction the **Sallie Howard Memorial Baptist Church** built in 1937 and now on the Alabama Register of Landmarks and Heritage. The chapel was built around a large boulder that serves as the back wall and part of the altar inside. Milford W. Howard, a U.S. congressman in the late 1800s, had the church built as a memorial to his first wife; upon his death, Howard's own ashes were placed inside the rock in the church.

From the church, go back and make the turn south to continue on the DeSoto Parkway. You'll then enter the main section of **DeSoto State Park**, which contains the information center, a country store, a campground, a lodge with a restaurant, chalets and rustic cabins, tennis courts, a swimming pool, and a picnic area. You can make reservations for the cabins and chalets and the lodge guest units. The lodge is an interesting construction that incorporates the old stone lodge built by the Civilian Conservation Corps in the 1930s; the state did not merely add on to the lodge, but built around it. The rustic cabins were also built by the CCC and contain original handmade furniture.

A half mile south from the state park, you can also find accommodations at **Adams Outdoors**, offering tent camping and rustic huts along with more plush cabins. Turn east on Gray Road, and then in another half mile at a sign turn right on Mitchell Road. Adams Outdoors also has canoes and rafts for rent and offers guided raft trips on the Little River.

Along the parkway south of the park, you'll pass **DeSoto Woods Preserve,** a 50-acre tract purchased by the Nature Conservancy to protect a 100-year-old stand of upland forest. At this writing, the location is not marked, but the conservancy intends to establish a nature walk through the area.

You can then continue south on the DeSoto Parkway to its end at AL35; turn east and follow AL35 until you come to the **Little River Canyon Rim Parkway** to the south, which follows portions of AL176 and county road 275. This 22-mile parkway follows the edge of the Little River Canyon through the national preserve with several overlooks that have picnic tables and impressive views of the canyon. **Little River Falls Overlook** lies near the beginning of the parkway. Rock climbing in the canyon is a popular activity, but only experts should try the 200-foot rock walls.

At the end of the parkway, the Little River turns east, leaving Lookout Mountain. Where the river emerges from the mountain, you'll find the **Little River Canyon Mouth Park Unit**, a national preserve day-use area that you can reach off the southern end of the Rim Parkway or off AL273 between AL35 and AL68.

From Little River Canyon National Preserve, you can head south to see other attractions along Lookout Mountain. **Yellow Creek Falls**, a large waterfall where Yellow Creek spills down the side of Lookout Mountain to join Weiss Lake, can be seen from AL273 south of the entrance to the Canyon Mouth Park Unit. Just as you cross a causeway over the upper end of Weiss Lake, you'll see the waterfall on the mountainside behind an old bridge of the Tennessee-Alabama-Georgia Railway that ran from Chattanooga to Gadsden.

Cherokee Rock Village is a wonderful maze of massive boulders. To get to this county park, take county road 36 south from AL68 between AL273 and AL176. In 1.5 miles, turn left on an unmarked road. You'll come to a T where you'll turn right and then drive 2.8 miles to the end of the road, where you'll find the rock village and views to the east off the plateau.

You can get to **Noccalula Falls** by continuing south along AL176/Co89, part of the Lookout Mountain Parkway, or by heading for Gadsden on I-59. You'll find the waterfall at Noccalula Falls Park in Gadsden, a city park that has a "world of things to do." All the development around the falls disturbs the natural setting, but if you're in the area, the falls is worth the visit. The park includes a campground with 250 sites that have water and electric hookups, a bathhouse, and a country store. You'll also find a swimming pool, tennis courts, a pioneer village, botanical gardens, and a scaled-down replica of a steam-engine train that offers rides around the park.

Trails

Standing at the top of DeSoto Falls and facing downstream, you'll see a bluff on the right where remains of stone walls mark the site of the old fort. You can hike the unmaintained 0.5-mile **Welsh Caves Trail** to get to that point. Go back along DeSoto Falls Road from the falls a half-mile to a small pulloff on the left. The trail enters the woods and follows the ridgeline around to the site of the fort walls, which are now only faint rock lines. The stone walls were once 4 to 6 feet high and 2 to 4

The Welch Caves

feet wide, but most of the rocks were scavenged to build homes in the area. Just before and also beyond the wall site, you'll have long-distance views of DeSoto Falls.

On this trail you can also see the "Welsh Caves." Several paths lead to the right over the edge of the bluff; the one you need is at 0.3 mile from the parking area, before the first DeSoto Falls overlook. You'll climb down the bluff's edge to a ledge and then walk left to find several caves in the rock wall; there are some dropoffs here, so be careful. One theory speculates that the caves were used by the legendary Welshman Madoc, who supposedly discovered the New World long before Columbus. The caves have been obviously enlarged with connecting tunnels and so must have been inhabited at one time, but most likely by native Americans that once frequented the area.

The main section of DeSoto State Park, where you find the campground and accommodations, contains 20 miles of scenic day-hiking trails, including the **Azalea Cascade Interpretive Trail** and the **Rhododendron Trail.**

The 12-mile **DeSoto Scout Trail** follows the West Fork of the Little River from the Comer Boy Scout Camp on the DeSoto Parkway through the state park to AL35, passing through the Preserve Special Use Unit. At this writing the trail is in disrepair but will likely be upgraded; check with the state park or the preserve headquarters.

Several miles of unpaved roads travel through the **Special Use Unit,** formerly the Little River Wildlife Management Area. You can use the roads for horseback and ATV riding; you must obtain a permit from the preserve headquarters for ATV use. Three primitive campsites accommodate four people each, first come, first served.

Along the Little River Canyon Rim Parkway, a short loop trail leads down from **Little River Falls Overlook.** Another short trail leads into the Canyon from the overlook at **Elberhart Point,** which is at the southern corner of the junction of Bear Creek Canyon and Little River Canyon. This trail is the primary route used by paddlers to reach the river. Only experienced paddlers should try the Little River, which has Class III–VI rapids. After July there's usually not enough water in the river to make a run.

The only other access to the canyon, other than at the canyon mouth, is the **Powell Trail** toward the southern end of the parkway; watch for a sign and small parking area. The trail drops from the parkway road to the river's edge in less than a mile. This is also an access for paddlers; the stretch of the river from here down is more tame than the upper sections.

A rough trail exists along the 5-mile stretch of the river between

Elberhart Point and the Powell Trail; this is part of the old **Little River Canyon Trail** that has been devastated by floods. The trail will be up-graded in time, but for now should only be tried by experienced hikers. From the Canyon Mouth Park Unit at the southern end of the preserve, you can walk an easy section of the trail that has been restored upstream along the river for a mile. At the end of that section, experienced hikers may ford Johnnies Creek and continue on a rough section of trail into the canyon.

The 36-mile **Lookout Mountain Trail** connects Little River Canyon Preserve with the city of Gadsden toward the southern end of Lookout Mountain. While at this writing the trail is a bit in dis-repair, the path is still walkable and volunteers should be upgrading it soon. On its way south, the trail passes by Yellow Creek Falls and through Cherokee Rock Village and ends at Paseur Park, a city park in Gadsden on Highland Street near Noccalula Falls. The path is marked with a white blaze.

An overall Lookout Mountain Trail is proposed as a system of trails to cover the entire length of Lookout Mountain from Gadsden to Chattanooga. At Little River Canyon Preserve, a rebuilt Lookout Mountain Trail north would overlap a restored Little River Canyon Trail and the old DeSoto Boy Scout Trail to the Comer Scout Reservation. From the Reservation, the trail would follow the DeSoto Parkway to DeSoto Falls. The way north from DeSoto Falls has not yet been designated, but the trail would pass through Cloudland Canyon State Park in Georgia and eventually link with the Bluff Trail to Point Park in Lookout Mountain Battlefield overlooking Chattanooga.

Once the Lookout Mountain Trail is built and when the Cumberland Trail is completed, you will be able to walk virtually the entire length of the Cumberland Plateau—south through Kentucky along the Sheltowee Trace National Recreation Trail from the northern limit of the Daniel Boone National Forest through the Big South Fork National River and Recreation Area; then switching from the western side of the Plateau to the eastern escarpment, south along the Cumberland Trail through Tennessee from Cumberland

Gap National Historical Park to Signal Point Park above the Tennessee River Gorge; then after crossing the river to Lookout Mountain, along the Lookout Mountain Trail through Georgia and Alabama from Point Park to Paseur Park in Gadsden.

References

Alabama Dept. of Conservation. "DeSoto State Park." Brochure. Montgomery, 1989.

————. "DeSoto State Park on Lookout Mountain." Brochure. Montgomery, 1989.

————. "Trail Highlights." Brochure. Montgomery, 1989.

————. "Welcome to DeSoto State Park." Brochure. Montgomery, 1989.

Benefield, Dennis. "The Caves: What Historical People Lived in Caves near DeSoto Falls?" *Fort Payne Times–Journal,* Oct. 15, 1978, 1–2.

Butler, Talmadge, park manager, DeSoto State Park. Conversation with author. Sept. 11, 1986.

————. Interview with author. May 1, 1991.City of Gadsden. "Noccalula Falls Park." Brochure. Gadsden, AL, no date. Crownover, Danny. Interview with author. May 12, 1991.

————. "Lookout Mountain's J. F. Kennedy Trail." Brochure. Montgomery: Alabama Bureau of Tourism and Travel, 1984.

DeKalb Baptist Assn. "Sallie Howard Memorial Chapel." Brochure. Rainsville, AL, no date.

Horne, Sandra, Little River Canyon National Preserve. Conversation with author. July 23, 1998

Walker, Robert Sparks. *Lookout: The Story of a Mountain.* Kingsport, TN: Southern Publishers, 1941.

Epilogue

While exploring Little River Canyon before it became a national preserve, I stood at one of the overlooks next to a stranger, an older man, about my size but chunky with a noticeable paunch—probably not a hiker. We both gazed into the deep canyon, where a silver ribbon of water made its way through green forest below tall rock bluffs.

"Somethin', isn't it?" he said without turning from the view.

"Yeah," I agreed as I looked his way.

"I come up here 'bout once a week just to look into the canyon. My wife wonders about me, doesn't understand why I come." He finally glanced in my direction with a smile at one side of his mouth. "I brought her here once," he said as he turned back to the canyon. "Said she liked it, but doesn't see the need to come all the time. But I still come."

We looked in silence again, both understanding why we were there.

He turned to me a second time and asked if I needed a place to camp. We glanced at the clouds that mottled the sky. I hadn't thought much about where to spend the night, so I told him I did. He gave me directions to a rock overhang on the edge of the canyon where I could take shelter.

I followed his directions to the place along the canyon he had indicated and parked my car behind some trees and bushes so it wouldn't be quite so noticeable to any joyriders that passed by. I grabbed my last peanut butter sandwich, an apple, and a water bottle; pulled sleeping bag and pad from the trunk; and then followed a faint path through the scrub pine forest along the lip of the gorge.

I found a gap in the rock just as he had said I would. Back from the canyon edge it was as if the rock had separated, leaving a rock incline that led toward the gorge and opened on the canyon wall. As I walked down the incline, the rock sides of the gap rose 5 or 6 feet over my head on either side before I arrived at the lip of the canyon.

Right at the edge was the overhang, open on two sides as if someone had hollowed out the left-hand wall of the passageway, creating a space the size of a small room that opened to the canyon.

It was not yet dark, so I dropped my gear and walked back to the top of the canyon rim where I had noticed a path that led among boulders down the canyon. I thought I might be able to get to the river. Scrambling down the rocks, I found I had guessed correctly and was able to climb down to the riverbank. In the solitude of the place, I stripped off my clothes and plunged into the water to wash off the sweat and grime I had accumulated while exploring that day.

Back in my shelter, I started a small fire with a few sticks that were lying about. As I sat cross-legged by the warmth, with the night coming on, I ate the snacks I had brought along.

With a final drink from my water bottle, I spread the pad and sleeping bag under the shelter and crawled in to watch the dying fire, my feet only a few inches from a 100-foot drop into the canyon.

Sometime during the night I woke, as I frequently do when sleeping on the ground. The fire was just a few glowing coals. I shifted to look from under my rock shelter up through the crack in the rock to the sky. The clouds had gone and left a star-studded night.

As I looked, my eyes caught a silhouette, a black object at the top of the opposite rock wall protruding into the space created by the gap in the rock bluff. Probably just a fallen tree, a log jutting over the edge. Trouble was I didn't remember a log being there.

I thought of the rumors of mountain lions, or cougars, that still roam the secluded coves and ridges of the southern Appalachians— "panthers," the local people call them. Despite several purported sightings, no one as yet has produced any physical evidence: no photograph, no paw print, no scat. The great cat's existence on the Cumberland Plateau or in the southern Appalachians remains a mystery.

If indeed what I was looking at was the head of an animal—an animal watching me—it must eventually shift position or draw back, I thought. So I resolved to stare it down, not knowing what I would do if I detected any movement.

As incredible as it now seems, I fell asleep while on watch.

When I awoke, the coals from my fire had grown dark. The sky remained bright with stars. And the silhouette was gone.

The head had been too large to have been that of a common cat or a 'possum. It had come and left too quietly to have been a dog or a human.

Whatever it had been, it had checked me out and left me in peace. Possibly it had planned on using my shelter for the remainder of the night. Possibly it wondered if I would make a decent meal. For whatever reason, it had decided not to roust this interloper.

Now when I sit and wonder about the occasional insanity of civilization, I like to think the presence of that night still roams in the solitude and mystery of the Cumberland Plateau. I wish for him, or her, shelter and good hunting.

Appendix 1

Conservation Groups

Chattanooga Audubon Society, Inc.
900 N. Sanctuary Road
Chattanooga, TN 37421
423/892-1499

Cumberland Trail Conference
Route 1, Box 219A
Pikeville, TN 37367

The Dogwood Alliance
P.O. Box 1598
Brevard, NC 28712

Friends of the Big South Fork
P.O. Box 5407
Oneida, TN 37841

Friends of the Obed, Cumberland
Co.
P.O. Box 220
Pleasant Hill, TN 38578

Friends of Scotts Gulf
16 W. Bockman Way
Sparta, TN 38583

Friends of South Cumberland
Recreation Area
Rt. 1, Box 2196
Monteagle, TN 37356

Lookout Mountain Trail
Association
615 Bellevue Dr.
Gadsden, AL 35904

National Parks & Conservation
Association
Southeast Regional Office
P.O. Box 930
Norris, TN 37828
423/494-7008

The Nature Conservancy
Alabama Field Office
2821-C 2nd Avenue S.
Birmingham, AL 35233
205/251-1155

The Nature Conservancy
Tennessee Field Office
50 Vantage Way, #250
Nashville, TN 37228
615/255-0303

The Nature Conservancy
Kentucky Chapter
642 West Main Street
Lexington, KY 40508
606/259-9655

Savage Gulf Preservation League
1589 Sparta Street
McMinnville, TN 37110

Save Our Cumberland Mountains
P.O. Box 479
Lake City, TN 37769
423/426-9455

Save Our Sequatchie
735 Broad St., #1107
Chattanooga, TN 37402

Sierra Club
Southeast Region (Alabama)
1330 21st Way South, Suite 100B
Birmingham, AL 35205
205/933-9111

Sierra Club
Midwest Region (Kentucky)
2460 Fairmount Blvd., #307
Cleveland Heights, OH 44106
216/791-9110

Sierra Club
Appalachian Region (Tennessee)
1447 Peachtree St. NE, #305
Atlanta, GA 30309
404/888-9778

TAGER
P.O. Box 4193
Chattanooga, TN 37405

Tennessee Citizens for Wilderness
   Planning
130 Tabor Road
Oak Ridge, TN 37830

Tennessee Environmental Council
1700 Hayes St., #101
Nashville, TN 37203
615/321-5075

Tennessee Native Plant Society
Department of Botany
University of Tennessee
Knoxville, TN 37996-1100
423/974-2256

Tennessee Recreation and Parks
  Association
226 Capitol Blvd., #500
Nashville, TN 37219
615/242-8772

Tennessee River Gorge Trust
Suite 104
25 Cherokee Boulevard
Chattanooga, TN 37405
423/266-0314

Tennessee Scenic Rivers
  Association
P.O. Box 159041
Nashville, TN 37215-9041

Tennessee Trails Association
P.O. Box 41446
Nashville, TN 37204

Appendix 2

Addresses and Telephone Numbers

Adams Hilborne Inn
801 Vine St.
Chattanooga, TN 37403
423/265-5000

Adams Outdoors
Rt. 1, Box 191-X
Fort Payne, AL 35967
256/845-2988

The Allardt Schoolhouse B&B
P.O. Box 115
Allardt, TN 38504
931/879-6560 or 931/879-8056

Barthell Coal Mining Camp
P.O. Box 53
Whitley City, KY 42653
888/550-5748

Battles for Chattanooga
1110 E. Brow Rd.
Lookout Mountain, TN 37409
423/821-2812

Bell County Chamber of Commerce
P.O. Box 788
Middlesboro, KY 40965
606/248-1075

Big South Fork National River and
    Recreation Area
Rt. 3, Box 401
Oneida, TN 37841
931/879-3625

Big South Fork Scenic Railway
P.O. Box 368
Stearns, KY 42647
606/376-5330

Bluff View Inn
411 East Second St.
Chattanooga, TN 37403
423/265-5033

Bone Cave State Natural Area
c/o Rock Island State Rustic Park
82 Beach Road
Rock Island, TN 38581
931/686-2471

Booker T. Washington State Park
5801 Champion Road
Chattanooga, TN 37416
423/894-4955

Bowater Inc., Calhoun Woodlands
    Operations
5020 Hwy. 115
Calhoun, TN 37309
423/336-2211

Breaks Interstate Park
P.O. Box 100
Breaks, VA 24607
540/865-4413

Buckhorn Lake State Resort Park
HC 36, Box 1000
Buckhorn, KY 41721-9602
606/398-7510,
Res. 1-800-325-0058

Canoe the Sequatchie
Box 211, Hwy. 127
Dunlap, TN 37327
423/949-4400

Carr Creek State Park
P.O. Box 249
Sassafras, KY 41759
606/642-4050

Carr Fork Lake
Park Manager
U. S. Army Corps of Engineers
845 Sassafras Creek Rd.
Sassafras, KY 41759
606/642-3308

Carter Caves State Resort Park
Rt. 5, Box 1120
Olive Hill, KY 41164
606/286-4411,
Res. 1-800-325-0059

Charit Creek Lodge
250 Apple Valley Road
Sevierville, TN 37862
423/429-5704

Chattanooga Visitors Center
2 Broad Street
Chattanooga, TN 37402
423/756-8687,
800-322-3344 (out of state),
800-338-3999 (in state)

Chattanooga Choo Choo
    Holiday Inn
1400 Market Street
Chattanooga, TN 37402
423/266-5000, 1-800-872-2529

Chattanooga Nature Center
400 Garden Road
Chattanooga, TN 37419
423/821-1160

Chattanooga Regional History
  Museum
400 Chestnut Street
Chattanooga, TN 37402
423/265-3247

Chickamauga and Chattanooga
  National Military Park
P.O. Box 2128
Fort Oglethorpe, GA 30742
706/866-9241

Cloudland Canyon State Park
122 Cloudland Canyon Park Rd.
Rising Fawn, GA 30738
706/657-4050

Cloudmont Ski & Golf Resort and
  Shady Grove Dude Ranch
P.O. Box 435
Mentone, AL 35984
256/634-4344

Cordell Hull Birthplace and
  Museum State Historic Site
The Friends of Cordell Hull
P.O. Box 455
Byrdstown, TN 38549
931/864-3511

Cove Lake State Park
110 Cove Lake Lane
Caryville, TN 37714
423/566-9701

Cowan Railroad Museum
P.O. Box 53
Cowan, TN 37318

Cragsmere Manna Restaurant
P.O. Box 200
Mentone, AL 35984
256/634-4677

Cumberland Caverns
1437 Cumberland Caverns Rd.
McMinnville, TN 37110
931/668-4396

Cumberland County Chamber of
  Commerce
P.O. Box 453
Crossville, TN 38557
931/484-8444

Cumberland County Playhouse
P.O. Box 484
Crossville, TN 38557
931/484-5000

Cumberland Falls State Resort Park
7351 Hwy. 90
Corbin, KY 40701-8814
606/528-4121
Res: 1-800-325-0063

Cumberland Gap National
   Historical Park
Box 1848
Middlesboro, KY 40965
606/248-2817

Cumberland Gardens
P.O. Box 95
Crab Orchard, TN 37723
931/484-5285

Cumberland Mountain State
   Rustic Park
Rt. 8, Box 322
Crossville, TN 38555
931/484-6138

Daniel Boone National Forest
1700 Bypass Road
Winchester, KY 40391
606/745-3100

DeSoto State Park Resort
13883 County Road 89
Fort Payne, AL 35967
256/845-0051

Dr. Thomas Walker State
   Historic Site
HC 83, Box 868
Barbourville, KY 40906-9603
606/546-4400

DuBose Conference Center
P.O. Box 339
Monteagle, TN 37356
931/924-2353

Dutch Maid Bakery
P.O. Box 487
Tracy City, TN 37387
931/592-3171

East Fork Stables
(Bruno Gernt House)
P.O. Box 156
Allardt, TN 38504
800/978-7245

Edgeworth Inn
Monteagle Assembly
Monteagle, TN 37356
931/924-2669

Fairfield Glade
P.O. Box 1500
Fairfield Glade, TN 38558
931/484-7521

Fall Creek Falls State Resort Park
Route 3
Pikeville, TN 37367
423/881-5298
Res. 800/250-8610

Fishtrap Lake
Resource Manager
2204 Fishtrap Rd.
Shelbiana, KY 41562
606/437-7496

Frozen Head State Park and
    Natural Area
964 Flat Fork Rd.
Wartburg, TN 37887
423/346-3318

The Garden Inn at Bee Rock B&B
1400 Bee Rock Rd.
Monterey, TN 38574
931/839-1400

Gordon Lee Mansion
217 Cove Road
Chickamauga, GA 30707
706/375-4728

Grayson Lake State Park
Rt. 3, Box 800
Olive Hill, KY 41164
606/474-9727

Greenbo Lake State Resort Park
HC 60, Box 562
Greenup, KY 41144
606/473-7324,
Res. 1-800-325-0083

Grey Gables Bed & Breakfast
P.O. Box 5252, Hwy. 52
Rugby, TN 37733
423/628-5252

Harrison Bay State Park
8411 Harrison Bay Road
Harrison, TN 37341
423/344-6214

Highland Manor Winery, Inc.
2965 S. York Hwy.
Jamestown, TN 38556-5334
931/879-9519

Historic Rugby, Inc.
P.O. Box 8
Rugby, TN 37733
423/628-2430

Holiday Links
1701 Tennessee Ave.
Crossville, TN 38555
931/456-4060

Homesteads Tower Museum
96 Highway 68
Crossville, TN 38555
931/456-9663

Indian Mountain State Park
Jellico, TN 37762
423/784-7958

Jefferson National Forest
Clinch Ranger District
9416 Darden Dr.
Wise, VA 24293
540/328-2931

Jenny Wiley State Resort Park
39 Jenny Wiley Rd.
Prestonsburg, KY 41653-9799
606/886-2711,
Res. 1-800-325-0142

Karlan State Park
Hwy. 58
Ewing, VA 24228
540/445-5091

Kingdom Come State Park
Box M
Cumberland, KY 40823-0420
606/589-2479

Laurel Creek Travel Park
150 Laurel Creek Rd.
Jamestown, TN 38556
931-879-7696

Levi Jackson Wilderness Road
    State Park
998 Levi Jackson Mill Rd.
London, KY 40744
606/878-8000

Lilley Cornett Woods
91 Lilley Cornett Branch
Hallie, KY 41821
606/633-5828

Little River Canyon National
    Preserve
2141 Gault Avenue N.
Fort Payne, AL 35967
256/845-9605

Lookout Mountain Incline Railway
827 East Brow Road
Lookout Mountain, TN 37350
423/821-4224

The Manor
P.O. Box 156
Altamont, TN 37301
931/692-3153

McCreary County Museum at
    Stearns
P.O. Box 452
Stearns, KY 42647
606/376-5730

Mentone Inn Bed & Breakfast
P.O. Box 284
Mentone, AL 35984
800/455-7470

Mentone Springs Hotel/Bed &
  Breakfast
6114 Hwy. 117
Mentone, AL 35984
256/634-4040

Monteagle Assembly
P.O. Box 307
Monteagle, TN 37356
931/924-2286

Monteagle Wine Cellars
P.O. Box 638
Monteagle, TN 37356
931/924-2120

Natural Bridge State Resort Park
2135 Natural Bridge Rd.
Slade, KY 40376-9999
606/663-2214,
Res. 1-800-325-1710

Noccalula Falls Park
P.O. Box 267
Gadsden, AL 35999
205/549-4663

North Gate Inn
Monteagle Assembly
P.O. Box 858
Monteagle, TN 37356
931/924-2799

Obed National Wild and Scenic
  River
P.O. Box 429
Wartburg, TN 37887
423/346-6295

Paintsville Lake
Resource Manager
U.S. Army Corps of Engineers
807 KY Route 2275
Staffordsville, KY 41256
606/297-6312

Paintsville Lake State Park
P.O. Box 726
Paintsville, KY 41240
606/297-5253

Pickett State Rustic Park
Rock Creek Route, Box 174
Jamestown, TN 38556
931/879-5821

Pine Mountain State Resort Park
1050 State Park Road
Pineville, KY 40977-0610
606/337-3066,
Res. 1-800-325-1712

Point Park
Chickamauga and Chattanooga
  National Military Park
1116 E. Brow Rd.
Lookout Mountain, TN 37350
423/821-7786

Prentice Cooper State Forest
Route 5
North Chattanooga, TN 37405
423/658-5551

Raccoon Mountain Caverns
319 West Hills Dr.
Chattanooga, TN 37419
423/821-9403

The Read House, A Radisson Hotel
827 Broad Street
Chattanooga, TN 37402
423/266-4121,
800/333-3333

Red River Gorge Geological Area
Daniel Boone National Forest
District Ranger, Stanton
705 W. College Avenue
Stanton, KY 40380
606/663-2852

Reflection Riding Nature Preserve
Garden Road
Chattanooga, TN 37419
423/821-9582

Rock City
1400 Patten Road
Lookout Mountain, GA 30750
706/820-2531

Rock Island State Rustic Park
82 Beach Road
Rock Island, TN 38581
931/686-2471

Ruby Falls
1720 South Scenic Highway
Chattanooga, TN 37409
423/821-6705

Russell Cave National Monument
3729 County Rd. 98
Bridgeport, AL 35740
256/495-2672

St. Mary's Retreat and Conference
   Center
P.O. Box 188
Sewanee, TN 37375
931/598-5342

Sequoyah Caverns
Route 1, Box 302
Valley Head, AL 35989
800/843-5098

Sgt. Alvin C. York State Historic
   Park
General Delivery
Pall Mall, TN 38577
931/879-4026

Simonton's Cheese House
P.O. Box 36
Crossville, TN 38557
931/484-5193

Smokehouse Lodge and Restaurant
P.O. Box 579
Monteagle, TN 37356
931/924-2091

South Cumberland Recreation Area
Rt. 1, Box 2196
Monteagle, TN 37356
931/924-2980

Southern Belle
Chattanooga Riverboat Company
201 Riverfront Parkway, Pier 2
Chattanooga, TN 37402
423/266-4488

Stonehaus Winery, Inc.
2444 Genesis Rd.
Crossville, TN 38555
931/484-9463

Tennessee Aquarium
One Broad Street
Chattanooga, TN 37401-2048
800/265-0695

Tennessee Valley Railroad Museum
4119 Cromwell Road
Chattanooga, TN 37421
423/894-8028

Wildwood Lodge Bed & Breakfast
3636 Pickett Park Hwy.
Jamestown, TN 38556
931/879-9454

Wonder Cave
Rt. 1, Box 466
Pelham, TN 37366
931/467-3060,
Bed & Breakfast 931/467-3521

The Woodlee House Bed and
    Breakfast
P.O. Box 310
Altamont, TN 37301
931/692-2368

Yatesville Lake
Resource Manager
U.S. Army Corps of Engineers
P.O. Box 1107
Louisa, KY 41230
606/686-2412

Yatesville Lake State Park
P.O. Box 767
Louisa, KY 41230
606/638-3267

Index

The Historic Cumberland Plateau was designed and typeset on a Macintosh computer system using PageMaker software. The text and titles are set in Adobe Garamond 3. This book was designed and composed by Kay B. Jursik and was printed and bound by Thomson-Shore, Inc. The recycled paper used in this book is designed for an effective life of at least three hundred years.